PERILOUS TIMES

ray d. brown

ISBN 979-8-218-18378-3 (paperback)

Inspirational

Vox Dei Books / rdb publishing

Cover design:

Interior layout and typesetting: waynekehoe.com

Contents

Also by ray d. brown:

authority

Not of the World

The Laying on of Hands

One LORD

I AM (Jesus)

I AM (He)
/ addendum to I AM (Jesus)

This book is dedicated to the elect of GOD,
Christians the world over,
facing Perilous Times
and the Great Tribulation.

Book 1

THESE THINGS

*These things have I spoken unto you,
that ye should not be offended.*

*They shall put you out of the synagogues: yea,
the time cometh, that whosoever killeth you
will think that he doeth GOD service.*

*And these things will they do unto you, BECAUSE
they have not known the Father, nor me.*

– John 16:1-3

The exposition of this Word of GOD will largely depend upon my understanding and apprehension of its prophetic nature – relative to faith.

There was a time when I believed this Word was spoken exclusively to the immediate disciples of the LORD Jesus Christ, and my faith fundamentally went no further. Moreover, I believed that this Word was spoken primarily *of* the scribes and Pharisees (and perhaps the Sadducees), and that bunch of haters and hypocrites that drove (even) Jesus out of their synagogues. And neither my faith nor my vision (perception and/or revelation) went any further.

Attempting to reference only myself as an example, I must speak of faith relative to the prophetic (eternally *living*) nature of the Word of GOD. My transformation, my conversion, my salvation depends upon it. Let me speak of my own personal growth in the grace and knowledge of GOD in Christ. This inevitably proves difficult, knowing that the preponderance of contemporary Christianity even now shares the same predicament that plagued me.

Not until I submitted (or capitulated) to the *commands* of repentance, did I also apprehend the impetus and *power* to repentance. Only then, did I begin to perceive and apprehend the prophetic nature of the Word of GOD.

It is beyond finite expression or articulation. My best is insufficient. Nevertheless, I must tell someone about Jesus.

I cannot peer indifferently around the portal to peek at GOD, to take his assessment, as it were. You know how we do it. To see (or evaluate) if his prospective or anticipated portion for me would be adequate. But let us look, instead, at what GOD has to say about himself.

✳

I AM the Door: by me "if" any man enter in, he shall be saved, and shall go in and out, and find pasture.
– JOHN 10:9

✳

It is (during the process) of entering in that I am evolved. Christ is the nucleus and dynamic of my radical transformation, and the miracle of my being born again. Not trying to be mystical or deliberately obtuse, but Christ is the chrysalis of my *becoming* a son of GOD.

✳

But as many as received him, to them gave he power to "become" the sons of GOD, even to them that believe on his name.
– JOHN 1:12

✳

Receiving (accepting) the overtures and espousals of the love of GOD in Christ Jesus, acquiescing to the adjudication of GOD that sin must be condemned in the flesh, gives me, or entitles me, to the authority and power to become a son of GOD. *"Even to them that believe on his name."*

Often (I like to say) that this believing (or this faith) positions me at the portal to the kingdom of GOD. There I stand with authority and power (and with faith) at the portal. But I must enter into the *Door* to be saved.

These things – these preliminary understandings, these fundamental gospel principles, must be addressed. Faith proves or validates its own necessary works. Frankly, this is why there are innumerable professing Christians – they believe in Jesus Christ – but they have never fundamentally and realistically activated (or validated) that faith by entering into the Word of GOD (*the Door*) to be saved.

I offer no excuse or expiation of my inclusion of these *"innumerable professing Christians"* except to say (that we all know), I was not the only one persisting in such an unregenerate, untransformed, unconverted state. These things must not only be addressed, but also confronted and withstood.

✸

But be ye doers of the Word, and not hearers
only, deceiving your own selves.
– James 1:22

✸

Only as I enter into the Word of GOD (the LORD Jesus Christ – the Door), do I begin to comprehend and apprehend this dynamic. As I acquiesce to the *"becoming,"* submit to the commands, yield to the transformation. In fact, (and/or unapologetically), it is ludicrous to presume myself saved, yet remain fundamentally unchanged. It is preposterous to assume myself born again and not having agreed to die unto lust and pride, and not yet having surrendered my comprehensive character to the transforming power of the Living Word of GOD. His name is Jesus.

His name is Jesus, and he is the Christ of GOD and the wisdom and power of GOD unto salvation. It is the Holy Spirit of the resurrected Christ who makes me a Christian from the inside-out. Concisely, he is the Gift of GOD of himself – the resident (or indwelling) Christ Jesus – bearing witness from the inside-out that I am a Christian.

His name is Jesus, and his is the power (and authority) that I receive to *become* a son of GOD (re. John 4:24). Of course, *"GOD is a Spirit"* (re. John 4:24), and I receive, welcome and accommodate him as such – the Holy Spirit of the Christ of GOD. This Holy Ghost (Spirit – same thing), is both the Spirit of the Father and the Spirit of the Son – One indivisible LORD. His name is Jesus, *The Word of GOD*, and he bears his own record.

✳

For there are three that bear record in heaven, the Father, the Word, and the Holy Ghost: and these three are One.

– 1 JOHN 5:7

✳

It is expedient *and* incumbent that we list the principals. And the *principles*, to use a sort of play on words. Statements, or scriptures that are indisputable, immutable gospel truths – I sometimes call the *absolutes of GOD*.

We enter into what John the beloved Elder, calls *"the doctrine (or teaching) of Christ."* The comprehensive Word of GOD teaches that GOD is (in essence and in character) One LORD who is both the Father and the Son by the Holy Ghost.

This is the composite teaching (or doctrine) of the Word of GOD – the LORD Jesus Christ – both Old Testament and New Testament. I must list the following scripture references consecutively, but for those who have ears to hear, they are also concurrent.

✳

Hear, O Israel: the LORD our GOD is One LORD.
– **Deut. 6:4**

The first of all the commandments is, Hear, O Israel; The LORD our GOD is One LORD.
– **Mark 12:29**

✳

We must let GOD speak for himself. And those who have cultivated (and labored by faith to have) ears to hear, let them hear.

We must not presume (or finitely) presuppose without a conscious (calculated) consideration, that the Word of GOD who uttered the Old Testament, is different or incompatible (any wit different) from the Word of GOD who spoke the New Testament into existence by the singular unction of the Holy Spirit of GOD. I must take a stand; I draw no such distinction.

We must not compartmentalize GOD at any time, (or in any dispensation) limit the *Holy One.* Or in any circumstance to make him less than Almighty by the doctrines (and/or teaching) of men.

(For decades), as a direct result of the teaching of my fore-fathers, I was debilitated by a conceptualization of a Savior, whom by nuance and innuendo and omission, was as less than Almighty (or less than *"all" GOD*). Bluntly (and unapologetically), my forefathers had not delved into the Word of GOD deeply enough and intimately enough to find the Father in Christ.

Our soul can be in peril of strange (or insufficient) doctrines, and that still not negate our own negligence. Indeed. In many aspects, I was the volitionally (merrily) lukewarm, the cheerfully self-deluded and self-indulgent. He who has ears to hear, let him hear.

✳

Here are some gospel *absolutes* (or indisputable truths) that the Holy Spirit of GOD has graciously and mercifully guided me into, faith to faith with due diligence.

- GOD is One LORD who is "both" the Father and the Son by the Holy Ghost.

- This One LORD is the Christ of GOD.

- This Christ of GOD is the indivisible and unvarying Father and Son by the Holy Ghost.

✳

As the LORD Jesus Christ concisely expresses it: *"I and my Father are One"* (John 10:30).

Or, as the Spirit of GOD spoke it (and wrote it) by the Apostle Paul: *"For it pleased the Father that in him (in Christ Jesus) should all fulness dwell."* - Colossians 1:19

Here is (what I personally consider to be) the preeminent expression of the doctrine of Christ in practical application, as it were, in the life of a believer progressing into a disciple of the LORD Jesus Christ. In my own life of Christian development, I have also likened this systematic progression as the transition from servant, to steward, to son – and then becoming GOD's kings and priests in the earth.

*

*If a man love me, he will keep my words: and my
Father will love him, and "We" will come unto
him, and make "Our" abode with him.*
– John 14:23

*

These things – these indelible and undeviating gospel principles – these collective, composite virtues which comprise the comprehensive character and essence of the Word of GOD (the LORD Jesus Christ), must be covered. Preeminent among them, for lack of a better term, and in an attempt to keep it simple, is the consideration of GOD's numerical value, (if I may express it like that).

Here is an observation. It is religious men, and I reference (primarily) *"Pentecostal"* religious men, who insist that GOD is either three or one, and we are then (or subsequently) separated into two (seemingly) irreconcilable camps. Personally, at different times and seasons, I have been found aligned with each camp or religious enclave.

In a quick aside, and to keep this as concise and uncomplicated as possible, I condense my decades of religious observation into a few compact statements.

The *doctrine of the trinity* did not (unambiguously) address or accentuate the deity of each *"member"* of the trinity to my soul's satisfaction. Specifically, the deity of the LORD Jesus Christ.

The *"oneness"* or *"Apostolic"* Pentecostal doctrine did not, and could not, familiarize me with the Father to my soul's satisfaction. Specifically, the *intimacies* of the Father and a Son (or son) [fellowship with Jesus] – for which my inner-child thirsts and hungers and cries.

These things (and others) are the innate perils of resting my Christianity upon what some man said about GOD. These are the predicament and paradox of peripheral (superficial) Christianity and allowing (or depending upon) the preacher to read and study our Bible for us. Kind of like the children of Israel depending upon Moses to bring them (or serve them) what GOD had said.

> *"That which hath been is Now,"*
> (SEE ECCL. 3:15).

Or some things never change. The denizens of contemporary *"surface"* Christianity intuitively know (in a sense) that to approach Mount Sinai on our own, and not be consumed, we will have to be *"holy."* Kind of like approaching the Baptism of John to flee the wrath to come, we will have to bring fruits unto GOD meet (or representative of) genuine repentance (re. Matt. 3:7-8).

(Relatively), depending on the preacher to serve me up the Word of GOD, but not reading my own Bible (or entering into Christ) is the same dynamic. It is an acute and qualifiable repentance that I am circumventing. Like the children of Israel at Mount Sinai, we instinctively know that we are unworthy to approach a most Holy GOD. We must forsake our sin to do so, entering into Christ Jesus, the Word of GOD.

Duh. It was not (so much) my dull comprehension of the Word of GOD that rendered my Bible so difficult to understand – it was my inherent recalcitrant reluctance to repent of my lust and pride.

These things being said – that is, the revelation of GOD relative to my (embarrassingly manifest) multi-faceted need for an acute repentance being internally accepted and assimilated, I entered into my own Bible and began a mystical miraculous heavenly odyssey. When we read with godly intent, the Word of GOD reveals and imparts (his) *living dunamis* to authorize and empower us to live the godly lifestyle the Word of GOD commands.

His name is Jesus.

The Word was *"with GOD"* in the beginning, and the Word *"was GOD"* in the beginning. His name is Jesus. But do we believe it?

Christ Jesus was with GOD in the beginning, and Christ Jesus *"was"* GOD in the beginning, and Christ Jesus is still GOD.

✳

Jesus Christ the same yesterday, and today, and forever.
– Heb. 13:8

＊

The Word of GOD is eternally and perpetually alive, and there ought not be any incongruity or degree of separation between the love we profess for the LORD Jesus Christ and a corresponding love for our own Bibles. Personally, I like a hard copy to touch and to carry, to caress, totally separated from some suspect electronic device. Well? Yes, I am *old-school*, just like that. But I do not want my Bible to be just another *"app"* on my phone.

It is not just a Bible, or a history book or self-help manual – it is the *Bread of Life* (re. John 6:35).

Physically carrying a Bible also makes a definitive statement. It makes our worldly friends and love ones palpably uncomfortable. The world considers the Word of GOD confining, judgmental, intolerable.

Concisely, the Holy Spirit of this Living Word of GOD reproves the world of sin (re. John 16:8).

All that the *Word of GOD* (the LORD Jesus Christ) has spoken in the past (is spoken in the present) and will be spoken eternally. It is forever settled in heaven (re. Ps. 119:89).

＊

*I AM Alpha and Omega, the beginning and the
ending, saith the LORD, which is, and which
was, and which is to come, the Almighty.*
– Revelation 1:8

＊

What GOD has said in the past is eternally relevant. What GOD has said in the past is applicable, pertinent to the present. (I often say) its urgency is *Now*, it is occurring *Now*, it is spoken *Now*.

The wisest man who ever lived addressed or described the prophetic (eternally occurring, eternally pertinent) nature of GOD as follows:

＊

That which hath been is Now; and that which is to be hath already been; and GOD requireth that which is past.
— Ecclesiastes 3:15

＊

This is a concise statement of the Omniscient, Omnipotent, Omnipresent nature of GOD relative to time and circumstance.

The prophetic (and immediate) nature of the Word of GOD is that it is front and center (in my face) and it is *Now*. Kind of like the air I breathe – its nature (and my necessity) is immediate and perpetual. It must be confronted . . . uh, well, because it has already confronted me.

The Word of GOD must be reckoned with; accepted and assimilated, or summarily rejected – although my rejection cannot alter its truth or perpetually occurring and constantly fulfilling (prophetic) nature. Children, we must remember that GOD rules and governs *Infinity*, and that he is without limitations or impossibilities.

According to Revelation 1:8, we might say (in general) that GOD exists and reigns within the three broad dispensations of *"which is, and which was, and which is to come."* GOD fills and/or spans eternity – this is the scope of his Omnipotence, Omniscience, Omnipresence.

We are living in the grace and auspices of the dispensation of the GOD *"which is."* What a comfort to know that he is *"a very present help in time of trouble"* (re. Psalms 46:1).

Concisely, we are living in the dispensation of *Now*, (and ideally) by every Word that proceeds out of the mouth of GOD. Christian, it is GOD who initiated this sovereign ministry of the reconciliation of fallen man through the gospel of this Word. His name is Jesus.

Dear children, consider the great lengths that GOD went to establishing and facilitating a conversation with man. GOD reached (as it were) into the innermost recesses of his heart and treasure and sent the best of himself as the blood sacrifice that would satisfy his own law. I had transferred my own apathy and detachment upon GOD and treated him as if he were the one who was aloof and dispassionate. Duh. We know that God went looking for man in the Garden of Eden. It was Adam that was hiding.

As a young (impressionable) developing Christian, mainstream religious teaching and preaching (broadly) left me with the perception of a GOD who was largely unapproachable, and very, very angry. He was hypercritical and disgruntled – just like the preponderance of adult Christians with whom I was transacting the business of life.

But the comprehensive gospel bears overwhelming evidence of GOD's ardent love for (yes) sinners and his passion to establish the most intimate relationship possible with humanity. GOD not only desires to make us One with himself in Christ Jesus, but *"perfect in One"* (please see John 17:21-23).

Let me share something the Holy Spirit showed me (and imparted unto me) that revolutionized my prayer life and brought the Breath of GOD *(Ruach Elohim)* into my Bible study. GOD showed me the level of intimacy he desired to have with me personally, and the place he desired for me to have in kingdom affairs.

This *place* is (of course) *'given"* in Christ Jesus, but it must also be (what I call) appropriated or pressed into. There are levels and levels. Christian, it should go without saying, that the devil does not want you to have this place of power as GOD's king and priest in the earth relative to kingdom (heavenly) affairs. However, it must be noted, and documented, that the most insidious and cunning adversary and opposition of this place in Christ Jesus, is spiritual wickedness ensconced within the hierarchy of high religious places.

It was my own *Church* that had held me back, the doctrines of men and the traditions of my forefathers obsessively and insanely limiting what I could have with GOD.

Dear child of GOD, it is the Holy Spirit of the Living GOD who initially spoke this following Word unto the man Moses, and this same Holy Spirit (whom GOD is) can also quicken your understanding and apprehension to receive its promises – and to take your appointed place.

✳

*And there I will meet with thee, and I will commune
with thee from above the mercy seat, from between
the two cherubims which are upon the ark of the
testimony, of all things which I will give thee in
commandment unto the children of Israel.*
– EXODUS 25:22

Christian, this goes beyond my being saved – into the arena of
GOD's kingdom affairs in the souls of the sons and daughters
of men. This is approaching maturity – the apprehension of
the believer's preordained place in the perfections and intercessions of Christ.

This is the gospel, and the believer's life being progressively
coalesced and assimilated into the sacrifices of Christ, becoming One with the Love of GOD (and the Lamb of GOD)
in the earth. This is a place of absolute abandon, [as inspired
by Oswald Chambers]. Where the cost has been counted and
freely capitulated to. This is a place for kings and priests, for
the disciples of Christ made One with the sacrament of life
upon the altar, the surrender of self-interests in the intercessions of the LORD Jesus Christ for the lost.

This is inside the veil, where the mysteries and wisdom of
GOD in Christ Jesus await the intrepid and the invested,
where dark and hard sayings come to life (and light) – where
the heart and mind of Christ are won in the reverent midnight
wrestling of sanctification, and the perfecting of holiness in
the fear of GOD.

The devil will say this is too high for you, that you cannot
hope for such heights – who do you think you are. And, as

you can receive it, his most effective (indirect, surreptitious) allies in the war against your faith are the envy and ignorance and unbelief of your professing fellow Christians.

How shall I say it. Concisely, your GOD is alive, and they are still clinging to a one-dimensional, flat-lined, form of faith, the religious ritual and regimen they cite primarily to themselves as evidence that they are saved. You have the internal abiding resident Christ Jesus dynamically and miraculously transforming you into a Christian from the inside-out; they have church attendance and ceremony to represent their Christianity.

You have moved beyond Religion 101 and Surface Christianity and have entered into the Word of GOD. You are not just a practitioner of religious tradition; you are being made a new creature in Christ Jesus. Frankly, the anointing of the Holy One upon you, and the grace and truth and virtues of Christ Jesus the LORD radiating out of you, has incited the envy and acrimony (and raw hatred) of the hypocrite ensconced within the sanctuary.

The schism within the body of Christ is explicit evidence of infidels and pretenders having infiltrated the assembly. Well? Someone has to say it. Dear reader, I know because I was once numbered among them. Or do we suppose that there were hypocrites and haters and Pharisees glutting the temple in Jesus' day, but none within the confines of the righteous congregation today. What? We are better than that? Different from them? Frankly, to assume there are no false prophets or wolves in sheep's clothing among us today is to be either blatantly deluded or volitionally ignorant.

Some of us started off well enough, we might say. Much like the Jews and Pharisees recorded in the eighth chapter of John, we believed on Jesus (please see John 8:30-31). But much like them, we did not *"continue"* in the Word of GOD to either become disciples, or to know the Truth so that we could be made free. It must be noted, that by the end of the chapter, those same, uh, believing (GOD-loving) Jews had taken up stones to cast at Jesus, and drove him out of the temple (see John 8:59).

Many of us (contemporary Christians), although not out-wardly – are of the same general genre – the same general unconverted unchanged unregenerate genre. It must be said (and confronted) just like that. Do we suppose that people have fundamentally changed, or that religious entities or institutions have evolved to be more generally tolerant or merciful, more civilized, more gracious or genuinely loving?

I submit to you that, *'there is no new thing under the sun"* (re. Eccl. 1:9), and that moreover, *"that which hath been is Now"* (re. Eccl. 3:15). Only the love of GOD can empower me and liberate me to love my neighbor as commanded.

The Holy Spirit shall substantiate these things relative not only to our text, but also show them pertinent to the working out of our personal salvation. Sitting among them, you shall know that it is so. He who has ears to hear, let him hear.

[Reader, I must presume somewhat upon your familiarity with the eighth chapter of the gospel as recorded by John.] The *dynamic* which bridges the gulf between my being a neo-phyte believer of Jesus Christ, and a mature disciple of Jesus Christ, is *"continuing"* in his Word.

*

As he spoke these words, many believed on him.

Then said Jesus to those Jews which believed on him, IF ye CONTINUE *in my Word, THEN are ye my disciples indeed.*

And ye shall know the Truth, and the
Truth shall make you free.
– John 8:30-32

*

Continuing in the Word of GOD (and reading and studying our Bibles), we might say, is indicative of the simplicity (and profundity) of Christ. It is as simple as continuing the conversation, but as profound as the cumulative encounters of the believer with GOD.

To be so critical a Christian exercise, and ostensibly so simple a means for the young Christian to grow in the grace and knowledge (and power) of the LORD Jesus Christ, what (seemingly) makes it so difficult a discipline to achieve and sustain? The very first reason the Holy Spirit gives me is that, while I am busy entering into the Word of GOD (the LORD Jesus Christ – *The Door*), the Word of GOD is busy entering into me, evaluating, assessing, refining. Duh. The Word of GOD *talks* to me; the Word of GOD reserves the right to *ask questions* of me.

The Word of GOD does not (relatively) care about my religious title, theological pedigree, or denominational elitism; the Word of GOD takes care that I am learning to love GOD with all my heart, mind, soul, and strength, and to love my neighbor as myself.

If we would make it our business to *know and to keep* the commandment of Love, we would need no other religious business. *Love* is all the law and commandment. Everything else is relatively religious posturing and inane, extraneous table manners.

Without a genuine love for GOD in all his holiness, and a comprehensive (or universal) love for humanity, what I espouse as a saving faith is reduced to a (superficial) religious form. Gold-star Sunday-school attendance, without a faith that works by loving GOD and loving humanity in the same breath, is just a facile work of the flesh.

Continuing resolutely into the wisdom and mysteries of the Word of GOD will daily wrest the command of my natural love and affections and allegiance from this world system, dedicating them to the honor of GOD. Believing on Jesus (relatively) does not cost me anything; but following him will progressively and methodically cost me everything. This is the acute reality and gospel principle of *"the life lost to find it."*

Each believer in the LORD Jesus Christ is fully intended to be irrepressibly and radically transformed into an incendiary disciple of the LORD Jesus Christ by the dynamic metamorphosis of the relentless Word of GOD. It is called being *born again.* Ah, you know more than your disingenuous religious affect suggests. I sometimes call the processing of the sons and daughters of GOD *"the becoming."* It is, concisely, a miracle and a supernatural phenomenon.

Hear me. I cannot read and study and meditate upon the Word of GOD with the genuine ardent intent of faith and remain unchanged. Faith is the catalyst which incites the

Spirit of this Living Word of GOD to quicken my understanding and apprehension. This is effectively entering into the Word of GOD – and submitting to what I have read and heard. Behold the manifestation of the sons and daughters of GOD. Do I believe what GOD has said?

✳

For unto us was the gospel preached, as well as unto them: but the Word preached did not profit them, not being mixed with faith in them that heard it.
— HEBREWS 4:2

✳

The life of Christ who quickens me is never static, never complacent or idle. The miracle of my metamorphosis will not be finalized while I am prisoner of this flesh, assailed by this natural (carnal) consciousness. The Word of GOD ushers me naked into his presence. I perpetually yield to the perfections of Christ, appalled, repenting of the abhorrent state in which I am found.

Each disciple of the LORD Jesus Christ is fully intended to progressively transition into a king and a priest, an overseer and an intercessor of evangelical affairs. Frankly, if the Word of GOD is abiding within me, he will be reaching and speaking out of me. This is (sadly) a gospel phenomenon that is increasingly becoming an endangered species. It is called *"Witness."*

The welfare of my neighbor's soul is laid to my care, seamlessly coalesced with the commandment of love. It is a refiner's fire, this love. Its nemesis stares dumbfounded from my mirror in the morning, irrepressible, inescapable – lust, pride, ego, et.al. What to do about me – and the truth I am circumventing by religious observation?

Continuing in the Word of GOD is the gospel correlative of following on to know the LORD. The inherent difficulty with the revelation of GOD in Christ is the reality and veracity it commands of me.

The truth that makes me free is unsparing of the natural man. Cancerous and gangrenous growth must be excised. Self-righteous garments must be summarily rent and discarded. Extraneous and ostentatious religious personas (and the traditions of my fathers) must be forsaken.

The truth reveals all my escape clauses and loopholes and volitional (and liberal) misinterpretations of the gospel as wistful and delusional human reasoning. There is no all-permissive grace. There is grace to forgive me of sin, and grace to keep me out of sin.

It is the *Truth* that will get you thrown out of the synagogue – the sanctification and holiness that GOD commands, which laissez faire Christianity cannot countenance.

❋

Sanctify them through thy Truth: thy Word is Truth.
– JOHN 17:17

❋

It is the LORD Jesus Christ (the Word of GOD) who is Truth. Concisely, he is every Word that proceeds out of the mouth of GOD. He is what GOD has to say (and to proclaim and declare) of/or about himself.

Child, when the Truth that GOD has given you runs contrary to the traditions of your fathers and forefathers, this is when you will experience difficulties in the synagogue. I mean, who do you think you are, to disparage the denominational tenets and bylaws of the Holy Brethren and Sisters of Sanctity?

We know that Jesus promised us that the Holy Spirit would lead us into *"all Truth"* (re. John 16:13), but some of our forefathers decided long ago that they would rather be spared "all" of it. You understand.

Frankly, *"all"* truth threatens our collusion and compromise with carnal delights and our occasional excursions into the shadows. You know precisely how the preponderance of us play it. *"All"* truth precludes, limits, and/or compartmentalizes our doctrine of *all*-permissive grace.

"All" truth precludes my having much of what the Jones's possess. It prohibits my love of the world and the things of the world, all the goods and services and suspect amusements and entertainments that I have grown accustomed to. Goodness, *"all"* truth commands me to be a Christian 24/7 – 365, the real me without the bells and whistles of my religious cosmetics. A person no one really knows because he does not really exist.

Well? The truth must be cleverly and systematically suppressed for a conciliatory Christianity to have what the world has. You know, with a minimally disturbed conscience and my Sunday-morning smiling face intact.

This repression and attempted quelling of the truth is called *"holding the truth in unrighteousness"* (re. Rom. 1:18) – the base and calculated covetousness of an idolatrous heart and an unsanctified mind.

*

Who changed the truth of GOD into a lie, and worshipped and served the creature more than the Creator, who is blessed forever. Amen.
– **ROMANS 1:25**

*

Not that any man can alter the Truth of GOD, but that we present the truth as something different than GOD intended, a doctrine amalgamated and attenuated by worldly wisdom and men's philosophies – convenient, accommodating, conciliatory to the flesh.

(Broadly) religion becomes about our comfort. I mean, who are we really celebrating on Sundays? Church (broadly) becomes about salving our corporate conscience – corroborating, convincing one another that we are saved.

*

How can ye believe, which receive honour one of another, and seek not the honour that cometh from GOD only?
– **JOHN 5:44**

*

(I mean) how does the honor one of another demonstrate love toward GOD or benefit my neighbor? Mature Christians ought to know that GOD prefers we redirect our love for him back into his love for humanity, aligned with his love for the world, one sinner at a time.

I submit that the preponderance of us (Christians) are sequestered within the sanctuary surreptitiously circumventing the commands of that love. Christian, the love of GOD is predominantly selfless, not self-celebratory. The love or GOD in Christ is unselfconsciously and munificently sacrificial, not secluded in a false sense of security guarding its own elitism and entitlement – hiding from the hunger and heartbreak of humanity in its own hometown, essentially cowering from the commandment of love.

This is the truth that makes men mad – and the reality and mechanics of my single-minded self-realization, that my religion is fundamentally about myself – a clever (and a cunning) clandestine "*form*" of faith that allows me to escape the dynamics of a genuine faith – a faith that works, and only works, as I am coalesced with the commands of GOD's love for my neighbor.

Disciple of Christ, vocally and/or demonstratively espousing this truth will get you ostracized from the assembly and eventually ejected from the synagogue. Sitting among them, you shall know it is so.

For your testimony of love, the Holy Brethren and Sisters of Sanctity (I call them), shall indict you with legalism, and attempting to set a standard of selfless love that they have (already) summarily refused to consider.

The love of GOD in Christ Jesus is the catalyst and impetus of my radical conversion. Only coalesced with this love will my Adamic nature be changed. Moreover, (*thus saith the Holy Spirit*), that Cain received his nature from Adam – that it cannot be otherwise. He who has ears to hear, let him hear.

Without the genuine love of GOD in Christ Jesus, neither humanity nor organized religion has changed (fundamentally meaning, repented), or been converted from covetousness and idolatry and self-seeking. Predominantly, it is still all about us. That is, those of us denominationally minded, gathered and cloistered within the four walls of our respective discriminatory sanctuary. Just another general religious genre gasping for grace and eschewing truth, well might the LORD say of us:

※

But I know you, that ye have not the love of GOD in you.
– JOHN 5:42

※

Once upon a time, we dressed so immaculately as a congregation and smelled so wholesome that it was difficult to perceive or discern the seething cauldron of bigotry and hostility, unforgiveness and resentments, envy and ill-will and covetousness simmering just beneath the surface of our superficial Christianity. Yet these days, we are so infiltrated (corrupted and spiritually emasculated) by worldly influence, that we look no different and act no different than the infidels and adulterers with whom we mindlessly frolic and fellowship (and fornicate).

By the Holy Ghost, I declare that the preponderance of mainstream contemporary Christianity is of the same general genre of religious spirit as the scribes and Pharisees and Jews who coerced the Romans into crucifying the Son of GOD. Hear the Word of the LORD: *The hour is coming, and is even at the door, that elitist denominational Christianity, who consider themselves GOD's elect, shall recommence to slay the prophets of GOD sent into their midst.*

Even now, the Truth we suppress and conceal our hatred of is the very same Holy Spirit of the LORD Jesus Christ, (the Word of GOD) i.e., *"Thy Word is Truth"* (re. John 17:17). Theoretically, we know this, yet in practical application (or in *reality),* we refuse, or deny, its power to convert our Adamic nature into the virtues and wisdom of GOD in Christ.

(Broadly) we make a profession of faith, and then finding the gate strait and the way narrow, we settle into the religious form handed down to us by our forefathers. Concisely, the cross we will not carry is the love of GOD in Christ Jesus that commands and directs and implements the conversion of our innermost character.

That incendiary love is the catalyst of a Holy GOD, and his very nature that commands the loss of my life, and my love of the world upon the altar. This is the truth we have denied in order to spare the heart, mind, soul, and strength of our natural man, and thereby withhold the love of GOD from our neighbor.

This is the Truth, that, if declared (meaning, cried aloud) within our elitist denominational enclaves, would subsequently and summarily get us cast out of the synagogue. The hour is upon us, and now is, that the radically converted are not welcome in the worldly conciliatory and gospel-compromised assembly.

Generally, we have a form of godliness that espouses and presents itself as a people who love GOD. We go to church to prove it. Sometimes we sing and dance and shout – and conceal our unregenerate mind, impenitent heart, and un-converted character beneath a supercilious religious cloak and affectation of piety – a Christian imposter and contemporary Pharisee. The LORD Jesus Christ called out such religious pretenders and prostitutes as fools and hypocrites.

If calling out such religious charlatans within the contemporary congregation today did not get you killed, it would certainly get you *"put out"* of the synagogue, and perhaps get you beaten in the parking lot. By the Holy Ghost of GOD, I declare and attest to this prophecy upon the horizon. By the mercies of GOD, my present portion is to chronicle the despite done grace and the denial and refusal of the virtues and character of the LORD Jesus Christ – the rejection of the love of GOD which quickens and empowers faith. Anything less is religious form.

(Incidentally), I speak as the occasion presents itself, and as GOD orders my circumstances in Christ. Prophetically, my platform is coming, and I shall cry aloud and spare not out of my portion (and my place) in the heart and mind of the *Holy One.*

For the record, I have alienated every pastor (to varying degrees) that the LORD has orchestrated (and/or ordered) my acquaintance with. But I have hope for one.

✳

And blessed is he, whosoever shall not be offended in me.
– MATTHEW 11:6

✳

Christian, we must each of us, answer the individual (miraculously and wonderfully unique) call of GOD upon our lives. Oswald Chambers said, *"Many are called, but few prove themselves chosen."*

We must press into place by the violence and tireless importunity of a radical, living faith, walking past (and through) things seen and the testimony of infidels – especially those ensconced within the hierarchy of our religious institutions.

It is *continuing* in GOD's Word that qualifies the discipleship of the believer in Christ. Rather than being consumed with the morbid introspection of the insecure, I will delve deeper into the mysteries and wisdom, and the virtues and gifts of the Word of GOD. Rather than busy myself with religious things and the inane finite expectations of the Holy Brethren and Sisters of Sanctity, I will occupy myself with the Truth, and submit to being made free, (inspired by John 8:31-32).

The intimacies (and *intricacies*) of abiding in the Word of GOD will tell (or signify) the disciples of Christ. That is, the LORD Jesus Christ shall speak for them, even as they speak for him. Defending oneself is a vain endeavor; expounding upon the doctrine of Christ to those in volitional denial is an exasperating, unavailing (futile) exercise. They will hate you for having what they would not deny themselves to have.

✳

Whence then hath this man these things?
– **Matthew 13:56**

✳

Alas. The ninety and nine have not considered that, while they were celebrating the honor one of another in the self-righteous reflection of their religious form, you were conducting an intricate (and exquisite) inquisition into the secret recesses of Christ by faith – having found greater grace for abandon.

The lukewarm and the uninvested fear the fires of passion; an infidel will not pay the wages of faith.

The worldly conciliatory (world-loving) congregation will hate you for the truth of your testimony, and for having a *Holy* Spirit that they cannot have. Someone must say it. They will despise you for the life that they would not die to have.

Be aware Christian, that when circumstances of tribulation and testing are increased, neither the illusion of love nor the form of faith of the righteous assembly shall stand in the evil day. Undisguised persecution of the congregation shall reveal the latent hatred of the hypocrite for the truth.

In hard times, religious ceremony shall not be adequate to sustain our surface Christianity. Consequently, the remnant of Christ shall be revealed. He who has ears to hear, let him hear.

Wars and countless rumors of wars have always been. And for them with eyes to see, famines and pestilences and earthquakes in diver's places are even now upon us.

✳

All these (things) are the beginning of sorrows.
– RE. MATTHEW 24:8

✳

The fabric of society and the illusion of its civility is waning perilously thin. The specter of Christian love is even now a gossamer cloak. Contemporary scribes and Pharisees shall seek a sacrifice to appease the world's salacious hunger for the heads of genuine Christians – true disciples, the fire-starters among the assembly.

✳

Then shall they deliver you up to be afflicted, and shall kill you: and ye shall be hated of all nations for my name's sake.
– Matthew 24:9

✳

Behold, it is Christ who is hated so virulently – the Truth, the reality of the innate depravity and murderous intent and exceeding sinfulness (and evil) of sin. The preponderance of Christianity has little to worry about, their testimony of Christ is so attenuated and enervated that it does not incite or attract the hostility of Satan.

Active combatants on the front line of faith are disciples aligned with the love of GOD in Christ for the worst of humanity. These are the soldiers of GOD whose testimony of truth shall sever them from the religious illusion of love. If they are not driven from the assembly by the increasingly overt hatred of the hypocrite, their own hunger for a real move of GOD will incite them into the streets.

The genuine disciples of the grace and truth of GOD will often be found where sinners congregate. The love of GOD in Christ Jesus must have souls in crisis.

Children, neither outward religious symbolism nor self-celebratory ceremony avails anything, but faith which works by love, (re. Gal. 5:6, interpretation mine).

The love of GOD in Christ cannot be sustained or suppressed (or satisfied) with cursory ceremony or superficial religious presentation. Disciple of Christ, this is the internal unrest of Christ you intuit sitting among them, and the animosity of devils aware of the unction of the Holy Ghost upon your testimony.

Child, it is okay that the preponderance of the general assembly does not recognize or discern the dynamic of the warfare raging beneath the surface of the average church ceremony. [Well, it is not *"okay,"* but the point is made.]

Do not be offended, the hatred of the hypocrite is directed at the holiness of the LORD Jesus Christ abiding or inhabiting your earthen domicile. Uh, you are hated (despised, rejected) obliquely, as it were. Collateral damage, they call it, in a military (or warfare) connotation. Indeed, to be an ancillary or indirect hatred, it is quite palpable.

Amazing, isn't it, how we presume that these inimical, noxious things are not still all about us? Jesus says these things are coming, that we should not be offended. Christian, if you think the assembly (or congregation) is too civilized (or sanctified) to put you out of the synagogue, then you may well be part of the problem.

Personally, neither can I quite see it from here – but I intuit its shadow and portend and believe its promise prophetically. The LORD Jesus Christ said it is coming. If we cannot believe this specific Word of GOD, what does this say about the comprehensive Word of GOD that we espouse to receive? Or rather, what does this say about our testimony of faith?

Meditating upon John 16:1-3 specifically, verse 3 reveals the catalyst which will eventually ignite the overt virulent hatred and lethal intent exposed and delineated within verse two. (Personally), what I even now feel (or intuit and discern) by the Holy Ghost sitting silently among the solemn assembly, is a hard and ominous prophetic foreshadowing of the promise.

A review (and an emphasis) is indicated, and the Holy Spirit cautions me explicitly not to allow my offense (at whom I often call "*the righteous congregation*"), to interdict or diminish my acceptance of the revelatory truth of this prophetic Word of the LORD Jesus Christ.

✳

These things have I spoken unto you,
that ye should not be offended.

They shall put you out of the synagogues: yea,
the time cometh, that whosoever killeth you
will think that he doeth GOD service.

And these things will they do unto you, because
they have not known the Father, nor me.
– John 16:1-3

✳

Notwithstanding the LORD's admonition that we should not be offended, the task is (as they say) easier said than done. Yet, the same Holy Spirit, that warns us and enlightens us to the latent hatred of the hypocrite for the Truth that is (even now) simmering beneath the surface of our superficial (uh . . . civilized) Christianity, is the very same *Comforter* who encourages and empowers and sustains us under (a very present) clandestine, cunning, covert assault.

This malevolent religious spirit is the schism and upset in the body. By the Spirit of the LORD, I intuit that the true body of Christ is the remnant (broadly) scattered and disenfranchised sitting quietly appalled within the pews of contemporary organized worldly compromised Religion.

Hear me. When we are incensed enough to speak out against our general pandemic misinterpretation of grace, and the congregation's growing abhorrence and hatred of the truth, we will (at first), be shouted down. But let us know, that the prophetic hour of our being put out of the synagogue is upon us.

The Word (at first) seems absurd. The LORD knows I mean no disrespect. There is no other way to express its incongruity with our perceived righteousness and civility, our presumptive piety, our affected (artificially assumed) Christian love.

Someone must get honest. This Word is so unbelievable of our refined and enlightened Christian congregations that we are desperate to place it within the context of someone else's reality – some other people and time, some other dispensation. The problem with that is (that) the Word of GOD is a living entity, and it is for every people and time and within any (and all) dispensations. His name is Jesus.

Granted, this dreadful Word was first spoken to the disciples of the LORD Jesus Christ who were present at what is commonly called *"the upper room discourse,"* chapters thirteen through seventeen of the gospel as recorded by the Apostle John. However, the prophetic (compulsory) nature of the Living Word of GOD (the LORD Jesus Christ) is that he is now, and he is eternal.

The context of the comprehensive Word of GOD spoken to the disciples in the upper room (and everywhere, for that matter), are the immediate milieu and responsibility of his disciples today and every day. Indeed. This is not the first hard and dark saying of the LORD Jesus Christ that Christianity has strived to circumvent, or to (alas) simply ignore.

The entirety of the Word of GOD is spoken in the immediacy and exigency of the entirety of humanity. Every Word of it. Children, the context of the Word of GOD is my immediate consciousness. Jesus is here, and Jesus is now. And he has much to say.

When I place one portion of the Word of GOD into the context of one people (in a specific place and time), I establish a discriminatory and precarious precedent. Frankly, when I excuse myself from the context of any Word of GOD, I am still looking for loop-holes – indemnity, escape clauses. Christian, none are qualified or authorized to rightly divide the Word of GOD except GOD. Indeed, the compounded comprehensive Word of GOD corroborates himself.

When I take the Word of GOD back to GOD in prayer and study, in meditation and in fasting, in watching(s) and waiting(s) and in hallowed silences, GOD is faithful to expound upon what he has said. Children, it is in sanctified, private audiences that I have been proven to hear best.

✳

And unto you that hear shall more be given.
– RE. MARK 4:24

✳

Dearest Christian disciple, the LORD Jesus Christ here in John 16:1-3 is instructing us to be prepared to be offended. Ah, but to be prepared is to also be forewarned and forearmed. How we respond to offense, trial, temptation, persecution, et al., proves (and exposes) character.

It is in the fire (and under fire) that we shall see what I am made of. Concisely, if my character has been converted to that of Christ, it is contrary circumstance that will tell it best. Anyone can render offense for offense – it is Christ in me (and in you) who can remain silent when smitten.

These things must be reckoned with, assimilated, settled before they get here. They are upon the horizon . . . and the Bridegroom, behind the door.

✳

The night cometh, when no man can work.
– RE. JOHN 9:4

✳

It is (fundamentally) the incendiary, the intrepid, the radically vocal and demonstratively sanctified disciples of the LORD Jesus Christ who will be put out of the synagogue – those who sound and look conspicuously like Christ. A compromised congregation (even now) cannot abide the fire of Christ within close proximity to their wood, hay, and stubble.

It is the Truth who makes us free, and who also transforms us into virulent and contagious disciples of the LORD Jesus Christ. Moreover, it is the same Truth who exposes and incites the hatred of the hypocrite. The latter half of the eighth chapter of John exemplifies it best.

Christian, the prophetic portend of our eventually being put out of the synagogue, hated, and perhaps even killed by (quote – unquote) religious persons thinking that they are doing GOD service, must be addressed. These things, precisely and specifically John 16:1-3, are *before* the (great) tribulation. Personally, I believe these things are incorporated into *"the beginning of sorrows"* (re. Matt. 24:8) – the *birth pangs* or *labor pangs* in the birthing and the foreshadowing of Christ's return. Indeed, and all of heaven getting to their feet.

For preparedness and empowerment, for wisdom and enlightenment, we look to the LORD Jesus Christ, the Living Word of GOD. First, he does not want us to be offended. Being offended, and all the accompanying negativity associated with subsisting in a perpetual state of being offended, is counterproductive. It does not work the righteousness of GOD or advance his kingdom on earth. An angry Christian is not a wholesome witness of the love of GOD in Christ.

At the close of the eighth chapter of John, we see the LORD Jesus Christ *"allowing himself"* to be put out of the temple (and/or synagogue). This was not the first (or the last) time the Jews and Pharisees sought to kill him.

The LORD Jesus Christ being our preeminent example and forerunner in all things pertaining to walking and living by faith, it behooves us to examine the dichotomy (or dynamic) of his inimical relationship with the Jews and Pharisees that persistently resulted in his being unwelcome in the synagogue. (I mean) for this prophecy to pertain to us (his disciples), what is going to be the catalyst that will eventually get us put out of the synagogue, and our very lives endangered?

First, and this is going to be as difficult to hear (and believe) as the Word of GOD we are considering; I believe (by the Holy Ghost), and as I have already alluded to, the LORD's remnant of true believers is going to come out (and be put out) of the organized corporate form of faith that we currently call the Church. That is correct. It is my revelatory premise that the LORD's true body of believers is scattered within multitudinous (world-wide) congregations of infidels and hypocrites who have persuaded themselves that they are Christians.

He who has ears to hear, let him hear. As iniquity has abounded and societal morality has decayed, there has been a corresponding weakening and compromise of the average congregation. Moreover, (primarily) by negligence from the pulpit, and worldly infiltration and influence into the Church, the ranks of the Spirit-filled among the Christian assembly is being (and has been) systematically and alarmingly diminished. Concisely, we have fewer soldiers – Christian disciples, Spirit-filled intercessors and prayer warriors, kings and priests.

We are the few. And we are going to be forced to gather elsewhere. This is strong language, I know. Please bear with me, as many as can trust that I write upon the revelatory edge of the Word of GOD, sequestered here in my home office before dawn, scribing under the auspices and unction of grace – as GOD is my witness. I did not know this exposition was coming.

Now, the following Word of GOD is indeed (primarily) end-time prophesy, but we must not presume that it has lain dormant. He who has ears to hear, let him hear. For clarity and emphasis (and to minimize distraction), I will begin in the middle of the first scripture – and the Holy Spirit will make his own point.

✳

Because they received not the love of the
Truth, that they might be saved.

And for this cause GOD shall send them strong
delusion, that they should believe a lie.

That they all might be damned who believed not
the Truth, but had pleasure in unrighteousness.
– RE. 2 THESSALONIANS 2:10-12

✳

(In an allegorical sense) we are lined up and pushing against one another wide-eyed and bare-assed to be the first to receive the latest lie and most recent technological toy. We are busy perpetuating and preserving the pleasures of our senses in our rabid lust and wanton love for the world in the pride and notoriety of our carnal lives.

The preponderance of the contemporary supercilious congregation arrogantly and impudently presume the prophetic (Living) Word of GOD listed above is for apostates and hard-boiled sinners, for incalcitrant reprobates and infidels and hell-bound heretics – ah, and so it is. This dreadful revelatory Word is even now being fulfilled and perpetrated, revealed in the phony self-righteous reflection of the contemporary congregation of haters and gluttons, fornicators and adulterers, perverts and pretenders who press into the devil's doctrine of all-permissive grace – the delusion of being forgiven for all I willfully allow.

✳

(Here) I must expound upon some fundamentals as I have learned them by the Holy Spirit. The *truth* of GOD is the reality of his Living Word (the LORD Jesus Christ), seeking a place of preeminence in my life – within my heart and mind and soul.

Whether a general or specific gospel truth, it is all the nature and essence and character of Almighty GOD revealed in his Christ.

The *truth* of GOD is always presented with the *grace* of GOD to enable me to bear its revelation and impact upon my natural man, to incite and comfort and encourage – to empower me unto reform(ation) or repentance. GOD has never expected (or *commanded*) anything of me that he did not also graciously empower me to perform.

There is *greater grace* available for the invested and intrepid seeker of GOD; it is only them with a skewed or self-serving agenda who go away sorrowful. (I have found) that there is a progressive revelatory methodology to the truth of GOD – that, introductions *happen,* but that an intimate relationship must *develop* over time.

"Learn of me" says Jesus.

＊

The Word of GOD (my own Bible) is the revelatory, kingdom portal of the *"person"* and character, and *deity,* of the LORD Jesus Christ. The *"Truth"* of GOD is the *"person"* of GOD, to use a finite, common term to describe the Infinite (indescribable) One.

Contemporary mainstream Christianity (broadly) presumes upon a ceremonial religious presentation (uh, Church service) to imply and assume proximity to GOD. A worship service in spirit and in truth, coupled with the preaching of the undiluted Word of GOD, is indeed pleasing to GOD – correlative to the relationship I have already established with him in Christ. The best of us espouse an intimate love for the LORD Jesus Christ with our mouth, but without a corresponding demonstrative love for our own Bible.

＊

Well hath Esaias prophesied of you hypocrites,
as it is written, This people honoureth me with
their lips, but their heart is far from me.
– MARK 7:6

＊

The Truth of GOD is the character and essence of GOD – *"Thy Word is Truth"* (re. John 17:17). When we will not receive and develop a love for the Truth, for GOD's Word – for the essence and character and virtues of the LORD Jesus Christ, then (it can be said) that GOD takes this rejection personally.

When we reject the truth, and refuse to amend our lifestyles accordingly – that we might continue to have pleasure in unrighteousness – then GOD is just in allowing us to accept the delusion (or the lie) that takes its place or fills its void. It should go without saying, that when we oppose or contradict the truth of GOD's Word by our impenitent (and impertinent) behavior, we are unequivocally rejecting the LORD Jesus Christ and renouncing his right to reign over our lives.

This egregious willful denial, as it progresses, warrants a corresponding delusion and further hardening of our heart toward a total apostasy. At the precise juncture that I stop following, or where I question the veracity of GOD's Word, murmur and complain of (his) precepts and refuse its application to my lifestyle, the delusion (or the lie) entered in and began the inexorable process of seizing the preeminence (or ascendancy) in the spiritual warfare for my soul.

When I will not give the Word of GOD (the Truth, the LORD Jesus Christ) the preeminent place of honor in my heart and mind and soul, then delusion and fallacy take its place. Satan takes his place and fills the void with deception (and erroneous or attenuated, watered-down doctrine).

The Apostle Paul, Silvanus, and Timotheus present this Word of GOD (by the unction and anointing of the Holy Ghost) to the Church of the Thessalonians, in what may be called an *"end-time"* prophetic context. And so, we have always viewed it. But, dear children, this same dynamic has been raging for the soul of humanity since Eve questioned and then rejected what GOD had said, and first reached for that forbidden fruit.

By the same Holy Ghost, I attest to this dynamic (both a noun and a verb), not only still being executed or perpetrated within the average contemporary congregation, but that this process is being accentuated and accelerated as we enter into the end-times. By the Holy Ghost, I declare that church-folk (or religious folk) have not fundamentally changed.

"That which hath been is Now" (re. Eccl. 3:15). We still claim our spiritual heritage and the traditions (and exclusive denominational doctrines) of our forefathers, sporadic church attendance and superficial service work, as evidence that we are the elect of GOD – uh, the descendants of Abraham, GOD's chosen.

✳

I know that ye are Abraham's seed; but ye seek to kill me, because my Word hath no "place" in you.
– John 8:37

✳

Christian, the Holy Ghost, in the ardent incendiary defense of the honor and glory of the LORD Jesus Christ, solemnly and urgently asks each of us . . . "What *"place"* have you given the Word of GOD?"

There is but one place the Word of GOD will assent to and ratify with the precious blood of Jesus Christ – and it is the freewill offering up of my life and comprehensive affections upon the same altar, and my love mingled and coupled with the love of GOD upon the same mercy seat.

When the *"Word"* of GOD has no *"place"* in me, I have not allowed the Grace and Truth of GOD, the LORD Jesus Christ, ascendancy and thoroughfare (and entitlement) to the throne of my life. I have not capitulated to his sovereignty or surrendered to his rule. I may dress it up with some indifferent participation in a religious ceremony or service, going through an outward show of surrender, and my heart and mind still not submitted to the Word of GOD.

Fundamentally, I either live a life of (what I call) self-realization, or GOD-realization. Generally, in a life of self-realization, I have not received, surrendered to, and progressively developed a love for the truth, but I still predominantly *"spend"* my life having pleasure in unrighteousness. GOD has allowed the delusion because it is I who prefer the lie.

It is the same gospel principle (from another perspective) that the LORD Jesus Christ presented to Nicodemus.

*

Men loved darkness rather than light, because their deeds were evil. But he that doeth "truth" (practices, accepts, lives a life of) cometh to the light.
– JOHN 3:19-21

*

This is the same gospel dynamic. Just as those who do not accept and develop a love for the truth will eventually be revealed to hate it, even so, them who will not receive the light and live in its illumination, will be exposed as haters of the light.

*

*For every one that doeth evil hateth the light, neither cometh
to the light, lest his deeds should be reproved* (exposed).
– John 3:20

✳

When we do not love and cherish (and guard and protect) the light and truth that GOD has graciously afforded all of us in its season, then he is justified in withholding the next level or gradient, or revelation of light and truth – the next revelatory grace and truth by which Jesus Christ (the Living Word of GOD) comes.

Although at times it may be incremental, if we are not progressing in the grace and truth and knowledge of GOD in Christ, then we have veered off into some side-eddy of illusory rest or leisure (or worldly entertainment or amusement).

(Personally), I was proficient at straying from the austerity and self-denial upon the strait and narrow, into the wide gate and broad way of self-indulgence (and self-realization) which leads unto destruction. [For me], the primary reasons for my wandering was most often a combination of a desire to circumvent the constraints and suffering association of the gospel of Jesus Christ and him crucified, and a desire (*or lust*) for what the world was doing – and the things they possessed, the illusion of wealth and happiness.

(Generally) we have not accurately assessed the gospel perspective of our circumvention (and clever evasion) of the commands of light and truth. It is not preached with gravity and authority (or the proper solemnity or immediate urgency), but the gospel commands of the Word of GOD are non-negotiable.

What I am trying to say is that we have not rightly esteemed, or even realistically considered, that our suppression of the truth and evasion of the light is actually a symptom of a pervasive active hatred of truth and light. (From GOD's perspective, either we are developing a healthy, burgeoning love for the truth, or we are actively hating it. We are either walking and living in the light of his holiness, or we are (for now) clandestinely hating the light because our deeds are evil.

There is fundamentally only one viable direction for the (disciple) and follower of Jesus Christ by faith – and that is deeper in love with the Truth, and into the light and holiness of the countenance of the LORD Jesus Christ.

✳

But he that doeth truth cometh to the light, that his deeds
may be made manifest, that they are wrought in GOD.
– JOHN 3:21

✳

GOD's children are, of course, not only of diverse (and of all-inclusive) nations, tribes, and tongues, but also of varying ages. But we have not apprehended and assimilated the startling gospel reality that every child of GOD, from the newborn to the aged matriarchy and patriarchy, are upon the dynamic continuum of the living Word of GOD – actively pressing into the mysteries and wisdom of the striations of his truth and walking by grace through faith in the light of his holiness in Christ Jesus.

There are no *lukewarm* Christians in the kingdom of GOD. We are either ablaze in/and for the LORD Jesus Christ, or we are acrid soldering ash beneath a formal religious bushel – dying embers, a great darkness.

There are distinctly and categorically servants and sons (and daughters) in the House of GOD. By the Holy Ghost, I attest to there being predominantly more (and even overwhelmingly more) servants in the contemporary House of Jacob (the Church), than viable sons and daughters. The entire eighth chapter of John is fundamentally about the differentiation (and the discord) within the House of GOD. He who has ears to hear, let him hear.

It is the LORD Jesus Christ who shall sever the servants from the sons and daughters of GOD in the House of Jacob.

*

And the servant abideth not in the house
for ever: but the Son abideth ever.
– John 8:35

*

Infiltrators and infidels parading as Christians in the Church of GOD shall prophetically and inexorably be exposed as haters of truth and light. And we thought they were simply listless and indifferent, and relatively harmless. But we have not adequately apprehended the prophetic implications of the Word of GOD – that these hypocrites and pretenders are latent haters of the truth and light of the LORD Jesus Christ.

They espouse an erroneous notion of all-permissive grace to presume themselves forgiven for the sin and lust and love for the world that they continue to willfully allow. They cite the religious heritage of their forefathers and their own spurious decades of church attendance to qualify calling themselves Christians.

These surreptitious servants of their own appetites call themselves the sons and daughters of GOD, covertly and cunningly circumventing and suppressing light and truth (and holiness) of the gospel (and cross) of the LORD Jesus Christ that would expose them for the posers and prostitutes they really are.

These imposters are not the elect of GOD. The sons and daughters of GOD are those who have allowed the truth and light of the LORD Jesus Christ access, ah, proximity, to their hearts and minds and souls, surrendering to his transforming power. The sons and daughters of GOD are the radically converted in character, who have aligned themselves with the purposes (and commandments) of his evangelical love for the worst of humanity.

The very same dynamic that is irrepressibly at work in the eighth chapter of John is prophetically at work in our primary text of John 16:1-3. That is, in both situations, an identical evil spirit of religious pride – and the identical hypocrisy, is prophetically at work. The LORD Jesus Christ told the Jews and the Pharisees and chief priests that they had not allowed the truth to make them free, that they were effectively servants in the House of GOD, and not the sons that they arrogantly presumed themselves to be.

This merits review. As we have already mentioned, the word *"because"* used in John 8:37 is the conjunctive adverb (I believe it is called, but please do not quote me on that – unless, of course, I am correct). A conjunctive adverb links a *"cause and effect"* dynamic. The word *because* here is a "causative or catalytic" adverb.

✳

I know that ye are Abraham's seed; but ye seek to kill me [because] *my Word hath no "place" in you. I speak that which I have seen with my Father: and ye do that which ye have seen with your father.*
– John 8:37-38

✳

As we (should) know, the conversation here in the eighth chapter of John progressively deteriorates. I want to make an observation, and I will cast it in a personal context, hopefully to minimize offense and encourage a closer assessment. For decades, when I read this particular Word of GOD, I was as equally dumfounded as these Jews initially were. *"Because"* I had not given the Word of GOD *"place."*

I had not given the Word of GOD (the LORD Jesus Christ) a *place* of preeminence and honor in my heart and mind and soul, in my affections – or in my circumstances. My understanding was a closed door, an occluded ear and a closed mind, a hardened, indifferent, impenitent heart.

I must value the Word of GOD as the personality and character of GOD. Until I collude with and partner with (and *covenant* with) the Word of GOD, it is essentially a one-dimensional document, a history tome, and a dead letter. Only as I *receive* the Word of GOD is it accompanied with a Living Spirit – who empowers and authorizes me to become a son of GOD. Only in the giving and taking. Only in the breaking of Bread.

I may appear to be a good or ordinary Christian, but it is only as I give the Word of GOD *"place"* that it converts my unregenerate character and births me into the family of GOD. For decades, I was a warm but spiritually lifeless entity, a somewhat sentient body, occupying space within the pew – with the Word of GOD essentially going in one ear and unimpeded out the other.

Concisely, and without watering it down, I intuitively knew that if I gave the Word of GOD *"place"* within my heart and mind and soul, that it (*He*) would commence to make demands upon my natural man and my indiscriminate appetite for carnal goods and services and corrupt amusements and sordid entertainments. You get the idea.

The change the Word of GOD commands is *"repentance."* With repentance of sin comes the remission of sin, and the (relative) opening of my understanding. And much more for the asking.

Frankly, previously (in my unregenerate state), I fundamentally had another father. This is what Jesus is telling the Jews and Pharisees in the eighth chapter of John. Moreover, it has been recorded for our benefit and perusal, and as an explicit example. He who has ears to hear, let him hear. *"That which hath been is Now"* - (re. Eccl. 3:15).

I am either abiding in the Word of GOD, and the Word of GOD abiding (and living and prospering) in me, or I am as lost and undone as I ever was – under the influence and subjugation of the god of this world system, with Satan effectively as my father. I may be sitting in the pew next to you, pretending to be a Christian, but resisting and rejecting the truth of GOD's Word in order to save my natural life for myself, embracing a lie.

I either receive and develop a love for Truth (the Word – the LORD Jesus Christ), or I am a hater and an infidel (dormant for now), but soon to be revealed or exposed in these rapidly developing end-times. The fact that we (mainstream Christianity) have not accepted the prophetic reality of the Word of GOD progressively transpiring and materializing in our midst, confirms us and reveals us in a pronounced state of unbelief.

If I do not hear the Word of GOD, accept his truth, and conform to his commands, it is because I (in reality) have another father than GOD.

※

He that is of GOD heareth GOD's Word(s): ye therefore hear them not, "because" ye are not of GOD.
– John 8:47

※

We must be born again of the same Spirit whom GOD is – to even begin this spiritual odyssey of getting to know GOD. My natural man must be made to submit to the authority and Spirit of GOD's Living Word. I must make a beginning. If I will receive this Holy Spirit of GOD in Christ Jesus – the Living Word of GOD – he will give me the power (and the authority) to become a son of GOD (re. John 1:12).

We must look at these Jews in the eighth chapter of John objectively and thoroughly – without prejudice or impartiality, and most importantly – prophetically. What can we, the elect of GOD in our era, learn from these Jews and Pharisees as the presumptive entitled elect of GOD in their corresponding era? After all, we both consider ourselves the religious elite of our respective eras or dispensations.

This is relative to our primary text of John 16:1-3, and the LORD Jesus Christ cautioning his disciples that the sudden exposure of the mendacity and perfidy of the hypocrite incites their virulent hatred. The Truth of GOD (as we shall see) unsparingly brings their murderous character out of the closet of religious misdirection and pious posturing, and into the light.

The Truth commands self-assessment and accountability.

Children, the dynamic venue or arena, the antagonism and the hostility, the mutual enmity between light and darkness, righteousness and unrighteousness, is relatively the same in any era or dispensation. The spiritual contenders for ascendancy are the same. We are either living a life by the effectual working power of the Holy Spirit which honors GOD, or we are living a life of self-realization and self-indulgence as aided and abetted by the god of this world system, Satan.

This discourse and interaction {between the LORD Jesus Christ and the Jews} here in the eighth chapter of John is revelatory and enlightening, and especially pertinent to contemporary Christianity (and/or the Church). As everything that befell Israel in Egypt and during the Exodus was an explicit example for the New Testament Church (*see 1 Cor. 10:6),* even so, both the Old Testament and New Testament narratives concerning GOD's people is correspondingly relevant to GOD's people today. This is expressive of the prophetic nature of the Living Word of GOD, the LORD Jesus Christ: Alpha and Omega, and the Ancient of Days – him *"which is, and which was, and which is to come, the Almighty"* (re. Rev. 1:8).

Humanity (or human nature) has not fundamentally changed; the character and essence of GOD (the Word of GOD) has not, and will not, change. We may presume to be more civilized, more intelligent, and we are obviously more technologically advanced, but our Adamic nature has not changed.

Now, this is cynical, but also an imperative reality check. Some of us – the Bible says a *few* – are the converted of Christ upon the narrow way which leads to eternal life. And *many* of us are still of the unregenerate nature of Adam and Eve on the broad way that leads to destruction (re. Matt. 7:13-14), but wearing a new shirt or a new dress, and maybe new shoes, (and maybe a supercilious Sunday-morning smiling face).

Yes, it is my assertion out of the mind of Christ, and as revealed to me by the Holy Ghost, that the kingdom ratio of the *"many"* and the *"few"* is relative to (and at work within) the Church of GOD.

Just like ourselves (contemporary Christianity), the Jews in the eighth chapter of John are relatively an accurate cross-section, sampling, or composition of ordinary or typical church-folk. Moreover, each population considered or consider ourselves the custodians of the Word of GOD, and his chosen people. Moreover, I am convinced that both the Pharisees and the Sadducees, each concluded themselves doctrinally inerrant, and the other religious enclave (or denomination) not only in grave theological error, but also irretrievably hell bound. He who has ears to hear, let him hear.

Notwithstanding these observations, and they have their use, we are not to compare ourselves with them, but rather with the Truth, the Word of GOD. We could say that he was in their midst *physically*, but that he is in our midst *spiritually*. His name is Jesus, the Christ of GOD.

Over the course of some years and a few manuscripts, and under the astute and explicit tutelage of the Holy Ghost, I have gleaned much wisdom from this acute interaction between the LORD Jesus Christ and these arrogant and presumptuous Jews in the eighth chapter of John. Indeed, of late, I have found myself looking forward to another review of this prescient (prophetic) oracular encounter, knowing that every audience with the Word of GOD (mingled with faith) leads me deeper into the familiarity and mysterious intimacies of him whom my soul loves.

This confrontation is a spiritual engagement of the highest order, expressive of the reality of spiritual wickedness, evil and hypocrisy, ensconced and entrenched throughout the hierarchy of the religions of men. He who has ears to hear, let him hear. The Word of GOD testifies to a truth that is redolent and illuminating of this population of church-folk.

*

*As he spake these words, many "believed" on him. Then
said Jesus to those Jews which "believed" on him.*
RE. JOHN 8:30-31

❋

This quote is, of course, the entirety of verse 30, and half of verse 31, as the Holy Spirit of this Living Word appropriates the occasion to make his own point. (Please, stay with me). The Word of GOD by James expresses it especially well: *"Faith without works is dead"* (see James 2:20).

We speak (relatively and realistically) of the same gospel dynamic expressed from different perspectives. As the Good Shepherd, the Word of GOD says: *"My sheep hear my Voice, and I know them, and they "Follow Me"* - John 10:27.

Returning to our primary (current) text, the LORD Jesus Christ equates the *following* of his sheep, as well as the *works* of a viable (or genuine) faith, as the equivalent of *"continuing"* in the Word of GOD.

❋

Then said Jesus to those Jews which "believed" on him, "IF"
ye "continue" in my Word, then are ye my disciples indeed.

And ye shall know the Truth, and the
Truth shall make you free.
– John 8:31-32

❋

The *working* and the *following* and the *continuing* are definitive evidence and substance of genuine faith. The Word of GOD emphasizes that these Jews in the eighth chapter of John *"believed"* on Jesus, but as the narrative progresses it quickly becomes clear that they had not continued in the Word of GOD to know the truth or be made free.

When confronted with (and convicted by) the Truth, they immediately become indignant and offended, and then hostile. In fact, by the end of the chapter, the covert hatred in their heart for the truth is overtly manifested by the stones in their hands.

We ooh and aah and tsk-tsk at the infinitesimally thin religious veneer of civility exhibited by the Jews and Pharisees – but I am unsure (to) what degree we consider the prophetic implications for contemporary Christianity. I mean, how thick is our religious veneer of civility, how refined our spiritual poise under fire?

For one thing, we have not experienced (or been subjected to) the acute confrontation of the Truth of GOD personified – nor have we encountered the manifestation of the Spirit of Truth (the Holy Ghost) strong enough or palpable enough to convict us of the sin in the sanctuary and subsequently drive us unremittingly and en masse to the altar.

We only posture as wanting revival, this is what religious people do. Ha! But a real visitation of the Holy One, and an abrupt and acute manifestation of Truth would necessitate a genuine repentance of sin and forsaking the lie, and the luxury of our religious life. Succinctly, how prepared are we to die?

To draw an accurate comparison, and to ponder how we might respond, we must apprehend (exactly) what the LORD Jesus Christ is saying to this population (or congregation) of elitist religious folk. This could get graphic.

At first, and then at various times over the years, I thought that, yes, Jesus was conceding that these Jews were indeed Abraham's descendants, but not legal heirs through matrimony. Concisely, I thought they were incensed because they perceived Jesus was effectively calling them bastards. But the gist of it, as they say, (and the Truth of it), is much worse than being Abraham's illegitimate children. Jesus was essentially and unapologetically calling them the spawn of Satan.

Contemporary (civilized) Christianity presume ourselves innumerable degrees (and generations) removed from this dichotomy (and this dynamic) of the Living Truth of GOD's Word initiating such a rift in the House of Jacob, and inciting (or instigating) a congregation of religious folk to violence. Why, this doesn't even pertain to us.

Christian, the doctrine (or teaching) of Christ reveals – that if we have not *"continued"* in the Word of GOD far enough to receive and develop a love for the truth (and subsequently be made free), that we are still in bondage to the illusion, clinging to the lust of our natural life and our love for the world. Still a prisoner of sin. We may well be ensconced in the House of Jacob, a tithing, smiling member of the Church in ostensibly good-standing, and still not be a son or daughter of GOD – but a servant in the House, and not an heir at all.

Here in the eighth chapter of John, present in the temple (or in the sanctuary, in the "Church"), parading and posturing as the children of GOD, is the surreptitious hatred and lethal intent of the pretender and the hypocrite for the Truth – going through the motions of religious form, impersonating faith. Them confederate with the illusion, and loyal and subservient to the lie which enables them to save their natural lives for themselves, have hardened their hearts to the truth. And their hearing is blunted, occluded, (and excuse me), retarded.

Embarrassingly, they appear to be a little slow on the uptake (as it were), that Jesus is (at first) alluding to them as being Satan's children. They cannot seem to grasp the spiritual implications of his doctrine. As we have discussed, they are of another spiritual heritage and genre. But then Jesus makes it unsparingly plain.

*

Ye are of your father the devil, and the lusts of your father ye will do. He was a murderer from the beginning, and abode not in the truth, because there is no truth in him. When he speaketh a lie, he speaketh of his own: for he is a liar, and the father of it.
— JOHN 8:44

*

Now, the Truth is the very essence and character of the Holy Spirit of GOD. Moreover, without differentiation or degree of separation, the LORD Jesus Christ (the Word of GOD) is the embodiment of Truth.

*

Thy Word is Truth.
— SEE JOHN 17:17

*

Christian, even the most erudite and discerning Biblical masters among us have not fully comprehended the malevolence and mutual hostility (the enmity) which exists between the Truth (whom GOD is) and the father of lies, Satan. Frankly, the preponderance of humanity (and to a lesser degree) even the Church, have had little insight or appreciation into the ferocity of the spiritual warfare that ceaselessly rages for our soul. Moreover, that we have little or no fear of hell, or that the term *"lukewarm"* applied to our general sentient (congregational) temperature is actually quite generous to describe us – that this causes us no disquiet, startlingly exposes us in a pronounced state of mortal unbelief.

Alas, if I capitulate to the truth, I must release the illusion and the lie to which I cling and enter into the irrepressible loss of my natural life, and the denunciation of my love for the world. It occurs to me that my previous blindness to the truth was so absolute – and I was so anesthetized and mesmerized by the pageant and the presentation – I never entertained a thought that in such a willful state of sin and lust and insurrection, I was a child of the devil.

My willful acceptance of this world system's conditions is a covenant transaction. The conditions of my servitude include (but are not limited to) my sitting dumbfounded and insentient, spiritually impervious and essentially paralyzed in front of a television or telephone or computer screen – spending my life for what does not and cannot satisfy. For technological narcotics and virtual fornication, I have effectively sold my soul. The most appalling aspect of the tragedy is that I take no thought of the loss.

But what are the LORD's conditions?

✳

> *He that is not with me is against me; and he that*
> *gathereth not with me scattereth abroad.*
> – **Matt. 12:30**

*

Alarmingly, in the lust and love pursuit of the goods and services of this corrupt world system, my consciousness was impenetrable and inaccessible to the truth of GOD's Word, effectually immune and unmoved to the tender grace and love overtures of the Spirit of Truth whom GOD is.

*

Even the Spirit of Truth – WHOM THE WORLD CANNOT RECEIVE – because it seeth him not, neither knoweth him: but ye know him; for he dwelleth with you, and shall be in you.
– JOHN 14:17

*

The spirit and course (and counsel and wisdom) of this world system, crucified Christ. He is the *"prince"* of the power of the air, *"the spirit"* that is still working in (guiding, motivating, driving) the children of disobedience (re. Eph. 2:2). Them allegiant to the spirit (and father) of lies who rules this evil world system cannot receive a Spirit who is Holy and True. The LORD Jesus Christ, in his teaching (or doctrine) draws no distinction and no degree of mitigation or extenuating circumstance – that is, no diminished degree of accountability. Either I am living a life that honors GOD as my Father, or Satan is my father.

And we thought we were just trying to get by. You know, trying to make a living, and party off the radar. Perhaps we had no religious convictions one way or another. Perchance we were (in effect) conscientious objectors.

But (alas) dear children, having gone to such great lengths of labyrinthine internal dialogue to establish and defend that we have made no such choice *"to be in bondage to any man"* (re. John 8:33), the Holy Spirit of the Living Word of GOD convicts us of sin and reveals us as servants. Indeed, what we have considered to be (at its worst) negligence, the Word of GOD adjudicates as a willful reprehensible rejection.

※

The lusts of your father ye shall do.
– RE. JOHN 8:44

※

The LORD Jesus Christ had no reservations and no compunctions about calling out hypocrites and impersonators of piety. He would have no qualms and no hesitancy confronting their contemporary progeny. He who has ears to hear, let him hear.

Children, the choice is one of twain, even as the governor, Pilate, referenced Everyman and Everywoman's inalienable and compulsory preference one dreadful day.

※

Whether of the twain will ye that I release unto you? Barabbas, or Jesus which is called Christ?
– (SEE MATTHEW 27:17, 21).

※

Either I make a resolute conscious choice to live a life of faith by the grace of GOD in Christ Jesus, or I am consenting in his rejection, and a (vicarious, if you must) participant in his crucifixion. I cannot plead an indirect culpability or a diminished capacity. It was as if I were there.

For GOD to give the crowd (or the mob) a choice *"that"* dreadful day, that he will not give me *"this"* portentous day, would make him unrighteous. Heaven forbid. Notwithstanding our convoluted circumvention, doctrinal and dispensational argument, or theological sleight of hand, the choice is still one of twain.

Loathsome the revelation, that for multiple decades, I had been living a life of self-realization and self-indulgence beneath a threadbare religious garment, glutting myself on grace while eschewing truth. Subservient to the religious *"form"* of faith that allowed me to save my natural life for myself – untransformed, (uh, *un-born-again*), and unconverted – with the god of this world system (Satan) effectively as my father.

Abhorrence of the truth and light of GOD's Word and holy character, and evading the exposure of my deeds, compels me to disguise my real self beneath a religious covering – primarily church ceremony and routine and superficial service works. It must be examined. The dynamic which incited me to hypocrisy was (in fact) my hatred of the Truth, the essence and character of the LORD Jesus Christ. Oh my.

Or are we mindless or shallow enough to presume that our contemporary hypocrisy is any less motivated by our hatred of the truth than was these good (or ordinary) church folk depicted in the eighth chapter of John? (In every era) it is the fear and horror of sudden exposure that makes the hypocrite mad.

We are willfully remiss and mindlessly hedonistic to assume that the spiritual dynamic of light and darkness, and the hostility of the Liar for the Truth, has changed over dispensations. GOD would have had to have changed, Satan would have had to have changed, and the Adamic nature of humanity would have had to have changed.

The hypocrite hates the Truth as much today as he ever did. This hatred entered into the comprehensive fellowship of a man with his brother along with original sin. And it did not take it long to manifest its innate murderous nature.

※

As Cain, who was of that wicked one, and slew his brother. And wherefore slew he him? Because his own works were evil, and his brother's righteous. [Marvel not, my brethren, if the world hate you.]
– I JOHN 3:12-13

※

Such a level of hatred (to manifest as murderous) has always been integral to the DNA of the unbeliever (or infidel). Notably, the Apostle John (above) correlates the evil works of Cain as a by-product (if you will) of being allegiant (and enslaved) to this world system – subservient to Satan, the god of this world.

It is very difficult to imagine and acknowledge that this level of murderous hatred for the truth is at work in the world, much less to receive (and/or assimilate) the revelation that the same malevolent dynamic is at work within the Church. However, it is less difficult to concede that there is a worldly element or population within the ranks of our congregations and assemblies.

The Apostle John echoes the LORD Jesus Christ's teaching and admonition not to be surprised (or marvel not) that the world hates us. That is, the obedient and sanctified, Spirit-baptized disciples of Jesus Christ.

Children, we know that the world loves his own. The LORD Jesus Christ says that it is *"because"* he has chosen us out of the world that *"therefore the world hateth you"* (see John 15:18-19).

This teaching in the fifteenth chapter of John exactly parallels our primary text for this specific notebook from John 16:1-3. I am moved to list then consecutively.

※

But all "these things" *will they do unto you for my name's sake,* "because" *they know not him that sent me.*
– JOHN 15:21

And "these things" *will they do unto you,* "because"
they have not known the Father, nor me.
– JOHN 16:3

※

By the Holy Ghost, I attest to the servants (the unconverted) in the House of GOD, drastically outnumbering the genuine sons and daughters of GOD. The world has infiltrated our assemblies and congregations (and we have ushered them in) under the guise of tolerance and the preaching of all-permissive grace. We have coveted attendance numbers and have subsequently and consequently diminished the ranks of the Spirit-filled within the Church of GOD and the Assemblies of GOD.

The preponderance of us have not followed on to know the LORD – neither the Father, nor Christ (or whom I often call *"GOD in his Christ"*). Being *"in"* the Church does not always equate to being *"in"* the catacombs of Christ where the Father and the Son are One LORD by the Holy Ghost.

The majesty and the relevance (or the imperative) of the revelation merits its own redundancy – that Jesus Christ is LORD, Old Testament and New Testament. {Please note both scripture references.}

✳

Hear, O Israel; The LORD our GOD is One LORD.
–SEE DEUTERONOMY 6:4 & MARK 12:29

✳

This is covered in the beginning pages of this manuscript. This reflects a truth that has been largely suppressed. This is neither the Doctrine of the Trinity nor the Oneness Apostolic doctrine. This is the *Doctrine of Christ.*

This is neither three nor one as understood by Trinity and Apostolic Pentecostal Christians. The *Doctrine of Christ* is, in fact, two as One – both the Father and the Son (Jesus Christ) as One LORD by the Holy Ghost.

✳

Whosoever transgresseth, and abideth not in the Doctrine of Christ, *hath not GOD. He that abideth in the* Doctrine of Christ, *he hath both the Father and the Son.*
– 2 JOHN 1:9

✳

Know you not, dear children, that our forefathers and elders (and pastors) suppressed this revelatory knowledge and doctrine – this Truth – so that they might cling to the doctrines of men, to wit, the Trinity and/or the Apostolic doctrines. We shape our religion to fit and accommodate our lifestyle.

As we have also covered, when men will not receive and develop a love for the truth – then for this cause – GOD sends them strong delusion that they should believe a lie (re. 2 Thess. 2:10-12). When we deny the truth to spare our flesh, and to have pleasure in unrighteousness, GOD is justified in allowing us to have what we want.

(It could be accurately said) that we suppress the Truth to spite our soul.

A *"few"* of us hear and apply the Word of GOD to our character and lifestyle; and *"many"* of us hear or allow what accommodates our carnal appetites. We are pitiful slaves to our own lust and pride. Christian, the character and spirit of Cain is within the congregation, doubly treacherous beneath a religious cloak: insecure and unpredictable, potentially violent, ruthless, merciless and murderous. As you can receive the truth of the prophetic parallel.

✳

That which hath been is Now.
– re. Eccl. 3:15

＊

Latent, self-righteous animosity, simmering beneath a thin superficial religious civility, Satan prospers among the assembly. The murderous spirit inciting the Pharisees and Jews to violence in the eighth chapter of John, is present and flourishing among our contemporary congregations. If you think not, you are part of the problem – helping repress the truth of the revelation.

It is not unprecedented that unclean spirits and Satan himself gather together with the solemn assembly – yes, right along with the saints.

＊

*Now, there was a day when the sons of GOD
came to present themselves before the LORD,
and Satan came also among them.*
– Job 1:6

＊

Two things that the Holy Spirit shows me as immediately pertinent are, one, when the LORD asked Satan where he is coming from, he unabashedly says, *"From going to and fro in the earth, and from walking up and down in it"* (re. Job 1:7, 2:2).

As befitting a prince, from one perspective, he brazenly says it twice, asserting that the earth is his domain of scrutiny and influence, with, of course the sovereign limitations placed upon him by GOD.

The second point (which I will call) a *rhetorical question,"* asked of Satan by the LORD, is *"Hast thou considered my servant Job* (re. Job 1:8, 2:3)? Now, we know, of course, that Satan has obviously had Job under an intense surveillance for some time. I mean, how does he (Satan) know that the LORD has placed a hedge of protection about Job, except that he had tried to breech it?

Christian, of utmost significance, is that Satan has (indeed) considered that the LORD has already hedged Job about on every side, blessed the work of his hands, and increased his substance in the land (see Job 1:10).

Child of GOD, when Satan sees you significantly and specifically blessed, he will indeed consider you. Your prosperity exponentially increases Satan's animosity toward GOD, and his hostility toward you, the object of GOD's security, blessing, health, grace, love et.al.

He especially hates the image and likeness of GOD being systematically restored and rejuvenated within you: the renewed hope in your eyes, the love blossoming in your heart, and the Witness of GOD upon your lips. Being a genuine Christian does not exempt you from trial and temptation, from tribulation and persecution – it makes you a preferred target. You are a soldier now. "Every" Christian is an active combatant in the spiritual arena they influence and occupy for the kingdom of GOD.

Let us consider him while he is considering us. Briefly here, but critically and minutely within the details of walking and living by faith and passing through this world.

We must never forget, not even for a moment, that the victory we claim over Satan in Jesus' name is (first) the LORD Jesus Christ's victory, given in the immediate context and accountability of an old rugged cross.

✳

*Now is the judgment of this world: now shall
the prince of this world be cast out.*
– John 12:31

✳

The Christian's victory is wrought and apprehended within the intimacy and fellowship of Jesus' perfections. In the concise and acute accountability of walking and living in the light of nothing hidden, under the Omniscient eye of the *HOLY*, above the mercy seat. I have no claim anywhere but here.

✳

*But if we walk in the light, as he is in the light, we
have fellowship one with another, and the blood of
Jesus Christ his Son cleanseth us from all sin.*
– 1 John 1:7

✳

Pointedly, this is inside the veil of the natural life and affections, delivered from the merciless servitude of lust and pride, sanctified from the love of this world and its commands for allegiance – in reverence and in worship, perfecting holiness and godly fear as we walk with the LORD.

Satan suffered an irreversible loss at Calvary. However, after his defeat, (I believe) his vehemence and unbridled hatred for all that is holy also exponentially increased. It would be a grave tactical error to underestimate his power, his cunning, or his trenchant determination in these latter days.

✳

Be sober, be vigilant; because your adversary the devil, as a roaring lion, walketh about, seeking whom he may devour.
1 PETER 5:8

✳

(I cannot imagine) that the devil might have a discriminating appetite; from one perspective, a soul is a soul. However (I am sure), that the godly, the sanctified, and especially Christians with a fiery, infectious evangelical witness of the saving grace of the LORD Jesus Christ, are his preferred and most regularly pursued diet.

The Apostle Peter, quoted above, perhaps experienced an unprecedented level of testing or sifting among men. Especially when we consider the immediate context of all of the disciples of Jesus Christ being scattered when he was arrested, except Peter, who followed from afar, and who I personally believe was John, who went into the temple court.

The LORD Jesus prophesied of Peter's (especially) personal (and ouch) repetitive denial. There is much to be learned of the LORD's piercing censure and warning directed personally at Peter. But in the very next verse, there is abundant hope and unparalleled revelation of the dynamics of faith and conversion within the ranks of the Christian congregation – for those who have the ears to hear, and the heart and soul of the intrepid to receive.

✸

*Simon, Simon, behold, Satan hath desired to
have you, that he may sift you as wheat.*

*But I have prayed for thee, that thy faith fail not: and
when thou art converted, strengthen thy brethren.*
– Luke 22:31-32

✸

Relatively (I suppose), we could speculate that the higher one's gospel calling in Christ Jesus, then the bigger the threat Satan surmises that man (or woman) of GOD to be. And he will specifically target that man or woman, though his main argument be with the anointing of GOD upon them.

Satan's (real) nemesis is the Holy Spirit of Truth exposing lies and hypocrisy – he hates the *Unction* of GOD and the *Voice* of GOD and the *Word* of GOD and the *Christ* of GOD. His name is Jesus.

Christian, if you bear GOD's anointing – and lo, how magnificent and terrible, moreover, to bear his marks upon your body, and his own suffering fellowship shared.

It ought need no remembrance, and go without saying (as they say), that if you are sustaining an incoming horde out of hell laying siege upon your love and peace and joy, and upon your home and your work and in your ministry, Satan has seen the imprint and image, the likeness and the radiance, and the authority of the Father being bequeathed to another son or daughter of GOD. The enemy has just understood that King Jesus is in your camp.

(Moreover, moreover) Christian, as a fully endowed representative of the kingdom affairs of GOD – dear child, everything you think you have belongs to GOD – like Job, like Peter, like James and John, spent upon the LORD's grace and love for the world.

Someone has to break it down for us (in certain seasons). That GOD ain't got no hybrid Christians – one foot in the world, and one foot upon an empty altar – waiting to see which way the wind is going to blow. You know, kind of checking up with Jesus on his way in, lingering – and malingering, for that last hit.

Someone must make it plain. All of GOD's sons and daughters are soldiers – and they are soldiers because their life is given them for a prey. We are all collateral damage within the runaway love of GOD for our neighbor's soul.

＊

GOD has special forces, (and as the Holy Spirit
of the LORD speaks), extremists and fire-starters
among the assembly. I AM the LORD.

＊

Because we have no fire, we cannot hear the siren song of a consuming fire – GOD's fire. Our souls are not knit like that. We are estranged one from another. Hear the Word of the LORD, Christian, the birth-pangs of the children of God has broken.

＊

But he that shall endure unto the end, the same shall be saved.
– MATTHEW 24:13

✳

Only the sanctified shall be saved in an evil day. Children, the betrayal (prophetically) is closer than we have thought; the hand of him that hates me is upon the table with mine own. The unadulterated unabbreviated hatred which drives hypocrisy to virulence and murder will define itself – unashamed to own its evil. As in the days of Jesus, and Barabbas, and Pilate.

Someone must tell us . . . that *"this beginning of sorrows"* is but the tip of GOD's wrath. The nations shall not even know . . . what they are angry about. As we watch an irrepressible tide come in, from the east and from the west – and all in One day. And my enemy shall know that I AM GOD, saith the LORD.

Ill will and ingratitude corrupt the Gift of my Grace, saith the LORD. And shall I not order my servants, edit and inventory my stewards, and bequeath my throne to my rightful heirs? Verily, and so I shall – and the nations intuit the majesty and the terror, and the significance of the transaction – and an everlasting overwhelming sudden destruction. I AM the LORD, and these are your wages.

Ire and malevolence manifest upon the skin, in the bones, and laid heavy upon thought and consciousness. This is the hidden way of leaven to corrupt, working, and who shall withstand it. Not the whole world, I tell you: I AM the LORD – and this copious weeping, the mere beginning of your wages I allow.

This is the shifting of foundations, the threshing of my floor in the night terrors and sifting of saints. I, even I, shake the House of Jacob, pacing over the determinations of my people with integrity and righteousness, afraid of my own wrath.

In the silent sorrows of your soul, and in the recesses of your inarticulate hurts; I shake the House as I close the Door. Run into me, and be safe, child.

※

I am pressed under the nations of the world like a hired, no-name ass; my people have plundered me. Indeed. These things must come to pass.

The kingdoms of the earth shall war, at stake, (every man) upon the earth, none escape the hatred and murder of an unregenerate soul. Even now, I am removing a veil.

※

Then shall they deliver you up to be afflicted, and shall kill you: and ye shall be hated of all nations for my name's sake.

And then shall many be offended, and shall betray one another, and shall hate one another.
– MATTHEW 24:9-10

※

Relatively, these church-folk above, the same persons who are going to be delivering up one another and betraying one another here in the twenty-fourth chapter of Matthew, suspiciously and synonymously (uh, and remarkably) sound a lot like those religious folk in John 16:2 that put their brothers out of the synagogues. Are we really truly surprised that church-folk (both the righteous congregation and the solemn assembly), can hate that virulently and that completely? Indeed. That blindly and that ruthlessly, mercilessly.

Angry and disillusioned, disenfranchised from myself, partly unfulfilled because I am not who I ought to be, incendiary and disquieted because of who I am. O dear children, within too many of us, *"hate"* is systematically becoming perfected (our no-fault setting), and our hypocrisy fine-tuned.

The nations are biding their time in wars and rumors of wars, busy about famine and pestilences and earthquakes (and the like), in divers places. Indiscriminate, mindless hatred and blind bigotry are even now breaking forth. We are relatively the same runaway religious travesty that coerced the Romans into crucifying the LORD Jesus Christ. Relatively the same murderous progeny of the devil.

So we could save the best of ourselves – for ourselves – we, as a species, rejected the Holy One of GOD in lieu of superficial considerations. Comprehensively, we are that One perpetual gap-toothed dumbfounded generation ever trying to wrest the Truth of GOD into a lie, (so that with good conscience) we can continue to worship and serve the creature more than the Creator – who is Blessed for even. Amen. (see Romans 1:25).

For just a moment, I want to project myself among them – to better understand them. They are (or will be) after all, that self-righteous acrid cloud revealed as hypocrisy – who will one day soon, rise up to cast the anointing of GOD out of the synagogues.

How coarse, how base their hatred. Theirs is the hatred of insanity and evil, strong delusion wafting among them, passing through the rifts in their self-righteous garments. How well (and how holy) they hate.

Sudden exposure for the hypocrite – that thing he feared most would come upon him – is here. This will be the implosion of the Church from a prophetic and realistic perspective. This merits review.

How readest thou, saint? Or you, Pastor? What of this upheaval in the Church prophesied by the Voice of GOD within the confines of the Upper Room (notably John 16:1-3)? This is Jesus speaking here. And his Words have taken me in.

In contemporary vernacular – I mean, who could have imagined that a bunch of ostensibly saved and sanctified and Holy Ghost filled Church-folk, would lay hands on other saved and sanctified and Spirit-filled church-folk, not only casting them out of the synagogue, but killing them, and counting it as doing GOD service?

Who could have imagined our enemy's hatred so starkly revealed, and so close to home and family? Prospering, each of us, in our own negligence toward our neighbor. Such mindless self-serving anonymity. You know, don't look too closely.

Children, if GOD removed that unseen hedge of protection upon the house, it shall not stand. And (GOD forbid) if he releases us unto Satan to be sifted for a sustained and especially arid season, we know that our faith is going to take a hit – but the LORD has spoken it.

✳

*But I have prayed for thee, that thy faith fail not: and
when thou art converted, strengthen thy brethren.*
– LUKE 22:32

＊

We did not believe that the sifting would rise up from the sanctuary floor – if I may put it like that. Well? We still do not believe it.

We thought it (meaning hell) might well rise up out of the midst of that denomination down the road, but we did not expect that he (and she) would be sitting together with us in the pew. Why, if we had any faith, we would know that Jesus is speaking to us here and speaking to us now.

＊

*And these things will they do unto you, "because"
they have not known the Father, nor me.*
–JOHN 16:3

＊

Frankly, to get to where the Father dwells in the recesses and hidden places of the wisdom of GOD in Christ, I am pummeled and disoriented, afflicted in the strait gate and narrow way which leads unto life.

As I delve like a miner for gold, and abide steadfastly in the Word of GOD, the teaching (doctrine) of Christ is systematically transforming me into a disciple of the LORD Jesus Christ. This process (and this *state*) of being miraculously changed to reflect the character and virtues of Christ is called *"conversion."*

Saints, without this radical (bone-deep) character conversion, I am relatively as the same genre of religious folk observing ritual (and worshipping the ceremony), having a form of faith but no fire, no forward momentum, no kingdom fruit. Without this conversion, we fundamentally function with our natural man, and with our own understanding.

(Bluntly) in such a state, I am unregenerate and deeply impenitent, capable of great feats of hatred. Are you hearing the Word of GOD, child?

*

Marvel not that I said unto thee, ye must be born again.
– JOHN 3:7

*

Before the Apostle Peter was converted, the LORD Jesus asserted that he did indeed have a *"little faith,"* but that he could still stand some sifting, and some comprehensive conversion. The sifting by Satan removed from Peter that which could be shaken, and it was the spark or impetus of his conversion. One, he needed to be pruned, or cut-back. He who has ears to hear, let them hear.

Children, this sifting is in the arsenal of Almighty GOD, and a purifying transforming consuming fire. The LORD Jesus Christ is preparing to place (and to set) the anointing within the Church of GOD (along with the Assemblies of GOD), to place his divine unction upon his Word – to say and to do – as one and the same. The schism is of light and darkness (and sadly) of love and hate – the animosity and rage of the renegade directed at the true heir of GOD, the servant's clandestine hatred for the son. Unto whosoever has the ears to hear, let them hear.

The very same persons who once pledged their brotherly and sisterly love for me, will be revealed as anti-Christ. We might just as well get it out there – just as it is going to occur – suddenly and fearfully.

The strains on society and government as order deteriorates during the end times will also be felt within the Church. Because the world is in the Church, and the Church is in the world. It must be confronted just like that. By the Holy Spirit, I see a remnant fleeing the rising disunity and disorder within the Church, to gather in smaller numbers – in homes, basements, garages, attics.

What frightens the world reveals the faith of GOD's people. Or not. I am either troubled with the denizens of this world because this world is my home and my source, or I have been progressively sanctified (or separated) from the world unto GOD, as commanded.

There are no *conscientious objectors* in the kingdom of GOD. I am aligned with GOD's purposes and converted to his character; or I am a hater of truth and light and all that is holy.

Christian, we must remember, that it is the world within the Church that (actually) hates the LORD Jesus Christ. The god of this world system (Satan) colluded with the Jews and coerced the Romans into crucifying Jesus Christ. They were (without question) the ruling majority which cried *"Crucify him!"* that dreadful day. Moreover, they comprised the overwhelming majority that repeatedly took up stones, threatening Jesus, and repetitively drove him out of the temple – as recorded in the gospel.

The god of this world system, the prince of the power of the air, has not changed. It would be naïve to presume that he has not infiltrated our contemporary houses of worship, systematically suppressing the image and likeness (and virtues) of Jesus Christ among our members, and methodically diminishing our liberty and authority to speak and rule in his name.

The LORD Jesus Christ frankly assessed this world system as an opposition to be summarily overcome, and he viewed its hatred of him (and his disciples) as a necessary or natural part of the process. To be vanquished. Still, let there be no misunderstanding, the hatred is not theoretical or ideological, but very, very real.

✳

If the world hate you, ye know that it
hated me before it hated you.

If ye were of the world, the world would love his own:
but because ye are not of the world, but I have chosen
you out of the world, therefore the world hateth you.
– JOHN 15:18-19

✳

The Word of GOD is prophetic – immediate and eternal, and perpetually applicable – alive. Them in love with this world system, and enslaved by its goods and services (and its amusements and entertainments), will instinctively hate them who are not. Moreover, the innate hatred of unrighteousness for righteousness is difficult to conceal. We have covered this, but them who will not come to the light will be exposed as actually hating the light and loving the darkness (see John 3:19-21).

If I have worldly constituents who favor and honor (and love) me, there is an incongruity or disparity to my Christian testimony. [If I have one.]

I primarily speak from a spiritual perspective, but that will commonly overlap into social, political, or economic arenas. Frankly, my affiliation with Christ Jesus – and the likeness of my character to reflect his virtues – ought to be undeniable. The world should know to whom I belong.

Not to be deliberately coarse or uncivilized, but let's stop kissing the world's ass to keep the sordid goods and services flowing. Satan uses our fraternization with the world to surreptitiously acquire a controlling interest in our soul.

Briefly, we are (in reality) spiritual beings in a physical body. How we spend our life (or our time) is the offering up of spiritual sacrifices – or, in other words, worship. I will cite only the literal hours the average American sits in front of a television or computer screen (or smart phone) enthralled and anesthetized.

How we spend our time has covenant implications. You have heard me say, We cannot evict the devil whose rent is paid. Whom we allowed entrance, whom we accommodated, aided and abetted while he was purloining the jurisdiction of our soul.

Christian, this world does not love you. If you are a genuine Christian, then this world hates you *"because"* the LORD Jesus Christ has chosen you out of the world to represent his kingdom interests. The devil hates you for the authority you have to cast him out. He hates you because you have the authority to speak healing and liberty into the lives of those he has suppressed and controlled.

The LORD Jesus Christ cautions his immediate disciples (and his prophetic disciples) by his timeless, Living Word. As we have ears to hear, and the faith to make it manifest, every Word spoken to the LORD's inner-circle (specifically Peter, James, and John), can also be ours. If we want it.

Admonitions and portends are promises too. Children, it is all part and parcel of the gospel of Jesus Christ and him crucified. It is all integral and inherent to his cross – that it is also our cross.

✳

> *Remember the Word that I said unto you, The servant is not greater than his LORD. If they have persecuted me, they will also persecute you; if they have kept my saying, they will keep yours also.*
> – JOHN 15:20

✳

We have not esteemed the suffering fellowship or the commands of conformity to the death of Jesus' cross. This only is the way to *"know"* him, and the power of his resurrection (see Phil. 3:10).

In the scripture above (John 15:20), the LORD Jesus is effectively telling us that we must go the same way he goes. The servant partakes of the LORD's portion – the same cup, the same table, the same cross. Ah, but then – the same Baptism.

In this dispensation of grace, we indulge ourselves – as if the cross was not eternal, perpetual. As if I did not have to press myself into the light at times. As if there were not giants in the promised land.

Here, if they have driven the LORD out of the temple with their virulent hatred (John 8:59), they will suffer no compunction casting the servant from the synagogue.

The latent hatred of hypocrisy cannot but manifest when confronted with the truth. The sudden exposure makes the hypocrite mad, in every sense of the word.

✳

If I had not come and spoken unto them, they had not had sin: but now they have no cloke for their sin.
– John 15:22

✳

The truth and light of holiness, of perfection, are unsparing of sin. The mere reflection of the virtues and character of the *Perfect One* – even cloudy, as it were, in his servants – is enough to incite and sustain an uproar from hell to suppress your testimony. Have you not known it to be so, child, that the Christ within you convicts of sin – that some must either clandestinely circumvent the light and truth of Christ Jesus in your presence, or find a way (often meaning manufacture a way) to have you abruptly removed from theirs.

If the Holy Spirit does not convict of sin, beginning with me, it is because he is not abiding with me. Christian, you and I are the temple of GOD in the earth, ideally filled and overflowing all the time, inundating our neighborhood (and our workplace) with the love of GOD, for the kingdom of GOD.

Though few will admit it, the presence of the *Holy One* in you reminds them that they are abject, bankrupted sinners in desperate need of grace. Their abhorrence of the Word of GOD confirms it. If you frequently use scripture quotations in your conversation (or testimony) with others, then you know this is so by some very clever evasion of your presence.

Children, it is (relatively) the same reason some folks do not go to church. They may like the music and the fellowship, but the Word of GOD – preached with veracity and power – shows them the reality of an unregenerate mind and un-converted soul. Shows them their sin.

Duh. The light and truth of the Holy Spirit of GOD reaches into that (the mysteries and wisdom and power of GOD in Christ) behind the veil, where (as they say), angels fear to tread. Such are the strictures of holiness and the abundance of grace in the balances of GOD.

The word "*cloke*" that Jesus uses in John 15:22 means that they are without excuse. Except the *"cloak"* they wore is representative of a self-righteous mien or aspect that (purportedly) hid their unregenerate character beneath or within a religious garment.

The light and truth of the Living Word of GOD pervades religious presentation, and reaches not only into our myriad excuses for repetitive sin, but also reaches beneath the cloak of our religious persona to the real sinner beneath.

Jesus gives emphasis to the Word he has *"spoken"* unto them as being the catalyst of their awareness of sin. It is a discerner of the thoughts and intents of the heart (see Hebrews 4:12).

Let us not take it personally. In fact, the LORD counsels us to *"not be offended"* (re. John 16:1), that the world hates you, Christian, primarily because GOD has *"chosen"* you out of this world (re. John 15:19).

Dear reader, to assist us in the apprehension and application of the next gospel truth, I beseech the LORD Jesus Christ for greater grace, as I like to call it.

We have looked at the following scriptures briefly, and as we consider the following Word of GOD, I am moved to list them concurrently.

※

But all these things will they do unto you for my name's sake, BECAUSE *they know not him that sent me.* – John 15:21

And these things will they do unto you, BECAUSE
they have not known the Father, nor me.
– John 16:3

※

Much of this has been covered. My redundancy is in response to the LORD Jesus Christ reminding me that the majority of professing (regular Church attending) contemporary Christians are woefully unprepared for his return. And it is soon. In my spirit man, I see and I know, that the LORD Jesus Christ is even now behind the door, pacing.

We have thought the criteria for salvation (if I may express it like that), is a fleeting superficial familiarity with the LORD Jesus Christ. We have predominantly and presumptuously decided that "believing" in the LORD Jesus Christ is sufficient to be saved, without going anywhere, without continuing in the Word of GOD, without works, without love, and without a profound character conversion.

Now, I do believe the vast majority of us did make the LORD's acquaintance some years ago, or at least the preacher tried to introduce us to him. In fact, a few of us may well have been on our way to a reciprocal fellowship, when the cares, the lusts, and pleasures of this life took us off the rails. Our Christianity fell through the cracks of a life consumed with other things.

Someone (obviously misinformed and enervated as ourselves) told us to just relax. You know, something along the lines of "just keep believing." The problem with this, is that you can believe without having to go anywhere. On one hand this is what makes it so attractive: All the Grace and none of the work.

Believing on Jesus is a good beginning, but it is in *following* the LORD Jesus Christ that I get to know him, spending quality time with him, conversing with him, laboring side by side with him in prayers and intercessions for saints and sinners alike. For decades, I believed in Jesus, and every morning (metaphorically), I placed him among the paraphernalia of my life. You know, in the junk drawer, or on the backburner.

These prophetic scriptures referenced above (John 15:21 & 16:3), allude to what I will call *"professing"* Christians hating *"genuine"* Christians, casting them out of the synagogue (temple, church); and even killing them.

These persons no doubt consider themselves GOD's chosen and ordinary, loving church-folk. Hear me. They believe they are hating on the devil and that it is fundamentally him they are ousting from the sanctuary – but what they are hating is the truth and light of GOD's holy Word and his anointing upon his messengers. This is strong delusion.

You have (most likely) attended church with some of them. There may be one or two (or several) ensconced along with you in the pew, stealthily suppressing your worship – in the spirit refuting your testimony, tempering your joy, upsetting your peace. If you are not persuaded of their rapacious lethal presence, perforce you are one of them.

The anointing of Christ, the unction and knowledge of the Holy One upon the messengers of GOD, immediately intuits the presence of antichrist. It is Christ within you who discerns them who hate and refute the truth of GOD.

✳

But I know you, that ye have not the love of GOD in you.
– JOHN 5:42

✳

Markedly, phenomenally from a finite perspective [but just another revelatory moment of truth for the Word of GOD], Jesus is addressing (ostensibly) "quote-unquote" normal church-folk.

This encounter merits review by its relevance paralleled in our primary text. We are talking (not only) about regular church-folk, but them that consider themselves religion's best.

Concisely, the Pharisees (and the Jews in a broader application), were convinced of their own elitism and the inerrancy of their doctrine. Ahem. Much like the specific denomination to which you or I may be a member. Hear me. Although their zeal eclipses our own religious fervor and exposes us as luke-warm by comparison, we are just as persuaded of our own pedigree and entitlement. We are resting upon the labors of our forefathers.

You know precisely how we do it – how we spin it and dress it up. But when all is said and done, and all the ostentatious religious affect laid bare, you know that we know over here, that all those denominations over there are going to hell for believing what they do.

Predominantly, (it seems, or I suppose) that we consider ourselves (if we even think about it) as the only enlightened gospel enclave on the market, and everyone else in grave (and mortal) doctrinal error.

By the Holy Ghost, I attest to these Jews and Pharisees in the fifth chapter of John as being neither fundamentally nor comprehensively different than our own preeminent religious factions today. Instead of Christ, we teach doctrine, denominational strictures, church tenets and table manners et.al. But those of us who care are just as opinionated, superior and arrogant, and just as defensive as the Pharisees.

There is to be no questioning of our elitist position in GOD's hierarchy. Opposition is summarily quelled, and troublemakers ousted. Disputing the inerrancy of our denominational church tenets is an unforgivable sin.

Please, do not read me wrong. Religious zeal, with wisdom and temperance, is admirable (and needed). We must tread circumspectly. For now, I will summarize the subject by saying, fanaticism is a strange fire. We must beware of legalism and religious pride.

Returning to our present text, these Jews and Pharisees in the fifth chapter of John are persecuting Jesus because he had not only healed a man on the Sabbath, but praise GOD! he had made him whole. Since it is so difficult to believe that these Jews sought to kill Jesus for healing a man (so surreal, so absurd), we must let the Word of GOD speak for GOD.

※

And therefore did the Jews persecute Jesus, and sought to slay him, because he had done these things on the sabbath day.
– John 5:16

※

The Word of GOD is inerrant and absolute, indelible and eternal, a living infinite mysterious entity. His name is Jesus. Christian, only GOD can forgive my sin and heal me from its residual evil, or in other words, make me whole.

This healing violated religious protocol and offended them that sat in Moses' seat: the interpreters, custodians, and administrators of the law. The LORD Jesus Christ neither asked the temple rulers for permission to administer healing to this anonymous fellow, nor did he give them a *heads-up* (as it were) that he was going to do so. Indeed. One greater than the temple is here.

He did not present before the deacon board or the righteous assembly to petition their blessing or wait upon a vote. He asked for no authority because he has all authority.

Set religious programs and ritualistic tradition do not suffer being interrupted with grace. Those who consider themselves the preeminent religious royalty of their specific dispensation will not tolerate being outshined, outperformed, or upstaged.

Frankly, there is no anger (or madness) quite like legalism defied, or like the religious aristocracy offended. Everyone from the choir director to the janitor and the parking lot attendant shall feel the tremors and shaking of the righteous indignation emanating from Moses' seat. Someone is going to be arrested (or stoned). Indeed. Someone is going to be cast out of the synagogue . . . well, and even executed if it appears to do GOD service. For violating the sanctity of the temple and the religious propriety (and piety) of the righteous assembly.

Being convinced it cannot happen in our singular civilized dispensation shall contribute to our not being prepared when it occurs. Until looking down, dumbfounded and faithless, we see the stones (or the pistols and knives) spontaneously appear in the hands of the pious.

By the Holy Ghost, I attest that the legalism and tradition and religious intolerance in our day is just as incendiary and lethal as in the era of the LORD Jesus Christ's ministry on earth, and as potentially violent and murderous as in the generation of the martyr Stephen.

Being full of the Holy Ghost brought the full attention of hell into the immediate circumstances of Stephen's ministry in the name of the LORD Jesus Christ. His presence was seasoned with salt, and his testimony was on fire for the glory of GOD, and for the honor of the LORD Jesus Christ. These things are pertinent to our primary text, and though we should know them well, they still merit a short review or aside.

✻

And Stephen, full of faith and power, did great
wonders and miracles among the people.
– see Acts 6:8

✻

The early Church was prospering, and suffering persecution at the same time. Multitudes of men and women were being added to their number daily and were transitioning into ardent disciples. The status quo of (what I will call) the ruling religious hierarchy was disquieted, upset, (mortally) threatened. The early Church's most virulent opposition arose from within the temple, spawned from the ranks of religious self-interests and the preservation of the status quo. Men's positions (and livelihood) were threatened.

✻

Then there arose certain of the synagogue, which is called the
synagogue of the Libertines, and Cyrenians, and Alexandrians,
and of them of Cilicia and of Asia, disputing with Stephen.
– Acts 6:9

✻

Jerusalem had one temple, the place of sacrifice, but many synagogues. The synagogue was school, meeting place, court-room, and place of prayer. (*Ray Vander Laan*)

In some towns, the synagogue may even have provided lodging for travelers. It began as the center of Jewish social life, and acted as the community center in the first century. Notwithstanding all these things, the synagogue was first a place of prayer and worship.

It must be (or can be) assumed that many of these persons present were regular attendees to this particular synagogue, and regular visitors to the temple in general. Dearest reader, I submit that this spirit of hostility was ignited by the anointing of GOD upon Stephen. The murderous rage of Satan rose up to defy the giver of life and breath.

There was an unseen warfare seething in the synagogue that dreadful day. Just beneath the surface of civility, Satan and his minions were desperately conspiring to stop the voice of truth in the sanctuary. When practitioners of religion and seekers of GOD mingle in the synagogue – the former to seek the honor one of another, and the latter to present themselves before the LORD, Satan comes also among them (re. Job 1:6).

The spirit of religious elitism was already present in the synagogue that day when they met for worship, and it is present today when we meet for worship.

(In an aside) I know that if you are a preacher, you do not want to hear that about your (Spirit-filled and Spirit baptized, GOD-loving, sanctified) parishioners. That does not move me as such, nor diminish the weight of the mantle upon me to cry aloud, and spare not. Someone must say it. Some of the

Holy Brethren and Sisters of Sanctity are full of the devil – full of hate, full of murder.

This message is because the remnant of GOD is among you, casting off your religious spirit and worldly critique, rising victorious above your oppression and repression, to proclaim the truth of GOD, standing down your religious illusion and ineffectual form of faith – calling out hypocrites and pretenders and worldly prostitutes.

For now, these spiritual things, specifically this warfare, is predominantly latent – hidden, festering. To think not is to be in a precarious, inimical denial and pronounced state of unbelief. The devil is already here, among us as we sing and smile and spread dubious religious smarm.

The demons (religious and otherwise), ensconced within the synagogue that day recognized in Stephen a man full of the faith and power of the Holy Spirit of GOD – like John the Baptist, like Peter, James and John, and like Jesus of Nazareth.

Christian, it was spiritual wickedness in high religious places that conspired and colluded with Satan to have John the Baptist imprisoned and beheaded. Peter and John were beaten and arrested in the chapter of Acts preceding the one that we have been considering. James was beheaded. And, of course, it was ultimately religious men who crucified Christ.

*

Then there arose certain of the synagogue
. . . disputing with Stephen.
(SEE ACTS 6:9)

*

It is not recorded specifically what the dispute was about. But (I believe) we can safely assume that Stephen was bold in his indictment of the Jews for coercing and persuading the Romans into crucifying Christ. We have his lengthy and scathing sermon recorded in chapter seven. Succinctly, Stephen preached that Christ came out of Israel (out of the seed of Abraham, Isaac, and Jacob) and that the Jews had crucified him.

They may have been arguing that Christ could not have come out of Nazareth. Perhaps they were denying all culpability or consent to his crucifixion. Notwithstanding, they became incensed, inescapably convicted of their own conscience.

(I suggest) that these things are what the dispute was about in Chapter six. (And, it can be said, or paralleled) that certain parishioners (or regular Church members) arose out of the synagogue and were disputing these things with Stephen. They were at a distinct disadvantage, however, for the Holy Ghost was speaking mightily through his servant and emissary, Stephen.

＊

And they were not able to resist the wisdom
and the spirit by which he spake.
– ACTS 6:10

＊

Verbal argument failed the antagonists. The Holy Ghost was resting mightily upon Stephen. Worldly wisdom, even aided and abetted and amalgamated with general Christian principals, is no match for the unadulterated Truth of GOD's Holy

Spirit. As mentioned in each manuscript that the LORD has me pen, the LORD Jesus Christ calls the Comforter and/or the Holy Ghost the *"Spirit of Truth"* three distinct times. (see John 14:17, 15:26, & 16:13).

It is a lying spirit, and the work of the devil, which refutes and denies the Truth of GOD. *Truth* is the essence and the spiritual DNA (if I may express it as such), of GOD's fundamental being.

Much like GOD is Love and GOD is Light and GOD is Holy – GOD is Truth.

The wisest of men are fools, the quickly dissipating vapor of a rancid, corrupt hand breath before a Holy GOD. There is a wisdom that is earthly, sensual, devilish – an envious, striving spirit of contention like unto witchcraft and divination.

✳

But the wisdom that is from above is first pure.
(SEE JAMES 3:14-17)

✳

As men losing their argument sometimes do, these men opposing Stephen became desperate, and resorted to suborning men and setting them up as false witnesses against him. They physically laid hands upon him to restrain him, taking him before the council, or the Sanhedrin, the Jewish ruling council (re Acts 6:11-13).

Christian, when the end times befall you and me, or the remnant who is alive and remain at the prophetic juncture in time, and the manifestation of John 16:1-3, we do not (yet) know what council we shall be brought before. But it behooves us to be mentally and spiritually prepared. The prophetic portend of these scriptures must be assimilated by faith, before they occur.

Our predicament shall prophetically parallel what befell Stephen and the prophets, and the Apostles and the LORD Jesus Christ.

✳

Then shall they deliver you up to be afflicted, and shall kill you: and ye shall be hated of all nations for my name's sake. And then shall many be offended, and shall betray one another, and shall hate one anther
– MATT. 24:9-10

✳

It takes faith to receive and assimilate the dreadful, just as it takes faith to believe the miraculous and the wonderful. Many of us, who do not believe ourselves capable of such treachery, shall lead the charge. Then shall the *few* of us, whose lives are given for a prey, begin to understand the conditions of our discipleship.

Chaos and mistrust shall rule in the midst of the solemn assembly. The (self) righteous cloak of many shall wax insufficient – thin, odious, repugnant.

The nakedness, the reality of our religious charade is unceremoniously revealed – gangrenous, gluttonous, insatiable flesh.

Sin is a merciless master.

[Note: *obstructed circulation of the blood leads to necrosis or the death of soft tissue, followed by decomposition and putrefaction.* (per Google].

Lawlessness and chaos (before and after) the great tribulation will have to infiltrate the Church, to provoke Christians to hate and betray, and to kill other Christians.

Several pages ago, I wrote that the *"strong delusion"* that GOD is going to send upon those who will not receive a love for the Truth, is already present and at work in the Church. Moreover, I also propose and concur with the Apostle Paul, that these worldly elements have infiltrated the Church. They, also, are here and now. *"The mystery of iniquity doth already work"* (2 Thess. 2:7).

The stage is being set, circumstances conspire to prepare the way for the Deceiver *(that man of sin),* (whoever he may be) to establish himself within the Church of GOD representing himself as GOD. I believe he is already alive and involved in the development of new technology. He monitors the socio-economic heartbeat of America, waiting upon his time. Metaphorically, he is stepping up even now. He who has ears to hear, let him hear.

Friend, you may not believe this, but not everyone in the pew believes and receives the truth of GOD's Word, and then goes on to develop a deep love for the truth.

The *many* and the *few* is GOD's ratio (re. Matt. 7:13-14). I was one of the many. I sometimes refer to myself when in that state as being *volitionally deluded.* That is correct, I was delighted with the deception (the lie) that allowed me to save (and spend) my life for myself with a minimally disturbed conscience.

It is imperative that we *get* these things that GOD has graciously allowed us glimpses (by what I call) *Greater Grace.* The dynamic that will incite Christians to hate and kill is simmering just beneath a threadbare *surface civility* and a superficial Christianity. The following admonition is so dreadful that it must be listed.

＊

*And with all deceivableness of unrighteousness in
them that perish; BECAUSE they received not a
love for the truth, that they might be saved.*

*And FOR THIS CAUSE GOD shall send them
strong delusion, that they should believe a lie.*

*That they all might be damned who believed not the Truth
(The LORD Jesus Christ) but had pleasure in unrighteousness.*
– 2 Thess. 2:10-12

＊

It will become a matter of survival for them living a narcissistic, idolatrous lifestyle, a desperate matter of the preservation and security of the status quo. When our pleasures and lusts are threatened; and when we believe that exposure and censure is at hand, we panic – and we can become quite mean.

Will we become as vicious as the hypocrites here in Stephen's time?

Why would we not? These were educated, civilized, (uh, religious) persons.

These things must be. The LORD of Glory ordered them. Of a necessity, these things must come to pass. For the LORD of heaven and of earth ordered them out of the good pleasure of his grace.

＊

*Suppose ye that I come to give peace on
earth? I tell you, Nay; but rather division.*

*For from henceforth there shall be five in one house
divided, three against two, and two against three.*

And a man's foes shall be they of his own household.
–Luke 12:551-51

＊

We bring this division into the Church, and then feign as if our fellowship was genuine and the congregation in a blissful state of perfect unity.

This division in the home shall parallel the disparity and disunity in the Church. Hear me. It is Truth that sanctifies (*see John 17:17*). A progressive love affair with the Truth (the LORD Jesus Christ) will distance me from the world- from those who have pleasure in unrighteousness.

It is Truth that separates (severs) the genuine Christian from the hypocrite. Hear me. The hypocrite does not just dislike the truth, he hates the truth – and this hatred is spawned by a murderous spirit. Satan is a liar and a thief, but his passion is murder.

When we reject the truth we are refuting GOD as Creator and Jesus Christ as LORD; we deny his sovereign right to rule over us, rejecting his character and essence, and his very *"person,"* to use a finite word.

GOD is justified in allowing darkness to propagate where light should dwell. When we prefer a liar to GOD's only begotten Son (the Truth), the rejection is a willful, most odious defamation that validates the existence of a terrible place called hell.

Moreover, it is as if, when we initially prefer a lie to the truth, that *"for this cause"* GOD sends us an even stronger delusion and allows us even more outrageous lies. It is reasonable to assume that when the deception gets stronger, then our hatred for the light and the truth also exacerbates.

When lawlessness increases within society, (I believe) the animosity of the infidel toward the believer will increase exponentially – both in the home and in the Church. The helplessness and the fear, the despair of the unbeliever will manifest as hostility toward the believer. Religious intolerance and the hate index (as it were) will be off the charts. Home and (the formal) Church will disintegrate along with the chaos and discord within society.

Christian, it is the LORD Jesus Christ who prophesied division in the home, and that, specifically, a man's foes shall be they of his own household (re. Mt. 10:36).

What may have started out as a difference of opinion will escalate until I consider those who disagree with me as my *"foes"* [n. a person who feels enmity, hatred, or malice toward another; enemy: a bitter foe.]

I find myself wondering, what will be the general temperament of humanity going through such great tribulation. It is difficult to visualize the state of the people's house as divided *"three against two"* and *"two against three"* (*re. Luke 12:52*), but, again, this is prophecy directly from the Living Word of GOD (the LORD Jesus Christ).

This is the closest you can get to division, unless you are the man and his wife. By this time, dissension will have flooded the nucleus of the family and pressed its way into relationships.

Civility will first evolve as a formality and then as terse communication – in some cases, the giving and taking of orders or commands. Emotional and mental stressors shall be on overload. Families will have lost one or more necessary components – there is no other way to interpret this prophecy.

(Excuse me), but I can envisage clinging to the acute edges of propriety and civility. The desertion of family members, and the disintegration of the family unit, shall shake the foundations of society. Untoward, adverse circumstances and dangerous situations will abound. Some families will camp on the sharp edge of violence and anarchy.

Society's consciousness and cohesiveness shall take a hit from multiple, adverse arenas. We are accustomed (perhaps) to our mind and energy being invested in our families. But, dear Christian, this tribulation is called *"Great."*

✴

For then shall be great tribulation, such as was not since the beginning of the world to this time, no, nor ever shall be.
– MATT. 24:21

✴

105

Alas, such is the general unbelief and apostasy of society (even now), that the preponderance of us do not believe the specific prophesies of the LORD Jesus Christ.

Them that will not believe One Word of GOD obviously do not live by *every* Word that proceeds from the mouth of GOD, do not value the Truth, deny the Reality of GOD, and cannot receive the Spirit of Truth that they might be saved.

✳

Even the Spirit of Truth; WHOM THE WORLD CANNOT RECEIVE, *because it seeth him not, neither knoweth him: but ye know him; for he dwelleth with you, and shall be in you.*
– JOHN 14:17

✳

As we discussed earlier, them who reject the truth are sent a strong delusion to take its place (see 2 Thess. 2:10-12). It is the same fundamental principal. Notably, of all the wonderful names that Jesus could have given the Spirit of GOD – hope, love, joy, et.al., GOD's Spirit is naturally called the *Spirit of Truth.* It is the LORD Jesus Christ who calls the Holy Spirit the Spirit of Truth three distinct times (please see John 14:17, 15:26, & 16:13).

The spirit of this world, the lust and love of this world, and the pride of life, are the nemesis of a Spirit who is a Holy Spirit of Light and Truth and Love. I do not see him or seek to know him (in my unregenerate state). I already have a lover who possesses each conscious thought and all my affections. I am driven and enslaved by my own lust and pride.

✳

Jesus answered them, Verily, verily, I say unto you, Whosoever committeth sin is the servant of sin (Lit. *slave*).
– JOHN 8:34

＊

A *"Holy"* Spirit will not cohabitate with an *"unholy" spirit.*

The flesh and the Spirit of GOD are antagonists one against another. Children, we are born into a fallen state – of which no man or spirit can free us but the Holy Spirit of Truth. This Holy Spirit, he is whom GOD is.

＊

Hear, O Israel (and Christianity); *the LORD our GOD is One LORD.*
– MARK 12:29

＊

How can we esteem the value of this Word, spoken once in Deuteronomy 6:4 by Moses, and spoken by the LORD Jesus Christ in the gospel according to Mark. Jesus is ostensibly quoting Moses here, but I present to you that the man Moses was quoting GOD generally, and quoting the LORD Jesus Christ specifically. I am trying to say that it was the Living Word of GOD (Jesus Christ) who spoke this Word both times.

Moreover, I propose that the LORD Jesus Christ said, *"Let there be Light"* in Genesis 1:3. You say, "That would make him GOD." And I say, "Precisely." You say, "That would mean that he is also *"Father GOD."* And I say, "The Father dwells within the intimacies of Christ." By the Holy Spirit, the Father and the Son are One LORD. And the Word of GOD (the LORD Jesus Christ) always speaks for GOD.

I could write another book, but for now let us return to our ponderings. This tribulation will be all of humanity beneath the hand of GOD's wrath. We are (all of us) candidates, witnesses, and partakers of *"the beginning of sorrows"* (re. Matt. 24:8).

Children, this generation and its progeny shall taste this sorrow. Yet, Jesus says, *"See that ye be not troubled . . . the end is not yet."*

– MATT. 24:6

✳

Let us put these things in their immediate context, for they are, indeed, upon us. The state of being immersed in these sorrows (lends to) or aids and abets the latent haters and hypocrites of an entire civilization (species: *Homo Sapiens*).

Matthew 24:4-5 warns us that many false prophets and false Christs shall arise, and deceive many. Even now, child, completely trust your own Bible; while dwelling in the bosom of Christ, and in the secret place of the Father, sanctified by the infilling *and* Baptism of the Holy Ghost.

✳

*And ye shall hear of wars and rumors of wars: see
that ye be not troubled: for all THESE THINGS
must come to pass, but the end is not yet.*

*For nation shall rise against nation, and kingdom
against kingdom: and there shall be famines, and
pestilences, and earthquakes in divers places.*

All these are the beginning of sorrows.
–MATT. 24:6-8

✳

Christian, this is the state of society: global anxieties and fears and anger manifested, secret hatred exposed, religious idealism and all-permissive grace waning toward extinction. These things are the beginning of horror and a great darkness, chaos, anarchy. This is just before the majority of the populace delivers true believers to affliction, hatred, and murder (as recorded in Matt. 24:9). We cannot ignore or deny this prophesy:

✳

*THESE THINGS have I spoken unto you, that ye
should not be offended. They shall put you out of the
synagogues; yea, the time cometh, that whosoever
killeth you will think that he doeth GOD service.*
– JOHN 16:1

✳

These people will be stressed and afraid to the last degree, and deliver Christians to the authorities in hope of some type government relief, financial or otherwise. Christians may well have a bounty on their head. They also may deliver us to be killed out of a raw and unabbreviated hatred for the Truth (the LORD Jesus Christ). Nevertheless, (I propose) that we shall be delivered up to the authorities, with or without reward due to a hatred toward GOD and toward believers, out of a religious madness against all things holy.

It will be enough that these people do not know GOD – perforce blaming their misfortune and the world's tragedies on GOD, transferring that fear, confusion, and hostility toward Christians.

But this is the LORD Jesus Christ (the Living Word's) perspective:

❋

And THESE THINGS *will they do unto you, BECAUSE they have not known the Father, nor me.*
– JOHN 16:3

❋

Jesus says these people do not know GOD. But let us establish something clearly. Truly, there are innumerable people who consider themselves fine, upstanding members of the Church that do not know GOD, nor his Christ. Among the multitudes that deliver up the genuine disciples of Jesus Christ to the authorities, will be a countless number of hypocrites throughout the crowd. They used to be members of the Church. Indeed, and so it was when the LORD Jesus Christ was marched through Jerusalem to Calvary's hill.

These people's rage against the Truth personified (the LORD Jesus Christ), became murderous. The societal, world system's hatred for the Truth today remains relatively unchanged. We must be converted.

Here. Because I do not know GOD, I have no viable or working concept of selfless Love – for this is how GOD loves.

We think we know *Love*, and then we marry and divorce and sometimes murder our significant other.

Life and *Love* has no sanctity, we give it no honor, and it is corrupted with our possession.

The Father resides between the lines of my Bible, the Word of GOD, (the LORD Jesus Christ) – especially the text in red letters. Not trying to be mystical here, but as I say, The Father dwells in the catacombs of Christ – from the ends of the earth and where the moon abides by day.

Children, Jesus can and will take us there, in fact, there is no other Way to get there except the Lord Jesus Christ presents me in the perfections of his own blood – and in the ransom for his life.

✳

I AM the Way, the Truth, and the Life: no
man cometh to the Father, but by me.
– John 10:6

✳

The genuine, intrepid and inquisitive disciple will leave no (figurative) stone unturned in the odyssey of getting to know GOD in his Christ. He will scour the Word of GOD (the Bread of Life) for a loaf or a crumb with the same determination.

My familiarity and my apprehension of the Father is correlative to my getting to know the Son, the LORD Jesus, the Word of GOD. He is in there. But where am I on the dynamic continuum of getting to know the LORD Jesus Christ?

※

Have I been so long time with you, and yet hast thou not known me, Philip? he that hath seen me hath seen the Father; and how sayest thou then, Shew us the Father?
– JOHN 14:4

※

A mixed multitude of infidels and hypocrites will comprise the crowd that delivers up the genuine disciples of Christ to be afflicted and killed. The infidels have never claimed to know GOD or Christ, or alleged themselves to be a Christian. But the hypocrites insist they know both the Father and the Son, and they are doing GOD service for turning you over to the authorities and opening the door to expedite your murder.

There is no way to know GOD outside the Word of GOD, the LORD Jesus Christ. Spending quality time with Jesus will get us there. But Christians that claim to know GOD and Christ, yet they do not read their Bible, will be exposed as liars and imposters. This may be the genre or sub-group of people that are incensed by an unstable society, and evolve into religious zealots . . . um . . . *murderous* religious zealots.

(I imagine) this multitude of "quote-unquote" Christians who say they know GOD but frankly, have only a passing familiarity with the Father, will be innumerable. (I imagine) and this is, of course, supposition, but I can almost see some preachers and deacons and Sunday-school teachers bearing the torch of our indictment – and killing us, presuming they do GOD service.

Christian, we must assume these people vicious, (and though it is hard to imagine), they will be full of hatred and murder. The LORD Jesus Christ said so. Specifically, I presume them quick to violence and mayhem. They care no more for the society that has sustained them than they care for Christ.

These people are (of course) unregenerate and unruly – and they will cast off whatever civility or grace that remains. Perhaps, driving their insanity, will be the acute realization that they have missed it. Being apathetic and indifferent toward GOD, they never established more than a *"passing"* familiarity with the Father or the Son, or the Holy Ghost, for that matter.

If we do not take the time (and make the time) to get to know the Father within the mysteries and wisdom of Christ Jesus, we will either be among their number, or perhaps a collateral victim. Notwithstanding how these things turn out or manifest, we must know the Father *Now,* by prayer and by an intense, personal Bible study. By asking.

✳

But all THESE THINGS will they do unto you for my name's sake, BECAUSE they know not him that sent me.
– John 15:21

✳

The things they will possibly do, and their potential for evil, knows no license or bridle. They will not be deferred or denied doing GOD service under strong delusion. From Cain, even until now, the unregenerate remain unchanged, unconverted. Humanity yields and men murder, but Satan is the spirit of murder since Cain.

Ah, in this I see but a glimpse of what the unconverted look like from a spiritual perspective.

✳

*Ye are of your father the devil, and the
lusts of your father ye will do.*

*He was a murderer from the beginning, and abode
not in the truth, because there is no truth in him.*

*When he speaketh a lie, he speaketh of his
own: for he is a liar, and the father of it.*
– JOHN 8:44

✳

We are speaking of a people full of the hate and murder of original sin, the spirit of Cain, (Satan's son, or so some have said). We have no perspective. We have not tasted of the exceeding sinfulness of sin. To esteem the cost of sin we must survey Calvary, and the preponderance of us do not go there, not even we "Christians." To go there is to reckon with the reality of sin – my sin upon Christ Jesus.

People, we are going to be discombobulated and vicious, inundated with rumors of war (and the reality of war), distraught and afraid, unable to take our eyes off the pictures of famine, pestilences, and earthquakes on CNN.

We are going to be immobilized by fear, by raw terror, by iniquity abounding. We know we need to do something, but we are *stuck like Chuck,* if you will allow the idiom. But when we do react, it will be in a rush and in a panic, and we will over-react.

Murder and mayhem in certain seasons – by the will of GOD – will be commonplace. Hatred will breed unchecked and insurmountable. Hear me. When we do not receive and develop a love for the truth, strong delusion overtakes us, and when our religious hypocrisy is revealed, it shall also be shown that we do not know the Father, nor his Christ. Hear me. It will be revealed that not only did we not know the Father and the LORD Jesus Christ, but that we hated them and the truth they represented.

Our rejection of the LORD Jesus Christ is an egregious abandon, and our ignorance of the Father is a willful negligence. More than indifference, our hostile resistance shall be a burgeoning hatred.

The *new normal* of each day of these beginnings of sorrows shall encompass, subdue, and enlist us, seamlessly integrating us into its methodology. If we do not know and love the truth, we will believe the lie, and see the *new normal* as it was, through rose-colored glasses. And this *new normal* is another day closer to the great tribulation.

Preacher, we are either converted, or we are unregenerate (of Adamic nature, which includes Cain's DNA). It does not matter how good they look Sunday morning, if beneath their thin casual Christian cloak they are seething cauldrons of malice, murder, and madness.

Many folk have not looked into the eyes of another person showing that hatred – *that* hatred being a present or incipient potential for murder. In this, these have rejected the truth and have been obliged to hide or suppress their true self. Closed off from the Word of GOD, removed from prayer, distanced from the altar, they have not and cannot change. But many of them (the unregenerate, the hater, the liar, the murderer) attend church with remarkable regularity.

Here is the early tribulation (the beginning of sorrows) from Mark's perspective and in its relevancy to our primary text of John 16:1-3.

✳

> *But take heed to yourselves: for they shall deliver*
> *you up to councils; and in the synagogues ye shall*
> *be beaten: and ye shall be brought before rulers and*
> *kings for my sake, for a testimony against them.*
> **– Mark 13:9**

✳

It behooves us to go ahead and cite the prophetic equivalent (if you will) of John 16:1-3 as recorded by Luke. Hear me. The end is not yet, but it is imminent – yea, even at the Door.

✳

> *But before all these, they shall lay their hands*
> *on you, and persecute you, delivering you up to*
> *the synagogues, and into prisons, being brought*
> *before kings and rulers for my name's sake.*
> **– Luke 21:12**

✳

Children, we have no precise timeline, nor do we have a precedent, we simply trouble the waters of the Living Word of GOD for prophetic implications and imperatives. We will know when *these things* are upon us.

GOD is setting us up, you might say. And he who has ears to hear, let him hear. GOD oftentimes wields an imperfect or flawed tool. He is revealed in what he allows, and in what he withholds.

✳

And it shall turn to you for a testimony.
– Luke 21:13

✳

We see circumstances conspire within the sovereign fist of GOD that he might set his emissaries before the face of his enemies. These Christian disciples shall appear to be victims, prisoners; but they are, rather, the sanctified, avenging instrument of GOD. Christian, when they beat you in the synagogue (as says the Word of GOD by Mark), then they beat the LORD once more vicariously. He who has ears to hear, let him hear.

The *"Church"* as an institution during the tribulation in America, may well evolve to more closely resemble the synagogue or the temple in the middle east. We cannot know. All three of the synoptic gospels declare that the true disciples of the LORD Jesus Christ shall be delivered up to the authorities to be afflicted; the LORD Jesus says by Mark and Luke that this will transpire within the synagogue.

Now, when the Word of GOD uses the word *council*, it is referring to the Sanhedrin, the religious and political rulers of Israel under the authority of Judaism. In these beginning of sorrows, the true disciples of the LORD are going to be delivered up to the *councils* and before *kings and rulers.* Seems (to me) that GOD desires a formal, indisputable indictment against them. By this time, the *church* or *synagogue* may well more closely resemble a courtroom than a sacred place of worship.

Dearest child of GOD, the LORD shall have his testimony against them that afflict you. GOD is going to orchestrate the circumstances of one of the darkest nights in the annals of Christianity, and (by the Word of GOD, or as Jesus says) grant his disciples an appointed opportunity to speak. *"And it shall turn to you for a testimony"* (Luke 21:13).

It appears that (perchance, or perforce) the occasion (at first) is one-sided. Disciple of Christ, you are a prisoner; the council and the rulers of the synagogue are in charge. Yet, some time during the course of these events, the dynamic begins to change (or turn).

This caused me to think of the phrase *"the worm is turned."* I share the following: Even a worm will turn is an expression used to convey the message that even the meekest or most docile creatures will retaliate or get revenge if pushed too far. The phrase was first recorded by John Heywood in a collection of proverbs in 1546. Shakespeare used it in his play Henry VI, Part 3. (funtrivia.com)

(If I may), when a Christian disciple begins to testify in the name of Jesus, he is not as powerless as he may have first appeared. His (or her) GOD is still on the throne, and he has a sovereign immutable itinerary and methodology. What may look like an overwhelming flood and undeniable victory of the enemy, shall begin to *turn* when GOD lifts up a standard against him (re. Is. 59:19).

GOD makes a way in the midst of contrary circumstance, to *turn* seemingly impossible odds into opportunity (and responsibility) for the Christian disciple to testify. Whether it be accident, tragedy, or sickness, GOD is sovereign. Child, your testimony of Christ Jesus can alleviate sickness or suffering; you are converted and anointed to speak the virtue and power of the LORD Jesus Christ into the lives of others.

When a disciple of Christ begins to testify under the auspices and anointing of the Holy Ghost, by the unction and Voice of the Spirit of GOD, devils become mute and impotent in his presence. Child of GOD, when you perceive that the Holy Ghost is upon you, seize the moment, redeem the time – speak in the name of the LORD Jesus Christ all he gives, no more and no less.

In the appointed moment of GOD's divine pleasure, occasion for anointed testimony shall arise out of the maelstrom, even out of the midst of the enemy's camp. For this time, and to seize this moment for the glory of GOD, you are chosen and anointed by greater grace.

Most likely, you will feel inadequate to the task, yet this is one of the chief reasons GOD has chosen you. You have the capacity to empty yourself and allow GOD to be all in all. In other words, you will not get in GOD's way. You needn't fear failure – GOD trusts you for this time. The events and circumstances of your entire life have shaped you and prepared you for this testimony.

Let us receive the LORD's instruction by faith, apprehend his promises by a deeper, refined, mature trust.

✳

*Settle it therefore in your hearts, not to
meditate before what ye shall answer.*

*For I will give you a mouth and wisdom, which all your
adversaries shall not be able to gainsay nor resist.*
– LUKE 21:14-15

✳

Christian, whether before the magistrate, or in the prison courtyard, or courtroom, you shall be prepared. It is GOD who orchestrates the environment and circumstances of his children. Your testimony of the power and grace of the LORD Jesus Christ to deliver and save is already in your bosom. Child, you are more prepared, and more adequate to the task, than you have imagined.

When GOD says, *"I will give you a mouth,"* he means you shall be speaking by the Holy Ghost. In *"real time"* the Voice of GOD shall speak through your mouth like a prophet and a priest, words of Spirit and words of Life. [I know, right? It is hard to wrap your mind around.]

The wisdom by which you speak is other-worldly: divine, prophetic, living, eternal. Personally, it will be quite liberating not to feel compelled to have a defense or an answer prepared beforehand. Naturally, we would want our response to be perfect for the LORD. Amazingly, miraculously . . . it shall be.

Now, verse 15 sounds remarkedly like Acts 6:10, where the martyr Stephen is giving his testimony before the council (the Sanhedrin), and before the Jews in the temple or (synagogue)

✹

*And they were not able to resist the wisdom
and the Spirit by which he spoke.*
– Acts 6:10

✹

This explains to me how Stephen preached such a lengthy confrontational, even scathing sermon without being interrupted. We know the Pharisees and the Jews were offended.

By the time Stephen delivered this lengthy indictment, the temple would have been standing room only, yet no one attempted to stop him until the moment GOD had chosen. Before they could silence him, or before they rushed him as an insane mob, Stephen formally indicted them as betrayers and murderers of the Christ of GOD (see Acts 6:52).

Indeed, GOD shall have the last word. Christian, we must resolve it within our heart and mind, at this moment, that some of us will be killed for the gospel's sake: for our testimony, our witness of the truth, and for the image and likeness (and righteousness) of Christ Jesus upon us and within us.

✹

*And ye shall be betrayed both by parents, and
brethren, and kinfolks, and friends; and some
of you shall they cause to be put to death.*
– Luke 21:16

✻

Behold the heartbreaking reality of Jesus Christ and him crucified. Many of us will protest that we did not sign on for this, but Jesus says that for some of us, this shall be our portion. Sometimes the light-bread that our soul loathes is the very thing we are served. Alas, many of us consider ourselves too entitled or privileged to suffer these things – but the reality of following GOD is that sometimes there is bitter water, and sometimes there is no water.

We know that all the original disciples of the LORD Jesus Christ were killed in diverse manner for the gospel's sake, that none died a natural death, except for John, and that was after torture and exile. Of note is how Jesus forewarned Peter of how he would die.

✻

*This spake he, signifying by what death he should glorify GOD.
And when he had spoken this, he saith unto him, Follow me.*
– John 21:19

✻

The first time that I read this scripture with understanding, it filled my soul with a deep foreboding and an acute dread. Peter's crucifixion (ostensibly upside-down) glorified GOD; the stoning of Stephen and the beheading of both James and John the Baptist, glorified GOD.

Christian disciple, this also we must settle in our hearts: some of us are appointed to such dreadful, (and in GOD's eyes – Glorious) testimony, to die with his name upon our lips.

(If I may), this is not Grandma's Sunday school or Religion 101, this is the reality of the cross of Jesus Christ and him crucified – the revelation of his cross as my cross, and as yours. The Word of GOD has tried to prepare (this generation) for *these things* – and the beginning of sorrows, and of end-times, but we have been primarily busy about all-permissive grace. The best of us feed the hungry once a week, or on holidays.

The LORD Jesus Christ (the Word of GOD),is petitioning us, beseeching us – to be prepared to die for our testimony. The gospels are filled with the prophecy and harbinger of *these things* – these terrible (and glorious) things. The indifferent and the undecided shall be summarily routed.

The Word of GOD has taught us and admonished us, it must be definitive whose side we are on. Only the sanctified and the converted will stand in the evil day. What troubles me most, is that previous tragedy and hardship has not significantly changed us.

Some of us, the *few*, will have the opportunity and honor of being martyred for our testimony of Jesus Christ and the power of his resurrection. *Many* of us do not have a testimony upon which to stand.

When confronted with evil we will capitulate.

Being betrayed by parents and friends will have a tendency to depress and immobilize us. Let us recognize the infidels in our own family, above all, let us dismiss them from our inner circle. Not only will they be no help, but they are (in reality) working for the enemy.

Yes, it has come to that. Whosoever has ears to hear, let (him) or her hear, and let him hear no more of the celestial burden. Perilous times are here. Whether in times of relative peace, or under fire, whether living or dying, is it not one either and the same? All these things ought occupy, and glorify GOD who made the heavens and the earth.

But let us be prepared, and not anesthetized – living a life of quiet but reckless desperation. And let us not be in denial of GOD's Word. But I fear for us, a people who have barely recovered. How shall there be Gold. But let us fear, a people that have not received the first thing GOD has said, how shall we (thoroughly) believe the next thing GOD says.

These things are at the Door. And I shall dissimulate and procrastinate, or I shall glorify GOD. He who has ears to hear . . . has already heard.

Yeah. The same person that was remiss to teach me that I must be sold-out for GOD, is the same wise man and witch doctor that was negligent to teach, that for some of us, it is going to cost us all.

I fear the gravity and the urgency of *these things* shall come upon us unaware and woefully unprepared. We have not trained the heart and mind and soul of our spirit man to receive a hard Word – we are still swilling milk.

Here is a brief excerpt of how the LORD Jesus Christ describes it as recorded by Luke:

※

*And there shall be signs in the sun, and in the moon, and in the
stars; and upon the earth distress of nations, with perplexity;
the sea and the waves roaring. Men's hearts failing them for
fear, and for looking after those things which are coming
on the earth: for the powers of heaven shall be shaken.*
– Luke 21:25-26

✳

Unprecedented, except in the days of Noah, and in the days
of Lot. Whosoever has ears to hear, let them hear.

Let us neither be distracted nor deceived: hypnotized or
misinformed. Indeed. And let us not be overly informed. The
heavens and the earth belong to GOD.

✳

*By the Word of the LORD were the heavens made, and
all the host of then by the breath of his mouth.*
– Psalm 33:6

✳

All the earth shall know that Jesus, he is GOD. Every tongue
shall confess that Jesus Christ is LORD (and what that means).
All men shall know that the sun and the moon and the stars
were created *by* him, and *for* him (re. Col. 1:16). Moreover,
they not only belong to him, they speak for him.

✳

*The heavens declare the glory of GOD; and
the firmament sheweth his handywork.*

*Day unto day uttereth speech, and night
unto night sheweth knowledge.*

There is no speech nor language, where their Voice is not heard.
– PSALM 19:1-3

❋

Indeed, the sun and the moon and the stars, and the firmament speak an international language. Children, when the powers of heaven are shaken, GOD has somewhat to say.

How presumptuous – how brazen and bare-assed arrogant to believe that GOD has ceased speaking when his nature and essence and character are *The Word.* His name is Jesus. Let us hear him out of the kingdom of GOD developing within our inner (spirit) man.

Isn't the New Testament an indictment and diagnosis of our hearing retardation, our rejection of the Word of GOD, our dishonoring him and spitting upon him and crucifying him? If you maintain you were not there, you have heard (grasped, realized, internalized) nothing.

Ah, let us not refuse (or deny) him that speaketh, for him that speaks from heaven is the Word of GOD.

❋

*Whose Voice then shook the earth: but now he
hath promised saying, Yet once more I shake
not the earth only, but also heaven.*
– HEBREWS 12:26-27

✳

Alas. Men's hearts shall fail them looking too closely into *these things.* Rather let me submit to the Voice of GOD, and become One with the shaking, as it were.

Am I prepared for everything except Christ to be rent from me, and my life, also? Some of us are being groomed for just that, a living sacrifice, and a death that glorifies GOD. Selah

✳

And when these things *begin to come to pass, then look up, and lift up your heads; for your redemption draweth nigh.*
– LUKE 21:28

✳

Feb. / '22

– rdb

Book 11

PERILOUS TIMES

This know also, that in the last days perilous times shall come.

For men shall be lovers of their own selves,
covetous, boasters, proud, blasphemers,
disobedient to parents, unthankful, unholy.

Without natural affection, trucebreakers, false accusers,
incontinent, fierce, despisers of those that are good.

Traitors, heady, highminded, lovers of
pleasures more than lovers of GOD.

Having a form of godliness, but denying the
power thereof: from such turn away.

– 2 Timothy 3:1-5

*

These apocalyptic and haunting scriptures are, of course, taken from the Apostle Paul's second letter to his young protégé, Timothy.

Paul spoke to Timothy as one would speak to his son, and so he was in Christ. The Apostle Paul was no ordinary mentor, but a man of GOD . . . who had seen that call of GOD upon young Timothy's life and called it forth. Neither was Timothy an ordinary or average student, but rising to his call. We will look at their gospel narrative, and seek to know the principals – who was Paul? and Timothy?

Paul was born in Tarsus but raised in Jerusalem at the feet of Gamaliel, *"taught according to the perfect manner of the law of the fathers* (the Pharisees) *and was zealous toward GOD"* (see Acts 22:3).

While he was still known as Saul, we know that religious elitism and bigotry had moved him to madness in persecuting and pursuing Christians, *"making havoc" of the church"* in Jerusalem (see Acts 8:3).

We should know the particulars of his radical conversion well. It is recorded for our posterity and admonition an amazing three times in the Book of Acts (chapters 9, 22, & 26).

Intolerance, and a sectarian religious spirit of superiority and self-righteousness had driven Saul to pursue Christians to Damascus.

As we covered in the last chapter, it is hatred for the Truth (and for righteousness) that drives men to madness and murder. It is the spirit of Cain and of Lucifer, of narcissism and religious bigotry, that moves men to murder their brother.

By the Holy Ghost, I advance that Saul of Tarsus was literally insane with religious idealism – convinced he was an agent of GOD, anointed (chosen) for the eradication of Christianity. He was persuaded he knew who GOD was . . . until he met him, that is, on the Road to Damascus.

Are we any less convinced of our own elitist denominational enclave? Don't we know who GOD is, to the disdain and exclusion of all other opinions (and denominations)? Indeed, though covert (or hidden), I submit that our imperialism and hatred is just as seething as the Pharisees. A man who knows all there is to know about GOD, unmoved and inerrant, is a dangerous fellow.

There is much to learn from Saul of Tarsus' encounter on the Road to Damascus. The other apostles (the twelve) had a different perspective of Jesus the Christ than the vision Saul was favored with, (and subjected to). The twelve (or 11) accompanied Jesus of Nazareth in the way: the Son of man, as he frequently referred to himself. On the Road to Damascus, Saul of Tarsus was favored with (and subjected to) what I like to call the *"reality"* of the LORD Jesus Christ, whose visage and countenance was *"above the brightness of the* (mid-day) *sun"* (see Acts 26:13).

No one had met the LORD in this manner. The LORD Jesus Christ personally introduced himself to Saul.

✳

> *Saul, Saul, why persecutest thou me? And he*
> *said, Who art thou, LORD? And the LORD*
> *said, I AM Jesus whom thou persecutist.*
> — **ACTS 9:4-5**

✳

The Holy Spirit is leading to a common thread in the narrative of the Apostle Paul and Timothy, and both of their occasions of receiving the Gift of the Holy Ghost through the laying on of hands. First, there is Saul of Tarsus, as he was still known then. GOD had an appointed (and anointed) disciple already in Damascus, prepared to do the LORD's bidding.

✳

And Ananias went his way, and entered into the house; and putting his hands on him said, Brother Saul, the LORD, even Jesus, that appeared unto thee in the way as thou comest, hath Sent me, that thou mightiest receive thy sight and be filled with the Holy Ghost.
– **ACTS 9:17**

✳

This is no ordinary encounter; this is an act of GOD (if you will allow the parallel), and a supernatural impartation.

If you believe it was happenstance that Ananias was dwelling in Damascus, you deny the wisdom and foreknowledge (and power) of GOD. Moreover, Ananias, as becomes a servant of GOD, gave Saul all he had of Christ Jesus, and then the LORD supplemented it with his own personal endowment and anointing. The Apostle Paul would speak of it later.

✳

Unto every one of us is given Grace according to the measure of the gift of Christ.
– **EPHESIANS 4:7**

＊

These wonderful and mysterious things are beyond our personal purview – beyond our paygrade, you might say. It is GOD who decides what a man shall have (of GOD), by Grace and through Faith – and a man hopes for (and pursues) increase.

Saul of Tarsus was blind in more ways than one, even before he left Jerusalem enroute to Damascus. Though he was in grave error concerning Jesus of Nazareth and this young Christian movement, his religious zeal was unequalled. Personally, I can understand why GOD had to have him. Moreover, his was a singular introduction to the LORD Jesus Christ.

There is no blindness quite like sectarian religious elitism, you know, spiritual superiority, heavenly entitlement and exclusivity. Only our selective denominational enclave has a proprietary (and divine) knowledge of the truth. Everyone else is in grave doctrinal error, and subsequently hell bound. Well? Isn't this what we believe, and what we are proud of?

Saul of Tarsus' conversion is an exemplary example of genuine repentance. (I imagine he immediately resolved to turn around and go the other way.) His was an unprecedented transformation, literally from one extreme to another. Frankly, GOD would have all his soldiers such – incendiary witnesses of the Resurrected Christ with an indefatigable personal testimony of the saving grace of GOD.

Saul of Tarsus met (up close and personal), a GOD who opens blinded eyes and gives enlightenment, and baptizes with the Holy Ghost. His name is Jesus, whose glory is brighter than the noonday sun.

In the grace and power of this supernatural encounter, and beneath the auspices and good pleasure of GOD, the Apostle Paul (by the Holy Ghost) would pen thirteen epistles of the New Testament.

This Apostle to the Gentiles would make five missionary trips. It is believed that he met Timothy's grandmother, Lois, and his mother, Eunice, on the first missionary trip, and they became believers. He met Timothy on his second missionary journey at Lystra, already a disciple with a sound reputation.

The Apostle Paul would later remark that Timothy had known the holy scriptures from a child, having obviously been schooled by his grandmother and mother (see 2 Tim. 3:15). Paul would remind him of his faith and encourage him in it.

＊

When I call to remembrance the unfeigned faith that is in thee, which dwelt first in thy grandmother Lois, and thy mother Eunice; and I am persuaded that in thee also.
– 2 TIMOTHY 1:5

＊

The Apostle Paul is invested in young Timothy's apprehending GOD's call upon his life as only a spiritual mentor and spiritual father can be. Paul is apprised of Lois' and Eunice's faith, and persuaded of Timothy's also – for that faith, that genuine faith, is borne witness by the Holy Ghost. As a foundational and guiding elder, the Apostle Paul knows this entire church family and has watched over them as a hen broods over her chicks.

Historians say that by the time of this second epistle, Timothy has been Bishop of the Church at Ephesus for four years. (No doubt) Paul has grasped every bit of news that has come out of there, uh, on the grapevine that religious folk seem to have, sadly and tragically much of it unfiltered gossip.

Timothy was with the Apostle Paul during his third missionary journey. By the time of this letter, Paul is in prison a second time in Rome. Notably, it is recorded that over the course of his lifetime, Timothy would minister to five New Testament churches. Tradition holds that he was later stabbed and murdered at Ephesus.

But at the time of this second letter, he seems to have been suffering or enduring some type of discord at Ephesus, most likely regarding his youth. The Apostle Paul firmly reminds Timothy of when he received the Gift of the Holy Ghost by the laying on of the Apostle Paul's hands.

※

Wherefore I put thee in remembrance that thou stir up the Gift of GOD, which is in thee by the putting on of my hands.
– 2 TIMOTHY 1:6

※

GOD uses men to minister unto other men. When Ananias laid hands on Saul of Tarsus, he notably called him Brother, and the LORD Jesus Christ poured his healing and delivering and saving grace (and power) through Ananias and into Saul, filling him with the Holy Ghost (Acts 9:17-18). In the scripture above (2 Tim. 1:6), the Apostle Paul is reminding Timothy of when GOD filled him with the Holy Ghost by the laying on of Paul's hands.

There are many instances in the New Testament of persons receiving the Gift of the Holy Ghost by the laying on of the hands of Paul, Peter, and John. However, it must be noted, that there are also many naysayers, wise men, and witch doctors – that attempt to deny and suppress the impartation and Baptism of the Holy Ghost by the laying on of hands. Dearest reader, I will recommend you to your own personal research in the Word of GOD as led by the Holy Spirit. All *truth* is in the Word of GOD for the faithful and the intrepid, and for the sanctified and obedient to find.

(I will say this), some folk seem to receive the Gift of the Holy Ghost, with the gift of tongues, at the moment of salvation; some folk have had to wait or tarry for the Gift of the Holy Ghost. It was true in the New Testament Church then, and it is true in the Church today.

Many of us have difficulty releasing that control, dictating to GOD what he can do and what he cannot, and when, and where, and to whom. But it is not GOD who is confused or discombobulated.

For many of us (wise men), we like to have our theological argument ordered just so, prepared and streamlined (and denominationally skewed). You know exactly how we do it. We like to tell you how much we love GOD, we recite our Church tenets flawlessly, and then we pronounce hell fire on the denomination down the road.

This merits an aside. I believe in the infilling of the Holy Ghost, and I believe in the Baptism of the Holy Ghost. They can occur, and often do, simultaneously; and sometimes they are separate and distinct events. And (as mentioned) some folk must wait or tarry for the Baptism of the Holy Ghost.

(Broadly) I believe the infilling of the Holy Spirit is the regenerative breath of GOD; mankind's initial breath of life that made Adam a living soul was sullied when Adam sinned. (I commonly say) that mankind's image and likeness to GOD was corrupted and clouded by lust and idolatry and disobedience (original sin).

This infilling of the Holy Spirit (which I call the Gift of GOD of himself), is to lead me and guide me into this Christian life, liberating and empowering me to walk and live a life of faith. This indwelling Holy Spirit of Christ Jesus is a Holy Spirit of a Living Word. It cannot be said any simpler. He makes me a Christian from the inside out.

(Broadly), and as spoken and delineated by the Word of GOD, the Baptism of the Holy Ghost is given to Christian believers and disciples to convert us into incendiary witnesses of the LORD Jesus Christ – to testify with power of his saving grace, redeeming blood, and his supernatural resurrection.

✳

But ye shall receive power, after that the Holy Ghost is come upon you: and ye shall be witnesses unto me both in Jerusalem, and in all Judaea, and in Samaria, and unto the uttermost part of the earth.
– Acts 1:8

✳

Some folk must wait or tarry for the Gift of the Holy Ghost for GOD's own sovereign purpose and pleasure – all else is speculation. However, from personal experience, I can offer or name one variable within the dynamic (and divine) phenomenon. Personally, I was unprepared (and uninstructed) as a novice Christian to be a faithful, loyal host of a Spirit who is above all things a Holy Spirit of Truth.

That is correct. More repentance was in my immediate future, and a transforming purifying fire of adversity and admonition - unconditional comprehensive conversion. Frankly, I was taught, contrary to my assumptions and religious pride and ego, that it was I who was at the services of the Holy Spirit, and that the Holy Spirit was at the services of Himself.

They say that a man with an experience of GOD is never at the mercy of a man with an argument (*Leonard Ravenhill*). Personally, I was filled with the Holy Ghost (or Holy Spirit) when I first made a public profession of faith in the LORD Jesus Christ; sometime later, I was Baptized with the Holy Ghost, along with the initial evidence of speaking in other tongues as the Spirit of GOD gives utterance. I cannot speak for anyone else; but I can speak to my experience.

The *sometime later* that I refer to, was after I was considerably more obedient to the Word of GOD, and more sanctified (or separated) from the lust and love of this world system, severed from the pride of life unto Christ.

We are not to be saved and set aside. Or, as I say, sitting quietly dozing in the corner of the pew, patiently awaiting the second coming. GOD intends that believers transition into disciples, and disciples are converted into kings and priests

– given *place* in the kingdom of GOD – relatively restored to the place from which Adam fell.

(Most days) I experience a renewed infilling of the Holy Spirit, or being *topped-off,* as it were, during (and after) prayer and meditation and study of the Word of GOD. Any vessel that can be filled, can also be emptied. Christian, our lives belong to GOD in Christ Jesus to be spent in the service of his kingdom. And GOD is extravagant. Have you ever been *spent* quite like that? Timothy had.

Sometimes we have to *"stir up the Gift of GOD that is in us."* We will fight for some kingdom things, or we shall not have them. Truly, there are giants in the promised land. We do not know (exactly) what young Timothy was experiencing that incited the Apostle Paul's fiery encouragement, but thank GOD for men *"like-minded,"* meaning men of GOD that have travailed to form the mind of Christ.

✻

*For GOD hath not given us the Spirit of fear; but
of power, and of love, and of a sound mind.*
– 2 TIMOTHY 1:7

✻

Even men of GOD get discouraged, depressed, depleted. Once again, I emphasize that it is not exactly clear what trial or tribulation Timothy was experiencing, but the Apostle Paul definitively knew the remedy for all adversity and woe that ails the Christian. It merits its own redundancy.

✻

Wherefore I put thee in remembrance that thou stir up the Gift of GOD which is in thee by the putting on of my hands.
– 2 Timothy 1:6

✳

There are times (and seasons) in the Christian's living and walking by faith when prayer and praise (and worship and meditation) comes harder, and with more opposition, than at other times. But it is in the midnight of the soul, in the crucible of faith and in the fires of adversity, that I am seasoned as a soldier, a warrior, a champion. Victory does not come without a fight.

The Kingdom of GOD begins *Now*, within me (see Luke 17:21). This is the methodology and processing of GOD unto salvation; the promised land begins here and now, and the giants are real. If you are a disciple of the LORD Jesus Christ, you already know that such are the ways and the means of living and walking by faith.

You might say (metaphorically) that these terrible encounters in the recesses of my soul are the systematic events of traversing (or crossing) Jordan. Walled cities and the sons of Anak await me on the other side. This is the dreadful (prophetic) juncture where many disciples go back and walk no more with the resurrected Christ. Its parallel is in John 6:66.

This is the flesh and blood reality of being intimately acquainted with Christ Jesus, the fellowship of his sufferings, the conformity to the death of his cross, (as influenced by Phil. 3:10). Welcome, Christian, to the promised land.

✳

This is the bread which cometh down from heaven,
that a man may eat thereof, and not die.
– John 6:50

✳

Episodic adversity is the bread of GOD in Christ preparing my soul for eternal salvation. Sometimes, I just do not feel like getting up and putting my armor on – I just want to lay here and wallow in the sorrows of yesterday's defeat. But it is the spirit of dejection and depression (and self-pity) which makes GOD feel dormant and far away. In fact, despondency oftentimes seems to be the next (bare-knuckled) fight.

The *Gift of GOD* within us (the Holy Spirit of the resurrected Christ) responds amiably and liberally to sacrifices of praise and worship, and to fervent prayer and meditation. The hearth is not as cold as you thought. Beneath the ash and acrid smoke lies a fiery ember, a bank (if you will).

For my good and for my maturity there is opposition and testing plenty in the promised land. GOD is not asleep to my circumstances – but has distanced himself from my complaining and negativity. Truly, sometimes this life of faith is a wilderness experience: either the ultimatum of fighting giants, or an aimless wandering of self-deprecation and murmuring. Christian, self-pity is of the devil – a barren and arid, interminable odyssey.

This is not a popular message, but it is the gospel, nonetheless – that hardship and persecution are a given. Christian, not only can we expect more of the same, but the prince of this world is going to turn up the index. You know, the flames, the extremity of soul.

✳

This know also, that in the last days
Perilous Times *shall come.*
– 2 TIMOTHY 3:1

✳

Relatively, Timothy might say (along with many of us): I presumed that perilous times were already upon us. Children, the kingdom of GOD is being manifested within us at great cost to Christ. This is emphatically not Religion 101, Easter-egg hunts, Christmas plays, or dinner-on-the-ground. This is the ingesting and imbibing the flesh and the blood of the LORD Jesus Christ.

✳

Then Jesus said unto them, Verily, verily, I say unto
you, Except ye eat the flesh of the Son of man, and
drink his blood, ye have no life in you.
– JOHN 6:53

✳

Behold the implications of such intimacy: a dreadful old-rugged cross, the drinking of suffering association like water. I must have this cross to be saved, to have any *Life* in me. Come what may, this is my meat and drink.

✳

Yea, and all that will live godly in Christ
Jesus shall suffer persecution.
– 2 TIMOTHY 3:12

✳

My fear is not from GOD, for GOD has given me a Spirit of power over adversity and opposition, love as the weapon of choice, and a disciplined, sober mind to countermand the enemy of my soul.

Christian, you have a resident dynamo representing you from the inside-out, an *expediency*, and a Holy host housed within your spirit-man or spirit-woman. We must tap into that power of GOD by faith, and trouble the waters, you might say.

＊

But ye, beloved, building up yourselves on your
most holy faith, praying in the Holy Ghost.
– Jude, vs. 20

＊

Do not be satisfied with the status quo, just going through the motions of religious exercise. The Word of GOD is not a fixed volume of history lessons and/or inane ceremonial religious events, but the Holy Spirit of a *Living* document, a last *Will and Testament*. Ah, our advocate, our defender, our strong tower – our armament for battle.

＊

My child, consider this; what I ask is not uncommon.
What I asked of Abraham, I had already given: my
only begotten Son, and much else besides. This is

*the purview of Alpha and Omega: him without
beginning of days, nor end of time.*

*Behold, I ask nothing of you that I have not
empowered you to give. I AM the LORD.*

✳

Perilous times and increased tragedy are global. The promise of intensified tribulation is overt and increasing for whosoever has eyes to see. Civil unrest has been a viable embryo, now pushing itself into full-term. The populace is (predominantly) volitionally deluded, our blindness is (largely) self-inflicted. Ah, but these *birth-pangs* are also indicative of a soon coming King.

Many of us are not going to survive on the status quo of Biblical knowledge we have depended upon. Charlatans and hypocrites (and thieves) are going to seize control of the Church that is not Spirit-filled and Spirit-baptized, obedient and sanctified. This I have of the LORD.

Indeed. Even now, many of us are being sifted as wheat, with little hope of having substance or evidence of our Christianity after the sifting. In short, we persist as the unconverted and unappeasable. We are bound and enslaved by the vanity of self-interests, the allure (and the lie) of temporal things. I must (without mercy), sever lust and pride and the love of the world from my life.

Timothy is the Apostle Paul's son in the LORD, he wants him to be apprised of these things, prepared as much as possible. These things are also manifesting and proliferating in our generation. Myself, I do not believe that we have ten years to the return of the LORD Jesus Christ, and the destruction of this present earth. It is with fire that he shall recompence the infidel and the hypocrite. We are in the shadow of our own destruction, under the weight and fury of the hand of GOD.

Sin cannot stand in the presence of GOD, all duplicity and deceit will be eradicated, and the sinner given over to the destruction and eternal perdition of hell fire, relegated to live eternally dying.

✳

*And if the righteous scarcely be saved, where
shall the ungodly and the sinner appear?*
–1 PETER 4:18

✳

It is time for a rigorous self-assessment, to ascertain where my soul stands in relation to sanctification (or separation) from the world, repentance from lust, mortification from pride. Many of us would agree that the end-times are imminent, that these perilous times are the prelude to the Great Tribulation, and then the LORD's return. But (I propose) that if we truly believed that the LORD Jesus Christ was returning soon, we would do our first works (as it were) in preparation for his return.

We say we believe, but faith without works is dead, (re. James 2:26). If we truly believed that Jesus Christ is at the door, we would be seen getting ready – primarily repenting of our sin. If we truly believed that the righteous are *scarcely* going be saved, we would be busy making our calling and election sure, (re. 2 Peter 1:10). *IF* we believed in hell.

✳

*And because iniquity shall abound, the
love of many shall wax cold.*
– MATTHEW 24:12

✳

A superficial love and a facile faith shall not stand in the evil day. Our love too often is a hollow, inflated effigy, and our faith supplanted by religious form and ceremony. Church attendance (broadly) is our qualifier for being saved.

Religion has (largely) become something we do to suggest we have a moral code, a righteous conscience, and an upstanding character. Our denomination (only) has a proprietary understanding of GOD, and we pity every other persuasion. We arrogantly adjudicate that every one else is going to hell.

Love is the catalyst and impetus of faith, the meat and drink of faith, the power of faith. Love is the purveyor and assessor of my faith, a gentle, but meticulous, divine methodology.

In perilous times there will be a dog-eat-dog social unrest. Our declaration of love shall be shaken, sifted, tried by fire. The brotherly love we espouse for one another shall be revealed for the self-serving platitudes it is. There will be chaos and great fear within the church community, suspicion, mistrust. But praise GOD, genuine love will have a remnant, a hiding place, a strong tower for the elect.

GOD is Love. The love of GOD in Christ Jesus is the genuine article – 1 must be in Christ Jesus (the Word of GOD), and Christ Jesus be in me, in order to know the love of GOD and the hedge of its protection. To love GOD and love my neighbor is heaven's standard and commandment, to be covered in love, surrounded, clothed, preserved, enveloped in love.

(Relatively) all other loves are vanity – a carnal, preening, superficial, self-serving, idolatrous, merciless, demanding, rapacious, insatiable entity. You get the idea.

Many of us have a dysfunctional love-hate affair with ourselves, and with the world in general. Only the love of GOD in Christ Jesus can save me from the tyranny of myself, as the progressive grace and truth of GOD's Word makes me free unto GOD. Love aligns me with GOD's purposes. Conversely, to be in love with oneself is idolatry.

In perilous times, the populace (broadly) becomes suspicious, paranoid. A dog-eat-dog, every man (and woman) for themselves ideology or dynamic pilfers our love. Just beneath the thin veneer of religious civility, hatred, bitterness, unforgiveness and resentments infiltrate our Christian testimony. Iniquity abounds and proliferates, while our Christian love wanes and grows increasingly cold.

Self-seeking and self-promotion skew and deplete our grace, narrows our love. We are (quite frankly) unaware of the insidious robbery and depletion of the love we boast of having toward GOD and toward our neighbor, and toward one another. We become busy about many things - finite, temporal things.

✳

For men shall be lovers of their own selves.
– 2 TIMOTHY 3:2)

✳

This is the manifestation of original sin and the enemy of our soul. He is the bewildered fellow who peers at me out of the bathroom mirror. That is correct – I am my own worst enemy. My heart and mind are willing conspirators in a rapacious plundering of my own spirituality.

My natural man, my unregenerate nemesis, my residual humanity, his lethal intent is to get me off my game, supersede and derail my salvation – in all the universe (in a personal, finite sense), only he has such power. Notwithstanding, he has only what I allow.

My natural man demands to be ministered to at all times, at the expense and depletion of my spirit-man, at the neglect of my neighbor and thoughtlessness toward GOD. A man in love with his own comforts and appetites is a runaway train, a deaf, dumb, and blind hog.

Pleasure, entertainments and amusements, are not inherently evil, until they choke the Word of GOD and it becomes unfruitful. Especially for a man of GOD, his pleasure follows duty to GOD's Word, while my natural man lusts to eat all the time – even when he is not hungry. We have touched upon the following ominous scriptures:

✳

And for this cause GOD shall send them strong delusion, that they should believe a lie. That they all might be damned who believed not the truth, but had pleasure in unrighteousness.
– 2 Thessalonians 2:11-12

✳

There are, as it were, many things that are not inherently sin, but which are nonetheless, not expedient for the Christian's growth in the grace and knowledge of GOD. There is time for pleasure when my salvation is sure – which itself is joy unspeakable and full of glory, and a peace which passes understanding.

The Word of GOD is prophetic, eternally *Now.* The delusion is here, prospering, proliferating. The Father seeks those children abandoned, the acute sacrifice of the whole animal. Anything less is a token, a vestige, surface Christianity.

GOD will fill every void I present to him with grace and glory, with the image and likeness of himself. Satan likewise seeks place, accommodation, and my natural man is a volitional collaborator in the lust of the flesh as this world system (and Satan) strives for ascendancy. You know. So I can have what the Jones's have.

It is Truth who sanctifies and makes disciples. His name is Jesus. The very nature of the light and truth of GOD's Holy Word is intended to separate me from other loves, specifically the lust of the flesh and of the eyes, and the pride of life. (see I John 2:16)

Indifference or neglect of my Bible is a parallel rejection of the LORD Jesus Christ. We need to be confronted just like that. Not to love my Bible (the Truth, the LORD Jesus Christ), is to be lost.

The truth and the lie which strive for preeminence are mortal enemies. We speak of what I call "Th Big Lie" upon which all other lies are predicated, upon which they have their foundation, as it were. That is *Ye shall not surely die"* (re. Gen. 3:4).

This world system is designed upon the philosophical appeal of the statement (in contemporary vernacular), "Oh, it won't kill you."

Truth displaces hypocrisy and duplicity; and if given a place of honor and authority, hypocrisy displaces truth. Either I resolutely evolve into a genuine love for the truth or lies and deception will fill the void. GOD knows of my covert rejection of the gospel of Jesus Christ, sending strong delusion, releasing me to have the lie I preferred over living a godly lifestyle.

GOD will not force me to love the truth; with his grace I am intended to develop a love for the truth. And, not making an overt choice, is reckoned of GOD as a choice just the same – and a reprehensible rejection of his only begotten Son, the LORD Jesus Christ.

GOD will not force me to relinquish those things which impose distance between us; GOD will not force me to renounce this world system and its corrupt goods and services and lurid entertainments.

Beyond men and women being lovers of their own selves, the Apostle Paul writes Timothy, that men will be *"lovers of pleasures more than lovers of GOD"* (see 2 Tim. 3:4). Now, we know that the denizens of this world system worship their own ambitions and appetites, therefore, I suspect that the Apostle Paul is referring to church-folk becoming progressively worldly as perilous times approach.

Children, perilous times are already here when I love and exalt myself above the grace and knowledge of GOD. Satan encourages me in this rebellion, aids and abets me in my insurrection. When I misappropriate the honor of GOD to spend it upon myself, I am a thief.

We twist the truth of GOD into a lie. We pillage and plunder the grace of GOD for self-realization. We deliberately (and with calculated intent), misinterpret grace and circumvent truth.

＊

*Who changed the truth of GOD into a lie, and
worshipped and served the creature more than
the Creator, who is blessed forever. Amen.*
– ROMANS 1:25

＊

We are spiritual entities housed within physical bodies. The offering up of my time and attention is likened of GOD as a spiritual sacrifice. Upon whom I spend my time is my master. (I like to say), You can't evict the devil whose rent is paid.

＊

*Verily, verily, I say unto you, Whosoever
committeth sin is the servant of sin.*
– JOHN 8:34

＊

And it is not as if we can change the truth of GOD into a lie or alter the Word that proceeds out of the mouth of the Almighty. Indeed. We cannot add one cubit unto our stature. But when we prefer a lie to the truth, we sell our eternal birthright for what does not satisfy.

My convoluted religious routine is a scurrying desperation to save my life for myself. I present a religious form or ceremony in lieu of the living sacrifice that a life of faith commands. I become a master of loopholes and misdirection, smoke and mirrors, dissimulation.

To worship and serve the creature more than the Creator is expressive of the insurrection of original sin. The human psyche wants what it wants, when it wants it: delicacies, special ministrations all the time. Satan sold the idea into our minds that what we want and need right now is what matters most in life, while he masks and suppresses the urgency and reality of the eternal.

With a continual rejection of Christ comes a progressive apostasy, strong delusion, chronic blindness. Perilous times come with (or originate in) the heart and mind of mankind before they are acted out in society to become deeds – evil, or good. Perilous times are the beginning of sorrows as humanity simply reaps what it has first sown. This is the season, that the LORD of the Harvest puts the sickle in.

The creature reaps the wages of serving self in preference to serving and worshipping the Creator. We usurp honor and authority that belongs to GOD alone – that is, in Christ Jesus. And we shall be ultimately judged for our thievery, and for our volitional camaraderie with a liar (that is, Satan).

Our claim to the gift of life and all its accoutrements (its credit and honor), is larcenous and preposterous. The breath in our lungs does not belong to us, but to the Omnipotent Holy GOD, the One True GOD, the LORD Jesus Christ.

These perilous times are the preamble to a great reckoning, the Almighty GOD balancing his books, we might say. Our negligence of Christ, and our malfeasance and wasting of Grace, is upon us.

Those of us who take the name of Jesus Christ unto ourselves for temporal gain shall also be assessed in the crucible of Christ – examined to the uttermost. We insist upon "forms" of faith to possess the things the world has, and what a genuine active life of faith will not afford or allow us.

*

Now the Spirit speaketh expressly, that in the latter times some shall depart from the faith, giving heed to seducing spirits, and doctrines of devils.
– 1 Timothy 4:1

*

(What I call) the doctrine of "all-permissive grace" is sweeping through our congregations and assemblies at an alarming and unprecedented rate. Its primary attraction is the erroneous notion that I can be forgiven for the sin I willingly (and eagerly) allow. So I can have the things the world has. I subsist on religious ceremony and gold star Sunday school attendance. I must have a *form* of faith to circumvent the austerity and self-denial that a genuine faith requires and commands.

Its seduction suggests that I can have what the world has and still be a Christian. This is strong delusion – the doctrine of devils, worldly counsel having infiltrated the Church. We have left our *first love*, fornicating with the prince of the power of the air for trinkets and accommodations, luxuries.

We are an alloyed and impure entity, a diminished, emasculated, lukewarm beverage whom the LORD Jesus Christ will spue (or spew) out of his mouth (see Rev. 3:16).

GOD would rather we be hot or cold than be hypocrites, hiding behind a perfunctory religious routine, (a cloak) - pretending, presenting as if we had been transformed, sanctified, converted. The ranks of our Spirit-filled are being progressively decimated, primarily because we are not teaching and preaching the Baptism of the Holy Ghost. Well? Someone has to say it.

It is the devil's doctrine – the presumption that I can have a passing desultory acquaintance with the LORD Jesus Christ, pompously declaring myself a Christian.

When ought (anything and everything) is preached, let it be the spotless blood of the Lamb of GOD shed for sin. Jesus' doctrine is the revelatory grace and truth of the *Living GOD*, imparting life and virtue unto the dead. Sin must first die in the flesh that I might taste the goodness of GOD, and resurrection life and power. Any thing less than the whole animal sanctified is devil's doctrine.

"For men shall be lovers of their own selves" (re. 2 Timothy 3:2). Underlying my Christian affect, and my feigning of submission of GOD's agenda, is the runaway appetite of a glutton with his own shady scheme. Using memories of my unregenerate and unconverted character as example, my natural man eats when he isn't even hungry.

My ego strives for supremacy, for shadows in which to proliferate. And, I must be exposed by the light and confronted with the truth, my natural man quelled, humbled, silenced, crucified.

There are many things that are lawful for me, but that do not work the righteousness of GOD or bring him honor. The Apostle Paul says: *"Not all things are expedient"* (re. 1 Cor. 6:12).

The LORD Jesus Christ is my consciousness, and I must be held responsible to this *living* relationship. Satan comes after my faith, after the image and Spirit of Christ Jesus within me. I must protect and nurture with the utmost vigilance that astounding tidal wave of Grace that has taken me under, into deep waters – waters deep enough in which to swim.

I am beyond the cacophony and the cataclysm – out of sight of the shore on glorious occasion. Beyond the voices of men and of devils, there is a soft echo in the bosom of the sanctified where a spiritual covenant is drawn – where by faith I make my way to the mercy seat.

The intimacies and wisdom of GOD in Christ must be in safe hands and given the first place of honor. The LORD Jesus Christ must not be compelled to sleep with one eye open, as it were. GOD's host shall be holy.

(If I may) express the phenomenon of Grace and the hidden treasures of wisdom, power and authority bestowed upon the sons and daughters of men, *inestimable immutable eternal Grace* upon the intrepid, infinite righteousness, heaven's wealth within an earthen vessel.

(I have said) that there is one throne in the midst of my inner man, and One GOD who sits thereon.

(Broadly), we want to be served, accommodated, ministered to all the time. We consume copious grace, and then circumvent the truth that could make us free (and free indeed) from the merciless bondage of our own appetites.

✷

*Hell and destruction are never full; so the
eyes of man are never satisfied.*
– Proverbs 27:20

✷

We (fundamentally) understand that all the Law and the prophets are fulfilled in the LORD Jesus Christ. Moreover, Christ both refined and fulfilled the commandments of GOD, condensed them, if you will, into loving GOD and loving my neighbor as myself.

If the first man, Adam, availed himself of a fruit that was forbidden him by GOD, how much more shall all men covet what their neighbor has?

For whom do I labor, or upon whom do I spend my time and energy (and money)? The thoughts that fill my mind (at any given time), and which are given expression by my mouth, are a good indicator of what fills my heart, *"For out of the abundance of the heart the mouth speaketh"* (re. Matt. 12:34).

What thoughts spill over into action or behavior; that is, what am I full of? Thoughts never cease to seek expression, with or without words. Take care harboring bad thoughts, aiding and abetting (and entertaining) the enemies of faith: fear, unbelief, general negativity, coarse language and unkind thoughts of my neighbor, et.al.

We strive for goods and compete with the Jones' for material wealth, for a temporal fleeting moment of self-satisfaction, for more electronic toys, and the latest, upgraded, stunningly expensive telephone to stupefy and anesthetize and blind us to the incremental loss of our own soul. Frankly, this is the wide gate and broad way to hell, and someone needs to confront us just like that.

※

Therefore hell hath enlarged herself, and opened her mouth without measure: and their glory, and their multitude, and their pomp, and he that rejoiceth, shall descend into it.
– Isaiah 5:14

※

In that day (using myself as an example), I shall regretfully and startlingly realize that the service and the ceremony and the celebration has predominantly been about me, and for me.

The LORD's intent (and his perfect will) is that every believer transition into a fiery disciple of the gospel of Jesus Christ. GOD would make me an intercessor, a king and priest unto the people within the orbit I occupy for the kingdom of GOD. But I circumvent the evangelical calling upon my life and hunker down in the corner of the pew (as it were), dozing, oblivious to the unrelenting loss of my soul.

How many of us, I ponder, have followed on to know the LORD in the power of his resurrection life, to form the mind of Christ and align our heart with kingdom purposes. We like to sing and dance and shout within the four walls of our exclusive denominational enclave, but the front-line fighting is in the streets, in the workplace, and in the marketplace.

Because we have no functional knowledge of the Father in Christ, our joy and peace and love are not full. We are prisoner to the merciless appetite of our own self-realization because we have not followed on to *know* the LORD, as such. *"Therefore my people are gone into captivity, because they have no knowledge,"* (re. Isaiah 5:13). Because we do not *know* GOD.

We essentially minister unto ourselves and perform for the honor one of another. A "look at me" mentality. We have our reward. Sunday morning smiling faces and fatuous (or asinine) self-righteous smarm abounds. Do we really understand, or accept, that hell has had to get larger to accommodate our hypocrisy and worldly collusion, our spiritual fornication with infidels?

Self-love and self-first philosophy is idolatry. Are we celebrating GOD or commemorating and memorializing ourselves? *"Men shall be lovers of their own selves, covetous"* (re. 2 Tim. 3:2).

Our surreptitious love of the world, its amusements and entertainments, its excess, its goods and services, has resulted in the world owning a controlling interest in our soul. You think I exaggerate, but your love and addiction for, and your obsession of, (and your panic when it is misplaced), that latest model smart phone testifies otherwise.

My worldly collusion checks and quells my witness for Christ – its design is to silence me. My covetousness of worldly pleasures effectively muzzles my witness for Christ, taking me captive, prisoner to my own carnal appetites – greed displacing grace.

*

*And the cares of this world, and the deceitfulness
of riches, and the lusts of other things entering in,
choke the Word, and it becometh unfruitful.*
– MARK 4:19

*

There is nothing eternal in this life except the resident spark of GOD which makes me a living soul, the one (and only) place where man is in the image and after the likeness of GOD. My natural man schemes to wrest the ascendancy (as I call it) from my spirit man. We know these things intellectually, but faith transcends both emotion and intellect. We do not walk by sight or by feeling, but by faith in what GOD says.

My striving for stature or position is not only vanity, and not only detrimental to my soul, but lusting beyond my portion is sin. A man (or woman) ruled by feelings is naturally unstable. To keep my body under (the auspices and direction of grace) is a perpetual endeavor and a divine wisdom. Every thought (and every desire) must be taken captive to the obedience of Christ.

There is always one more thing I need, what I call my "must-haves." Uh, I must have one because the Joneses have one. Clever (and cunning) advertising suggest that I cannot live without one.

*

*Hell and destruction are never full; so the
eyes of man are never satisfied.*
– PROVERBS 27:20

✳

The LORD Jesus Christ counted this world as something to be overcome, not something to be placated and indulged and made partners with. Prophetically (or figuratively) we still reach for that forbidden fruit right alongside Adam and Eve. And it is still the serpent (Satan) who aids and abets and encourages our covetousness.

The following Word will present as redundant to many, and Spirit and Life to a few.

✳

Love not the world, neither the things that are in the world. If any man love the world, the love of the Father is not in him.

For all that is in the world, the lust of the flesh,
and the lust of the eyes, and the pride of life,
is not of the Father, but is of the world.
– 1 John 2:15-16

✳

These scriptures (I call) John's *short list* of all that is in the world. This is an appropriate place to include the Word of GOD by James. We might just as well get the indictment out there.

✳

Ye adulterers and adulteresses, know ye not that the friendship of the world is enmity with GOD? whosoever therefore will be a friend of the world is the enemy of GOD.
– James 4:4

✳

Christian, it could not have been said any plainer. How do we reconcile our surreptitious love affair with the world, with this explicit Word of GOD? Someone must call us out just like that – that we are whores and whoremongers, prostituting ourselves for shiny ephemeral things.

We are, concisely, spiritual beings, living souls; this is an eternal reality. How we spend our lives (our time and energy and emotions, and money and other resources) is, in effect, the offering up of spiritual sacrifices. The Gift of Life, I liken to the principle we invest. Nothing is without meaning.

My perspective ought to be that this beautiful gift of life bestowed upon me by GOD (and how I *"spend"* it), should bring glory and honor to GOD the Father in Christ Jesus – as I grow in the grace and knowledge, and the apprehension of the deity of the LORD Jesus Christ. Indeed, do I know the Father in Christ Jesus as One LORD by the effectual working of the Holy Ghost?

Note: I take the time to review the following because the revelation is liberating and empowering. We have missed it so grossly that it cannot be repeated enough.

✳

> *The first of all the commandments is, Hear, O Israel; The LORD our GOD is One LORD.*
> **– MARK 12:29 (SEE ALSO THE EXACT WORDS IN DEUTERONOMY 6:4)**

✳

It is GOD who gives his essence and character, his being, or (if you must, his numerical identification), preeminence over the commandment. As I write in every volume, I consider the admonition above to be the *preamble* or *preface* before the commandment to love GOD and love my neighbor. It is that important. We are instructed to *"Hear."* To hear that this is what GOD says about himself – that he is One LORD.

(As a quick aside), when GOD establishes my portion of the life more abundant, I will not be compelled to covet what my neighbor has – and be set free to love him. In fact, I will have surplus, and grace for grace.

Notably, the commandment of love follows this preamble. The LORD Jesus Christ consolidated all the commandments into one – loving GOD and loving my neighbor. He is One Love as he is One LORD. He admonishes us to *Hear* this: and that one Word means (for me) to give this revelation a *place of honor* in my consciousness.

When GOD says *hear,* he wants me to pause, and meditate, and pray about the sentence that follows: *"Hear, O Israel* (and O Christianity); *The LORD our GOD is One LORD"* (re. Mark 12:29, Deut. 6:4).

We do not get to place restrictions or limits or conditions upon GOD. It is his prerogative and (I say), by his Omniscient foreknowledge, to give and to withhold. As GOD says it: *"I will be gracious to whom I will be gracious, and will shew mercy on whom I will shew mercy"* (re. Ex. 33:19).

When GOD told Moses, *"I AM THAT I AM,"* he is (in part), telling Moses that more important than my name or title is what I do, or how I treat others. I AM THAT I AM: GOD is Love, (re. 1 John 4:8)]. More important than being called

Reverend is how I minister unto others . . . uh, how I wash the feet of humanity, touch the heart of the leper for GOD.

When GOD says *hear*, I prepare for some dynamic character transforming Truth – and the Grace to be able to bear it and implement it.

The mystery of the Father in Christ is the correlative mesmerizing revelation of the LORD Jesus Christ in the Father.

✳

I and my Father are One.
– John 10:30

✳

Many of us say *"Jesus Christ is Lord"* that have no working revelation of the divine glory of One LORD – that is, The Father and the Son (the Word, Jesus Christ), as One LORD by the Holy Ghost.

GOD taught me this. It was other men who, attempting to inculcate me into the disciplines of their own specific elitist denomination, taught me that GOD was three *persons*. While the *other* Pentecostal *faction* taught me the apostolic doctrine of *Jesus-only*, and did not have much to say about the Father.

Only (the Word of GOD – the LORD Jesus Christ) can lead me into the mysteries and wisdom of the Father and the Son as One LORD by the Holy Ghost. It is mine, as I continue to plumb the Word of GOD: the liberation and empowerment of my spirit-man, delivering me from the denominationally skewed doctrines of men.

I must know who Jesus is – that in the intimacies and fellowship of the Word of GOD, the Father is found to have been there all along. Many of us feign to know Jesus Christ as Savior; few of us have followed far enough to encounter the Father, and to know Jesus Christ as LORD. There is much more in this vein to be mined by the intrepid disciple, but I must return to our text. When I know Jesus Christ as LORD – that is, as both GOD and Creator and the Source which upholds and sustains all things by his Word, I will trust him with my every need – and to covet what my neighbor has becomes a foreign concept. GOD decides my portion, and his divine love seeks my highest good.

✻

For men shall be lovers of their own selves, covetous, boasters.
– 2 Tim 3:2

✻

(Broadly), men given to boasting tend to be preoccupied (and even obsessed) with position and personal possessions. Boasters (in general) are inquisitive and greedy, manic for the next acquisition; they sometimes present as hoarders. They are motivated in part by (what I call) one-up-manship; they live to have something the next fellow does not. Their self-worth is enmeshed and enslaved (and defined) by material goods.

A man given to boasting is also prey to suspicion and paranoia. [Let me switch to first-person narrative].

The more material wealth and goods I possess, the more afraid I am of their loss; and the more suspicious I am of you. This is not ideal for any type of meaningful fellowship – other than what concerns mammon and wealth, and how to defraud the next guy out of his. I speak (generally) of the unconverted of the congregation who casually call themselves Christian.

The majority of contemporary Christians present a religious effigy on Sunday morning, a theoretical (paper-thin) Christian, a fellow that does not actually exist – or a least no one sees the same guy during the week.

I tried to emulate the persona of the righteous congregation, you know, their demeanor or carriage: new dress, new shoes, new suit, spouting all the latest buzz words and religious platitudes, signifying – we used to call it. Oh, was I the only one that studied the preening and the pomp (and the prostitution), and the soliciting the honor one of another – the boasting and the pride of the preeminent righteous congregation?

This pride of life, of status and station and surfeit, is not of the Father, but of hell and perdition. The Apostle John specifically includes it in (what I call) his short list of all that is in the world and not of GOD. It bears repetition in every chapter till we take it to heart.

✳

> *For all that is in the world, the lust of the flesh,*
> *and the lust of the eyes, and the pride of life,*
> *is not of the Father, but is of the world.*

> *And the world passeth away, and the lust thereof: but*
> *he that doeth the will of GOD abideth for ever.*
> **– 1 John 2:16-17**

✳

Pride, and boasting . . . in a gift, that is – well, it is unseemly. Worse is the purloining of its value as one's own virtue and acumen. Think about it. Is this life a gift, or did we spontaneously evolve from the flotsam and jetsam of some slimy mudhole?

No; you were chosen for the life you have been given. That spark that gives you life, that spirit which comes with the breath of GOD that makes you a living soul, is the DNA of GOD (if you will allow the finite comparison). The one place where you are in the image and after the likeness of GOD because you possess, you house, you quarter something that belongs to GOD: his own eternal life – making yours eternal also.

You did not evolve from another (lower) lifeform, you were created, given an eternal footprint in the annals of human history, recorded in the ledgers of the Almighty. You will live forever somewhere – it is the earth that passes away, the shell – dust to dust, all that. You are a biological and a physiological masterpiece, as much an enigma as all creation – but eternal life is the miracle and conundrum of energy. You matter.

Really. All is vanity except that *Breath of Life* who is GOD – one breath at a time of the grace and mercy and longsuffering love of GOD – all else is vanity, all you shine and polish and accumulate, dust determined to return to where it came from. Every one of us, as unstable entities, even now hasten toward dissolution – dust to dust; and the *Breath of Life* that makes mankind a living soul unerringly returns to the One who gave it. Conclusively, the body, the shell (if you will), was not mine (per se), to begin with – though I am responsible for its care and maintenance, and behavior.

Notwithstanding these distasteful temporal things, (personally) I believe my consciousness (or my awareness) is indivisibly linked to the *Breath of Life* which makes me a living soul. You may disagree, but while folk argue logistics, I am preparing for eternity. When I pass, I fully intend to wake up in the presence of GOD. For simplicity's sake, and to be as accurate as I possibly can, I call him *Jesus.*

In short, Life is a Gift. And (technically) so is the body which houses the Gift of Life. This is why pride is so odious to GOD. We know that *"a proud look"* heads the list of seven things that the Bible says GOD hates (see Prov. 6:16-17). And as already noted, the *pride of life* is on the Apostle John's (short but comprehensive) list of all that is of the world, and *"not"* of the Father (see 1 John 2:15-16). James and the Apostle Peter concur that *"God resisteth the proud, and giveth grace to the humble"* (see James 4:6 & 1 Peter 5:5).

Pride in all its forms is cunning and larcenous: malfeasance and pilferage. My misappropriation of the praise and acclaim for status or wealth or accomplishment is blatant misrepresentation and oblique (if you will) impersonation. The Gift of Life (any success I have, acumen and endeavor, health and wealth), *all* things, must be attributed to the grace of GOD.

This word system, and the god of this world (Satan), has convinced us that our life is fundamentally ours to spend as we see fit. The Truth (GOD's Word, the LORD Jesus Christ) is available, light (and enlightenment) has come. If we will not receive the truth, Satan fills the void with clever deception, illusion, worldly counsel.

※

But if our gospel be hid, it is hid to them that are lost. In whom the god of this world (Satan) *hath blinded the minds of them which believe not, lest the light of the glorious gospel of Christ, who is the image of GOD, should shine unto them.*
— 2 CORINTHIANS 4:3-4

※

A multitude of mainstream Christians say their life and substance belong to GOD, and then they live wantonly and extravagantly unto themselves. We are prisoners of our appetites.

We cannot reverence GOD while living unto ourselves – unto spurious acquisition and questionable amusements and entertainments – and then posturing as if we (alone) are responsible for whatever wealth or status we have been favored with. GOD likens it to blasphemy, and this I have of the Holy Ghost. Purloining GOD's praise is like unto blasphemy, and taking the LORD's name not only in vain, but in hope of gain, a Christian without Christ in their Christianity.

We are willfully blinded to the implications of living unto ourselves; we are meant to be spent in GOD's love for the world. We are making the wrong choices, delightfully oblivious to the eventual consequences.

※

*For in that they hated knowledge, and did
not choose the fear of the LORD.*

They would none of my counsel: they despised all my reproof.

*Therefore shall they eat of the fruit of their own
way, and be filled with their own devices.*
– Proverbs 1:29-31

✳

Because we were not taught any better by our forefathers (generationally) that anything less than the whole animal as a living sacrifice is a token offering, an empty gesture, a form. Mainstream Christians today (relatively) have no effectual (vocal) testimony of the grace of GOD, much less a public behavioral witness. Inviting someone to church is not (in itself) witnessing; telling my neighbor where the grace of GOD found me and redeemed me, and quickened me, is to witness.

A Christian is intended to be a public, overt, undisguised, observable light in the midst of this current, dark and depraved society. We hide our light under a bushel because this world (and its goods and services) does not favor a Christian outspoken about their faith. You know this is so. But here is the LORD's injunction:

✳

*Whosoever therefore shall confess me before men, him
will I confess also before my Father which is in heaven.*
– Matthew 10:32

✳

Whosoever therefore shall be ashamed of me and of my words in this adulterous and sinful generation; of him also shall the Son of man be ashamed when he cometh in the glory of his Father with the holy angels.
– Mark 8:38

✳

We are that (perpetual) prophetic generation – but we sure look good going through the motions of ceremonial religious form. We surreptitiously hide our Christianity to solicit the world's favor. This is spiritual fornication, whoredom – adultery.

The pride of life and the covetousness of worldly things and considerations has carried us away. The prophet Ezekiel, by the Holy Ghost, says that Israel's (and by prophesy, Christianity's) uncleanness is to GOD as a menstruating woman: *"Their way was before me as the uncleanness of a removed woman"* (Ezekiel 36:17).

Getting back to our primary text of 2 Timothy 3:1-5, the Apostle Paul goes on to say that in the last days men shall be *"disobedient to parents."* Concisely, our seniors (our moms and dads, grandparents), warehoused within questionable (sketchy) elder homes attests to our neglect: our disrespect, indifference, delinquency – our distaste and disdain.

Frankly (predominantly), we cannot be bothered. We conveniently forget their contribution, their care for us, the sacrifices they made so that we can have a better life – which we then wantonly spend coveting worldly affluence and acceptance, and oftentimes lusting and striving for the very things our elders warned us about. Experience, wisdom unheeded, silenced and abandoned.

The word *disobedient* is also interpreted as unpersuadable or *"contumacious,"* which, in turn, means: alienated, contrary, disaffected, estranged, haughty, inflexible. Essentially, we put our old folks away, and then cannot be bothered with them.

Each generation ought to surpass the previous one in the grace and knowledge of GOD in Christ, but we often cast off what our elders have prayed and fasted for; we settle for quick-fixes and shortcuts because greater faith is always a fight.

There is revelation, blessing and abundance untapped into, because we will not get alone with the Word of GOD and wrestle for them (like Jacob). Sadly, it is too often our preachers who are first to occlude the portal to the kingdom of GOD, knowing there is greater revelation available – but that we must live what we preach.

Neither we (the congregation), nor the preacher, are amenable to the self-denial and austerity, the fasting and the praying and the tarrying at the altar, all which ushers in fresh vision and greater faith – the next Breath of GOD, the next *"mighty rushing wind"* (re. Acts 2:2).

Here (in a quick aside), I must confess my own malingering and complacency, just going through the motions of my life (and my religious ceremony) like some mindless and emotionless automaton. If I am out of breath and blessing, out of grace, out of fresh revelation of the *Infinite One*, it is because I did not go after it: did not call upon the name of GOD, or stir myself up to take hold of him (see Isaiah 64:7).

Because it has been a while since I laid on my face and wept into the floorboards, heartbroken for my country and my government, for my family and my neighbor, or for myself. How long since I have foregone a meal and pushed myself back from the table to go pray for a soul in need? How long since I have allowed the Holy Spirit to quicken me to lay hold upon the mantle of intercession, and taken my *place* as a king and a priest in the earth?

Unthankful, unholy, (and me first). Am I living my life openly and demonstratively as being *"set apart"* by GOD – and for GOD? This is what it means to be a Christian. Are my life and resources upon the altar for GOD to spend in the kingdom interests of the next sinner's soul?

To be unholy is not exclusively sinning (per se) but living my life and using my resources for something other than GOD's divine service. To be *worldly* (by default, if you will) is concisely and definitively to be unholy – frankly, of no use to GOD in his kingdom endeavors . . . uh, fruitless. Someone must say it.

✳

Without natural affection, truce-breakers, false accusers, incontinent, fierce, despisers of those that are good.
– 2 Timothy 3:3

✳

As you can receive it, the Apostle Paul received vision and revelation of end times. (I dare say) the Apostle Paul rivals the Beloved Elder in familiarity and proximity, (in spiritual intimacies) of the LORD Jesus Christ.

John, indeed, laid his head upon the bosom of GOD; Paul was afforded (and subjected to) a glimpse of the glory of GOD in Christ Jesus above the brightness of the sun. (I like to say) that, on the Road to Damascus, he glimpsed the *Reality* of GOD in the glory and majesty of the LORD Jesus Christ.

This I have of the LORD, as you can receive it. We must not assume that the three days Paul was blind in the disciple Ananias' house, that he saw nothing, or stared at the wall. Rather, I suggest that he saw marvelous and dreadful things in his spirit-man, as it were.

Moreover, (I propose) that the Apostle Paul saw this genera-tion. Yes, this unholy godless generation living now.

Using adjectives and interpretations from several versions of the Bible (if you will allow it), the Apostle Paul tells Timothy that we are implacable and unappeasable, heartless and un-forgiving, irreconcilable, slanderous and brutal and cruel. He said this generation are malicious gossips, without self-con-trol or neighborly regard – *"despisers of those that are good"* (re. 2 Tim. 3:3).

The following I have said many times, but not for a while: If I do not suffer some type of persecution for being a Christian, it is because the world does not know that I am one. Obviously, by my behavior, speech, and appearance, the world thinks that I am one of her own.

To confess Jesus Christ as my LORD and Savior before men, is to let them know when the opportunity presents itself, who and what I stand for. My time and substance are not mine; I am an emissary and an evangelist in the earth for the kingdom of GOD. This is the *Good* that evil men hate and disparage and deny, the *Good* whom the Christian represents – his name is Jesus.

Them that are volitionally deceived have no desire for illumination of the truth, and when their illusion is challenged, they become quickly defensive and potentially violent. Christian, you are despised because of the light and truth within your bosom, and for the name (and reflection) of Christ you bear.

Later in the same chapter, the Apostle Paul references a *promised* persecution for Christians, and he speaks again of these persons who despise those that are good:

＊

Yea, and all that will live godly in Christ
Jesus shall suffer persecution.

But evil men and seducers shall wax worse and
worse, deceiving, and being deceived.
– 2 Timothy 3:12-13

＊

This is one of those promises of GOD that we are (generally) not too eager to claim. If you have been a Christian for even a short time, you can probably testify to the veracity (and the agony) of this promised persecution. And the Apostle Paul says that these despisers of them that are good, these deceivers, these evil men (and women), are just going to get worse and worse.

Christian, as bad as it is now, what are you going to do when Satan turns up the index of persecution, when demonic activity becomes increasingly prevalent, when evil men take to the streets, and then house-to-house?

Perilous Times are here. This I have of the LORD: only the sanctified and obedient will stand in the evil day. Those Christians definitively separated from this world system, and obedient to the Word of GOD.

There are multitudes of us (mainstream Christians) woefully unprepared to meet a *Holy* GOD. We must forsake the world and prepare our souls for heaven. We must rise out of this current mentality of complacency and mediocrity, and (what I call) being a minimal and nominal Christian: GOD forbid, <u>lukewarm.</u>

*

Traitors, heady, highminded, lovers of pleasures more than lovers of GOD.
– 2 Timothy 3:4

*

The Word of GOD by the Apostle Paul says these evil men in the last days shall be quick to betray friends and family, especially Christians. They cannot be trusted or brought into agreement; they cannot be reasoned with – they have no honor, no grace, no mercy. They are arrogant and conceited, blinded by a skewed estimation of their own self-worth. They are treacherous and rash, puffed up by pride.

In the end days (and even now) the preponderance of us (mainstream Christianity) are hedonistic and selfish, given to sensual self-indulgence. We seek amusement, distraction, entertainment, rather than seeking the will of GOD and his righteousness, and aligning ourselves with his sovereign purposes in the earth.

We must forsake the world for Christ.

✳

For we ourselves also were sometimes foolish, disobedient, deceived, serving divers lusts and pleasures, living in malice and envy, hateful, and hating one another.
– TITUS 3:3

✳

Paul writes to Titus that we, too, were once blinded by the god of this world, enamored of the things of this world, mesmerized and anesthetized by mammon: insensible, ignorant, oblivious in the pursuit of wealth and status. Who am I living for; my own perverse appetites, or fulfilling the will of the LORD, perfecting holiness in the reverence and fear of GOD?

I look to Moses as the prototype Christian faced with having to choose between living for GOD or living for the world: for wealth and position in the unrelenting clutches of the pride of life.

✳

*By faith Moses, when he was come to years, refused
to be called the son of Pharaoh's daughter.*

*Choosing rather to suffer affliction with the people of
GOD, than to enjoy the pleasures of sin for a season.*

*Esteeming the reproach of Christ greater riches
than the treasures in Egypt: for he had respect
unto the recompence of the reward.*
– HEBREWS 11:24-26

*

As the child of Pharaoh's daughter, Moses may well have been in line to be the next Pharaoh, we do not know. But he was certainly surrounded by affluence and could have lived a life of royalty and luxury – to perhaps become the second wealthiest individual in Egypt, or even become Pharaoh. GOD moved him to identify with his own oppressed people.

It was GOD who raised him up to be a deliverer. Pharaoh, and Moses' own (adopted, providential) mother, Pharaoh's daughter, entertained great things and a powerful future for this singular, enigmatic man found as a babe floating among the reeds and bulrushes of the Nile.

It was *"by faith"* that Moses refused to be called the son of Pharaoh's daughter. *Faith:* that fiery living catalyst that incites all of heaven to its feet. Faith, that *divine* faith that gives man vision above his peers – that sovereign other-worldly persuasion which makes man fearless and single-minded for GOD's glory and good pleasure.

We see in the epistle of Paul to the Hebrews, that it was *"by faith"* Moses:

✳

When he was born, was hid three months of his parents, because they saw he was a proper child; and they were not afraid of the king's commandment.
– Hebrews 11:23

✳

It was *"by faith"* that his parents *"saw"* . . . well, we do not know exactly what they saw, but I propose that they saw hope and deliverance and liberty from the chains of bondage – representative for you and me as deliverance and freedom from the clutches of sin and its inexorable wages of death.

In the sight of GOD, it is *faith* that makes one man different from another, and not status or wealth or the color of his skin. That is:

✳

According to your faith be it unto you.
– Matthew 9:29

✳

"GOD is a Spirit" (re. John 4:24). GOD's essence and character is the Holy Spirit of a Living Word. Therefore, from GOD's perspective (and for our highest good), it is imperative that we believe what the Word of GOD says: says, *perpetual present tense.*

Faith in what GOD says is the currency of heaven. It is the Word of GOD who separates (or sanctifies) me from the clutches of this world system, liberating and empowering me unto GOD.

✳

Sanctify them through thy Truth: thy Word is Truth.
– JOHN 17:17

✳

It is faith in the Word of GOD that distinguishes the Christian from the infidel. We might venture to say that GOD's coin of exchange for every kingdom transaction is faith in the Word of GOD.

✳

Without faith it is impossible to please him.
– HEBREWS 11:6

✳

We profess to know these things. And many of us (contemporary Christianity), neither read our Bibles nor listen to the man of GOD preaching. This precludes our pleasing GOD.

Because when I look into the Word of GOD with intent, the Word of GOD looks into me relative to my purpose or agenda. Its heavenly design is to separate (or sanctify) me from this evil and adulterous generation. But, alas, not many of us want to be separated from our lust and pride and worldly affiliations.

The Word of GOD plainly declares that Moses *"chose"* to identify himself with GOD's people, and to suffer the same afflictions with them, *"rather than enjoy the pleasures of sin for a season"* (re. Heb. 11:25).

He came out of Egypt. This is the prophetic equivalent (or type and shadow) of Christians separating themselves from sin. We must deliberately and willfully identify with this Word of GOD:

※

For unto you it is GIVEN in the behalf of Christ, not only to believe on him, but also to suffer for his sake.

※

This is an integral aspect of being a Christian, and part of the Gift of GOD, that we are not enthusiastic about receiving. In fact, we go to great lengths to avoid and reject it.

If we really *believed*, then we would see the prophetic implications of Israel's deliverance from Pharoah as the correlative of our own deliverance from sin. If we had any genuine faith, we would realize that everything that befell Israel is written as our prophetic model and pattern:

※

Now these things were our examples, to the intent we should not lust after evil things, as they also lusted.
– i Corinthians 10:6

※

The Word of GOD has a powerful (and liberating) message of sanctification that we have not generally preached, and have not lived by:

※

*Wherefore come out from among them, and
be ye separate, saith the LORD, and touch not
the unclean thing, and I will receive you.*

*And will be a Father unto you, and ye shall be my
sons and daughters, saith the LORD Almighty.*
– 2 Corinthians 6:17-18

✳

The Holy Spirit has shown me that the *"unclean thing"* is fundamentally this world system and its philosophy – me first, or self-realization rather than GOD-realization: representative of a people who are lovers of themselves (and pleasures) more than lovers of GOD.

We wander in the wilderness of a corrupted world without a clue, much like the children of Israel. Everything that befell them is for our example:

✳

*And they are written for our admonition, upon
whom the ends of the world are come.*
– 1 Corinthians 10:11

✳

Christian, (I believe) that we are that generation upon whom the ends of the world has come; the Bridegroom is at the door. If we will not come out of the world, then we will perish with the world. Either I live a life of sanctification and holiness which honors GOD, or I live unto myself, pursuing pleasure in a narcissistic wantonness, blinded by my own ambition and appetites.

✳

*Having a form of godliness, but denying the
power thereof: from such turn away.*

✳

We presume to have successfully avoided the austerity and
suffering fellowship of the cross, and of the LORD Jesus
Christ. Fundamentally, we have ceremony and church ser-
vices, but do we have intimacy with GOD? Do I have a cross?
Children, the gospel of the saving grace of the LORD Jesus
Christ comes with a cross.

The word *"form"* in the scripture above is best interpreted as
"appearance" or *"semblance."* Genuine faith commands the
death of my natural man, and the cessation of my covetous
and idolatrous lifestyle. Only the dead (as it were) can worship
in spirit and in truth; only the converted, only the radically
transformed, can GOD use in his evangelical enterprise.

We serve appearances, meaningless and ostentatious religious
personas – essentially a person who does not exist. We are
a *semblance* of a Christian, without love and without mercy,
without spirit and truth – we gather for the honor one of
another.

The poor in my community cannot eat the semblance of love,
cannot feel appearances or see Jesus among us. I know how
to dress like a Christian and how to talk like a Christian, but
spirit and truth is far from me. Beneath my self-righteousness,
my self-interests rule.

I have a *"form"* of godliness, but *"deny"* the power of GOD
that could transform my heart into a reservoir of love and

mercy and grace. The word *"deny"* in 2 Timothy 3:5 means to contradict: to disavow, reject, abnegate.

Saving my life for myself has consequences. The power (and authority) is present to convert my life into a channel of GOD's love, but I resist the metamorphosis so that I might have what the world has. I become insentient to love, ignore (or stuff) my own awareness, reject the enlightenment of Christ. I will not pick up my cross; I am a religious effigy going through the motions.

GOD wants a *living sacrifice,* and I offer him dry religious routine, smiling faces, unwashed hands. The power and authority to become a son of GOD is present, but I prefer the darkness because my deeds are evil; I serve my unregenerate natural man, prisoner of my own aberrant appetites.

(Broadly), the contemporary congregation serves its own self-righteousness, captive of its own volitional ignorance. We have a self-celebratory ceremony and go home unchanged – unconverted.

If the following is a redundancy, it is not mine; it is the Holy Spirit's.

※

*I hate, I despise your feast days, and I will
not smell in your solemn assemblies.*

*Though ye offer me burnt offerings and your meat
offerings, I will not accept them: neither will I regard
the peace offerings of your fat beasts.*

*Take thou away from me the noise of thy songs;
for I will not hear the melody of thy viols.*

*But let judgment run down as waters, and
righteousness as a mighty stream.*
– Amos 5:21-24

*

It is pretense (*and* presumption) that GOD hates: the hidden evil of hypocrisy. Many of us are Christians . . . only in Church, our attendance the only substance of our faith all week. Father wants (and seeks) worship in spirit and truth, but many of us worship in the flesh; that is, we have not submitted ourselves to the power of GOD that could transform our irascible character.

Someone must say these things. This Word of GOD penned by the prophet Amos is a *Living Word* – spoken *now* into my Christianity. But have I *heard* the indictment? The Bible is full of the misrepresentation of our forefathers; and we did not fall too far from the tree.

When my heart is not surrendered (and taken captive) to the commandment of *Love,* then my worship is perfunctory, and my attitude is indifferent. My church attendance is not my whole duty to *love.* When my heart and my mind are not taken captive to love, when I do not present the *whole man* unto GOD, then I have offered a token sacrifice, uh, with which I presume to clothe myself – a form of faith.

The LORD Jesus Christ reaches behind my religious facade to find the natural man cowering there, subsisting on worldly counsel, a slave to my appetites and proclivities. The piercing reality of my religion is that all my presumptive righteousness is filthy rags (re. Isa. 64:6). The very best of us are sinners saved by grace, the highest gospel calling.

GOD is not attracted to the pageantry, the parade, (the spectacle); GOD is moved by genuine repentance. We predominantly offer the LORD platitudes and prayers of self-interest.

Regarding these Christians with a *form of godliness,* but having resisted the power of GOD that would have otherwise transformed their character, the Apostle Paul instructs Timothy, *"from such turn away"* (re. 2 Tim. 3:5).

How am I supposed to read this, friend, but that given time and space (and place), these nominal and minimal Christians will form in me a lukewarm mentality, as well.

Persons who claim to be filled with the *power* of GOD (the Holy Spirit), and/or to be baptized into the Spirit of GOD, but remain principally unchanged, are a contradiction to their own testimony. Frankly, their old behaviors and old (bad) attitudes deny their being *born again*: this is the *gist* of it – as if the power of GOD is unable to transform them.

The conclusion must be drawn that they have not *submitted* themselves to the power of GOD; from a Biblical perspective, meaning, that they *"deny"* the power of GOD. This word *deny* when used other than to denote total apostasy, can mean "to place oneself against, oppose, resist" – "to hurl off, despise, depreciate (devalue): to renounce, to avoid, to break faith with, to spit out."

Now, to pretend, or posture as if I have been converted, but I still cling to my old prejudices and bad attitudes, makes of me the basest hypocrite. There was a time that I hid my real self behind service work and immaculate church attendance. This hypocrisy is an especially effective instrument of the devil used to undermine the works of true righteousness and unity of the Spirit; it is the cancer in the *body.*

As the last days settle down around us, this genre of (compromised) *Christian* will become more and more prevalent. [These are not to be confused with novice or immature believers.]

*

Nonetheless the foundation of GOD standeth sure, having this seal, The LORD knoweth them that are his.

And, Let everyone that nameth the name of Christ depart from iniquity.
– 2 Timothy 2:19

*

There is a great difference between a young Christian that is struggling under the assault of the devil, and the soul set upon total apostasy – or those determined to have the best of this world's lust and attractions yet insist upon calling themselves by the name of Christ simultaneously. We must allow the Holy Spirit to differentiate between pretenders and true proselytes (or disciples).

The Apostle Paul addresses *"youthful lusts"* and the necessity of living a sanctified lifestyle, and of giving every opportunity for these young believers to continue to submit themselves to GOD. Here is how he instructs Timothy to treat these young believers:

✻

In meekness instructing those that oppose
themselves; if GOD peradventure will give them
repentance to the acknowledging of the Truth.
– 2 TIMOTHY 2:26

✻

It is the Holy Spirit who draws the distinction between youthful lusts and attitudes, and them who have hardened their heart by repetitive rejection of biblical instruction. Pastor, if Timothy had both genre *"Christians"* among his parishioners, then you can bet they are also glutting the pews within your congregation. Ah, but let us always ere on the side of *Grace*.

We are so generally (and comprehensively) riddled with worldly compromise that the LORD's ratio of the *"many"* and the *"few"* is applicable here. You know, the many and the few of the *"broad"* gate and the *"strait"* gate. This is not my equation or arithmetic; this is the *sanctification* of him whose name is *HOLY*.

The Holy Ghost attests to there being an large element within the contemporary congregation that has a zeal for GOD, but nonetheless oppose their own good to have what the world has:

✻

*Ever learning, and never able to come
to the knowledge of the Truth.*
– 2 Timothy 3:7

❋

The reason I am stuck in some side-eddy of Christian growth is (perforce) I have been presented with (or have come up against) some gospel truth that I am not prepared to sacrifice my natural man to possess. It is a liar and a deceiver who keeps me earth-bound (we might say) so that I can have what the Jones's have of this world's goods and services, and hopefully a newer model than they currently have.

Three distinct times, the LORD Jesus Christ calls the Holy Ghost (or the Holy Spirit), *"the Spirit of Truth"* (see John 14:17, 15:26, & 16:13). This *Holy* Spirit (whom GOD is), is not going to cohabitate with a lying and deceiving spirit.

❋

*Even the Spirit of Truth; WHOM THE WORLD CANNOT
RECEIVE, because it seeth him not, neither knoweth him: but
ye know him; for he dwelleth with you, and shall be in you.*
– John 14:17

❋

This is not my first sermon or dissertation of this specific Word. If I am in love with the world, or even friends with the world, this infidelity (or spiritual adultery) precludes my having the *Holy* Spirit of GOD.

The spirit of this world system, the prince of the power of the air and the god of this world, is *Lucifer*; and he has *"blinded the minds of them that believe not"* (see 2 Cor. 4:4). The *prince* of this world system is Satan, *"the spirit that now worketh in the children of disobedience"* (see Eph. 2:2).

Though he reigns and works havoc and murder, the earth belongs to GOD. Satan is a trespasser whose day of reckoning is drawing nigh.

I am to live a life that honors GOD, not one of self-indulgence and dissolution, of wantonness and covetousness and idolatry. Hear me. This I have of the Holy Spirit of the Living Word of GOD: *The world owns a controlling interest in the lives of most church-folk.*

Our values are so closely related that (relatively) there is little or no degree of separation from worldly folk and church folk. Someone must dare say these things, yes, and cry them aloud.

❋

*Ever learning, and never able to come
to the knowledge of the truth.*
– 2 Timothy 3:7

❋

Always attending church (and revivals and hymn-sings and church camp) but never getting any closer to GOD or more intimate with the LORD Jesus Christ.

GOD is a Spirit (re. John 4:24), and he is a *Holy Spirit of a Living Word* intent upon saving and sanctifying the children of GOD.

❋

Sanctify them through thy Truth: thy Word is Truth.
– John 17:17

✳

The truth that I could have had has passed me by again (this year), because I will not make the lifestyle amends to possess it.

It is as I come out of the world that understanding comes, as I make myself available – revelation comes – as I stop watching those sordid television shows, stop surfing those sexually explicit internet sites, uh . . . as I stop coveting my neighbor's wife, oh my (not sure who that was for), and as I stop coveting what the world has.

The Word of GOD is a Living Spirit whom Jesus says *the world cannot receive*. The worldly are allegiant to another spirit (Satan), and receive it or not, he commands your silence about the LORD Jesus Christ in exchange for this world's goods and services, amusements and entertainments, wealth and status. This is predominantly why most Christians have no viable testimony of the resurrection life that is in Christ Jesus. We are compromised.

The Holy Spirit will not cohabitate with an *unholy* spirit, nor fellowship with the spirit of this world (who effective-ly) crucified Christ. The Holy Spirit will not share quarters with a lying, thieving, murdering spirit. Concisely, this is the austerity of the gospel of Jesus Christ and him crucified. This is how I can *"ever learn"* but never quite get there; this is why I have attended church regularly for forty years but am still the same old malcontent and covert hater.

From our pastors and deacons, on down, we court the world's favor and approbation. We join ourselves to them more corrupt and more covetous than ourselves.

These (*carnal Christians*) are not only incapable of possessing the Spirit of Truth, but they clandestinely oppose him. They occlude the portal to the kingdom of GOD, and the revelation of GOD. He has not finished speaking to them who have ears to hear.

This I have of the LORD: The body has no vision beyond the head, no greater revelatory grace. The head decides what the body shall have.

⁂

Therefore my people are gone into captivity, because they have no knowledge: and their honorable men are famished, and their multitude dried up with thirst.
– Isaiah 5:13

⁂

Ever learning but unable to retain knowledge. The LORD Jesus Christ came by Grace *and* Truth (re. John 1:16-17). Grace to save my soul, and grace to withstand my regeneration, my radical conversion, my transformation.

The truth about GOD is the agonizing correlative truth about myself. For me to apprehend (cumulative) gospel truth that has been presented unto me, I will need greater grace. For all that GOD requires, he has made a way in Christ Jesus. I walk and live by faith.

When our *"honorable men are famished"* then the whole *"multitude is dried up with thirst."* Hear me. When the priest (and the preacher and the deacons) are not petitioning the LORD for *Living Waters*, then the whole congregation is spiritually dehydrated.

We have a fixed (oftentimes stagnant) body of knowledge handed down to us, and using the same H2O metaphor as Isaiah, no one is digging deeper. Where are the fresh wells? Where, then, is the river? The fountain of *Living Waters* is hidden from the perfunctory and the casual, from them with appetites and thirsts only for themselves.

And so we sit through another dry and desultory church service. These priests and pietists stand watch over knowledge that has no life, no *Spirit.* None are moved to the repentance that ushers in the revelatory grace of *Living Waters.*

The preacher stands upon the well, occluding the water, complaining that the congregation is not thirsty. Because we have no genuine faith, we are captive to (and dependent upon) a religious *form* that does not quench our innate thirst for GOD. Religious form is the black hole where the next revelation of GOD is suppressed, where the well is capped.

✳

> *The priests said not, Where is the LORD? and they*
> *that handle the law knew me not: the pastors also*
> *transgressed against me, and the prophets prophesied*
> *by Baal, and walked after things that do not profit.*
> **– JEREMIAH 2:8**

✳

The preacher feigns and pontificates as if we had genuine faith: that holy catalyst of revelatory grace and (fresh) (moving) *Living Waters.* But none among us remonstrate or protest of thirst – sated, glutted with strange beverages.

✳

*Hath a nation changed their gods, which are
yet no gods? but my people have changed their
glory for that which doth not profit.*
– JEREMIAH 2:11

✳

We serve mammon and technology and worldly fashion. We are indentured to the next pay raise, bent down beneath the weight of our credit cards and car payments – this world's aggregate extortion payments in exchange for the illusion of life. I would say that we serve ourselves, but that is only the face of our volitional delusion; the evil and iniquity we perpetuate serves Satan in the destruction of our neighbor's soul

✳

*Be astonished, O ye heavens, at this, and be horribly
afraid, be ye very desolate, saith the LORD.*

*For my people have committed two evils; they have
forsaken me the fountain of Living Water, and hewed them
out cisterns, broken cisterns, that can hold no water.*
– JEREMIAH 2:12-13

✳

We (figuratively) sit at the feet of Hollywood, salivating for the next travesty upon decency; the more perverse, the more we slaver till Satan serves the next portion. Television has supplanted our vision for GOD. [I would say *"stolen,"* but you cannot steal what I have *given* away.]

If we loved GOD, would we run bare-assed and brazen seeking distraction upon which to spend our substance, thinking to escape his presence and scrutiny? Religious drudge has become another duty, just another brick upon my back and a broken cistern.

There was once water here; I can remember the high-marks, and the river flooding her banks. We have forsaken waters in which to swim for dregs in the bottom of the cup; we deny the bitter aftertaste of our treason.

We have professional (and adult) amusements and entertainments, so we do not have to ponder or reckon with eternity. And thank goodness for the tragedy (over there): the child abuse, the starvation, the war, the earthquake, the mass shootings – so the rest of us have somewhat to tsk, tsk about.

✳

(inspirational)

*The heavens are astonished, saith the LORD, at
the resilience of Sodom and Gomorrah.*

*Judgment is at the door deliberating, seeking,
soliciting repentance; his rod is in his hand.*

*From the harbor in the east, unto ocean beaches in
the west – calamity, impending desolation.*

*Since you will not turn your television off, or lift your
eyes from your cellphone, I shall do it for you.*

I AM the LORD.

✳

*But evil men and seducers shall wax worse and
worse, deceiving, and being deceived.*
– 2 Timothy 3:13

✳

There is a (certain) progression to evil, as there is a progression unto godliness. This is why stasis is so dangerous for a child of GOD; when my learning and fellowship with GOD wanes, Satan is roused (encouraged) to fill the void. Evil is to Satan, as Good is to GOD.

The love of GOD in Christ Jesus, the salvation of GOD, extends its tender overtures and endearments to all men. To those who accept GOD's appeals unto righteousness, the love of GOD inundates them with more grace, favor, strength; to those who reject the gentle petitions of GOD in Christ, the grace that they have will become depleted, and reluctantly depart. And then Satan eagerly fills the void where grace once was, inciting men to even more evil than they currently perpetrate. If a man is ultimately evil, it is because he *chose* evil.

Unfortunately, these evil men (and women) are in positions of authority within society (and within the Church) where they have the opportunity to lead others astray. Neophyte or novice believers are especially susceptible to the subtle evil underlying otherwise sound doctrine. Many persons in authority do not teach or preach evil (*per se*); they teach and preach compromise: doctrine distinctly lacking in sanctification and holiness. This is attractive because I can justify having what the world has (and doing what the world does) with a relatively clear conscience because the doctrine emanates from the pulpit.

These men and women progress from evil to evil, seducing and being seduced, until their hearts are hardened against the truth of sound doctrine as they proceed headlong into an eternal perdition. The (doctrinal) error may have appeared as a small matter initially; but compromise aides and abets compromise – until the whole body is filled with darkness and worldly lusts.

*

A little leaven leaveneth the whole lump.
– GALATIANS 5:9

*

Unless evil and compromise are dealt with quickly and hardily, they proliferate unto more and more evil until the whole body (the Church) is thinking and speaking and living as the world (in general). (What I call) the doctrine of *all-permissive grace* is the pattern and prototype which first comes to mind: the erroneous notion that I can be forgiven for the sin I willfully and regularly allow. Hear me. This is evil begetting evil after its kind: seducing and being seduced, deceiving and being deceived. [But our attendance (and our tithe) is up.]

Them not progressively sanctified by the truth will eventually be exposed as enemies of the truth, tainted by the world: fornicating, copulating proponents and defenders of adultery with the world – enemies of the faith. Here is an example taken from our primary text:

✳

Now as James and Jambres withstood Moses, so do these men also RESIST THE TRUTH: men of corrupt minds, reprobate concerning the faith.
– 2 Timothy 3:8

✳

It is historically believed that these men were the leaders of the magicians and sorcerers that opposed Moses before Pharaoh, mainly the men that encouraged Pharoah to pursue Moses and the children of Israel into the Red Sea.

I will progress or advance in the knowledge of GOD grace for grace, truth to truth, and faith to faith, or I shall begin an inexorable season of backsliding and/or lukewarmness. There is no status quo that can sustain and prosper a child of GOD.

There is no specific or fixed body of Biblical knowledge, that once obtained, affords me the leisure or license to *sit down.* I am to cultivate the Word of GOD that I presently possess, and from (where I call) the precipice of the next revelation of GOD in Christ, by faith, command (or commandeer) it to manifest. Otherwise I will become stale and apathetic.

There is no ethereal Christian nirvana of perfection while I am bound to this body – that is a place called heaven. The following depicts the danger of not growing in the grace and knowledge of GOD and in the nurturing of his Word:

✳

And even as they did not like to retain GOD in their knowledge, GOD gave them over to a reprobate mind, to do those things which are not convenient.
– Romans 1:28

✳

My obedience (to the Word of GOD) under correction elicits the grace of GOD and the peace of a relationship maintained with care. Ideally, unbroken fellowship, and a virtual constant dialogue with the Holy Spirit of the Living Word of GOD.

✳

Turn you at my reproof: behold, I will pour out my Spirit unto you, I will make known my Words unto you.
– Proverbs 1:23

✳

Indeed, we ought to know that to *obey* is better than sacrifice (re. 1 Sam. 15:22). Frankly, to repent when corrected is better than burying myself (and hiding myself) in service work: better than my tithe and spotless attendance, better than a fraudulent self-serving testimony and hypocritical presentation.

Solomon, in the first chapter of Proverbs, indivisibly links obedience with a greater understanding of GOD's Word. Relationship is preeminent; obedience is better than my comprehensive (oftentimes) ostentatious religious persona.

Where is that one (small) area that I have been disobedient, feigning as if GOD was not speaking to me? Because that is the precise juncture where my growth in the grace and knowledge of GOD was unceremoniously halted. Other Christians may seem to accommodate the same behavior without negative consequences. But it is never about Sister Sally or Brother Bob – it is about me alone with GOD in the midnight of the soul. Indeed, I may not have had to wrestle so vigorously (and interminable), except for that one (small) thing.

The dangers of ignoring GOD's counsel and correction are starkly portrayed in the first chapter of Proverbs. It is especially pertinent to our Christianity here in these perilous end times, where many of us appear to be stuck in some religious byway of perfection – some erroneous presumption of all there is to know about GOD. It behooves us, therefore, to list the more needful (and cutting) correction; perchance some of us might find a place of repentance.

✴

Because I have called, and ye refused; I have
stretched out my hand, and no man regarded.

But ye have set at naught all my counsel,
and would none of my reproof.

I also will laugh at your calamity; I will
mock when your fear cometh.

Then shall they call upon me, but I will not answer;
they shall seek me early, but they shall not find me.

For that they hated knowledge, and did
not choose the fear of the LORD.

They would none of my counsel: they despised all my reproof.

Therefore shall they eat of the fruit of their own
way, and be filled with their own devices.
– **Proverbs 1:24-26; 28-31**

❋

Grace shall have the recompense for her overtures not returned. How shall I say it. The goodness of GOD is much like seed corn, it is not to be greedily and immediately eaten, but planted, sown into the earth – into my neighbor's life, if you follow.

GOD speaks to be heard, to be heeded, to be harrowed into the soil of my natural man – to edify and transform my spirit-man into his likeness, even as a Father girds and dresses his children. Hear me. We are the *progeny* of GOD, for his profit and posterity (first).

Lo, but we are leafless and fruitless spiritually and full of plumage and vanity naturally – we do not take his cautions to heart, his Word does not reach unto the root, to the marrow. But we are dangling marionettes of Christians, shadows, bond slaves to natural appetites, puppets of the prince of the power of the air – and not the progeny of a great King; but we are beggars, heedless gatherers of blighted, accursed fruit, decayed, dead-men walking.

Children, GOD still calls, and is refused; he still stretches out his hand, and no man reverences it. The best of us are unprofitable servants; the worst of us drink strong delusion like water. We despise counsel and abhor wisdom; we eat like sows in the wallow – never full, never satisfied.

Reproof rolls off our back like rain; we reject our own highest good; we renounce, repudiate, reject Words of Life – preferring slop, corruption, decay. We sink in the mire of our own scat; in the refuse of a ruined life we sit.

We stampede for that which does not sate our thirst or fill out hunger; an alloyed and infectious all-permissive gospel. We are the mega-church: the young executives of America, the future pastors of your children.

The eyes of the flesh preclude our ears from sound gospel. This is (relatively) our end-time calamity and a perilous time of no open vision; we are perniciously and chronically blinded to the reality of eternity and the value of our own souls. It is pride that will not permit us to petition a greater grace in these times of unprecedented need.

✳

He that is unjust, let him be unjust still: and he which is filthy, let him be filthy still: and he that is righteous, let him be righteous still: and he that is holy, let him be holy still.
– **REVELATION 20:11**

✳

These are dire, perilous times; and they are already upon us. How many of us *"will come to ourselves"* as the prodigal son feeding swine, and realize the urgency and corruption of these present conditions? Frankly said, we must come out of the hog pen; out of both the trough of willful sin and sedition, and out of the trough of erroneous compromised (men's) doctrines? We eat what we want, when we want it. We must abandon these indiscriminate appetites: offering our thirst and hunger to GOD, yielding our souls to be sanctified by the Word of GOD.

✳

Redeeming the time, because the days are evil.
– **EPHESIANS 5:16**

✳

Mindless of the time, many of us are effectively asleep in the pew; and the remainder (or those of us with the energy), are wanton and self-indulgent, servants of our senses.

✳

Wherefore he saith, Awake thou that sleepest, and arise from the dead, and Christ shall give you light.
– **EPHESIANS 5:14**

✳

First (our preachers), if they are essentially reciting from memory the same stale doctrine without fresh revelation, then they are effectively asleep at the pulpit and helping occlude the portal of revelatory grace and truth – or they have capitulated to the whims and demands of a compromised congregation.

The Apostle Paul is not just referencing physical sleep in the scripture above, but (first) spiritual sleep or worldly narcosis. If I am asleep (or indifferent, or selective) to the Word of GOD, then I am spiritually asleep to the consequences, and effectively dead - the gospel going in one ear, and passing (unimpeded) out the other.

We must rise up out of this dormant, inactive, unproductive state, (and smell the coffee) some would say. That is, look to the times. If I really want to know the state of my own soul, and the truth of these perilous times, GOD will give me light and grace for the odyssey and the revelation.

Christian, Christ in you is the Light of the World that exposes and denounces evil, and freely disperses illumination and understanding. Neither the world, nor my neighbor, will see Christ except through the children of GOD – we are that light of the world now.

But I ask you: Why are we smoldering ash and dying embers beneath a regimented religious routine, burning out within the four closed (and elitist) walls of our singular denominational rampart? What is to be said for Christians hiding beneath a bushel, groveling in the valley when we should be casting light from the hill – sharing the hope that is in us?

Who told you, Christian, that you do not have to bring the whole animal to the sacrifice? or that you could keep back the best for yourself?

This radical, miraculous and agonizing process called being *"born again"* asks everything of my natural man. And frankly, I transparently confess that I am the first to fall short of the abundance of Grace afforded me. Bringing the old-man into a state of perpetual submission is kind of like a leopard changing his spots (re. Jer. 13:23). Beginning with me, we must keep the miracle of redemption alive; because the transformation is not over, the conversion is not complete . . . until I endure unto the end.

❈

But if ye will not hear it, my soul shall weep in secret places for your pride; and mine eye shall weep sore, and run down with tears, because the LORD's flock is carried away captive.
– Jeremiah 13:17

❈

Pride (both carnal and religious), is rampant and unbridled among GOD's people, mingled and complacent, pressing against one another to obtain and accumulate this world system's goods and services. Our collusion and fellowship is (in reality) a covenant agreement; an open unashamed spiritual adultery. As I have often said, we sell our soul for shiny things and technological toys, eager for the devil's next distraction to blind us to the eternal consequences of our complicity.

We are the volitionally blind to the unfolding prelude of these perilous times. No one wants to hear it, we suppress it and drive it from our consciousness with the next upgrade, with the next rumor from Hollywood – or next season's *"reality"* show. Judgment is not only promised; it is imminent.

We have been led to believe (through omission and poor example) that a surface Christianity shall suffice, that a casual acquaintance with Christ will meet the criteria for my *knowing* the LORD Jesus Christ. Hear me. There is but one legitimate explanation for our not heeding and implementing the warnings in the Word of GOD concerning our worldly confederations and friendships – and that is *unbelief.*

Well? We do not really believe that GOD rained down fire and brimstone on Sodom and Gomorrah for sexual deviancy, or we would immediately stop indulging in our own. We do not really believe that GOD will judge America and contemporary Christianity for ordaining homosexual priests and legalizing same-sex marriages or we would have never allowed it. We would have unconditionally and summarily succeeded from this ungodly *Union.* We would have taken to the streets, preached it from the housetops, and voted those devils out of political office; we would not have cowered in the corner of the sanctuary, tsk, tsking. We, GOD's people, would have humbled ourselves and prayed and sought the face of GOD, turning from our wicked ways, and GOD would have healed our land (re. 2 Chr. 7:14).

We claim to be those people – GOD's people – called by his name: that is, by the name of Christ. Once more:

※

Nevertheless the foundation of GOD standeth sure, having this seal, The LORD knoweth them that are his. And, let every one that nameth the name of Christ depart from iniquity.
– 2 Timothy 2:19

✳

Once again, I am the first (and the basest) of sinners in abject need of such amazing grace and power that is in the name (and blood) of the LORD Jesus Christ – the all-sufficient sacrifice of GOD. It is not inherent within my fallen (Adamic) nature to depart from iniquity or alter my irascible character one bit. Moreover, in my own strength I am powerless to do so. I must submit my life and my will at the cross of Jesus Christ, and receive by faith that innocent blood that can transform me from a sinner into a saint – not sinless, but guiltless.

The old nature must be eradicated, unceremoniously crucified with Christ; for it has no capacity (and no desire) to either love GOD or my neighbor. My sin is primarily insurrection, treason, or serving the creature rather than the Creator. All the other accompanying sin (bad attitudes and bad behaviors, ad infinitum) is symptomatic of the original sin of insurrection and disobedience.

To be a Christian is to be totally dependent upon that name and that spotless blood, obedient and committed to the Word of GOD without reservation. I must allow the Holy Spirit of that Living Word to perpetually search me for strongholds of my own will and pride; I must step into the fire of him, if you will.

This is my portion, and the accumulated weight of my own personal cross, to keep my body under authority and my character exposed to the transforming blood and power of Christ – my wood, hay, and stubble constantly upon the altar, tarrying for the fire to fall. This is not religion, this is life and death – to share the crucifixion and death of Christ, that I may also share his resurrection power and glory. This I have of-tentimes called the agony of my grace.

This is not playing church or surface Christianity – this is the reality of the cross of Jesus Christ, the truth about the radical militant enigmatic process called being *born again.* This few of us suspect, or have searched out among the ash on the other side of the fire.

Children, this is the preparation of the Christian for perilous times. Only the invested and the resolute shall stand in the evil day and power of darkness unleashed in these end times.

These preliminary days, if you will, ought be a serious season of soul searching, of unremitting submission to the will of GOD – I must make my salvation sure, and be found on the right side of the bloodline bearing up the cross of Jesus Christ, a servant and a steward and a son, and a soldier. I must search out my portion, and my appointed *place,* and then take it by faith. There is some urgency to my task for there is much opposition: the fickleness and compromise of other Christians, an encroaching darkness, the desperation of evil – and of Satan knowing his time is short.

I must be found in Christ Jesus, and Christ Jesus in me, One with GOD in the crucible of his suffering association and in the fellowship of his death, if I am to share in his resurrection life. By all means, he must be mine, for the times are indeed perilous – my work and my testimony are tried by the fire of untenable circumstances and things beyond my control. I seek the perfect will of GOD as my hiding place, both my defense and my offense against a foe with nothing to lose in the midst of unparalleled and unprecedented times.

How shall I say it. We must come to terms with these untoward circumstances and perilous times; this is but the precursor (and prophetic promise) of an impending and progressively *"Great Tribulation."*

✳

For then shall be great tribulation, such as was not since the beginning of the world to this time, no, nor ever shall be.
– Matthew 24:21

✳

These are increasingly desperate times (June, 2022), the cross is heavy, Christian; this is the reality of salvation, the manifestation of evil, the unveiling of the powers of darkness, the unseen and the seen – a time of terror and terrible revelation. The price of your redemption (and the exceeding sinfulness of sin) is exacted and exposed: inescapable progressive revelation, hidden veins of knowledge laid bare for the intrepid.

Circumstances conspire to silence your testimony, persecution designed to have you capitulate your allegiance to Christ. Your mind must be made up before greater darkness falls. We will need more tenacity; we will require more resolve than we have demonstrated. Someone must rise up from our ranks to speak in the name of Jesus Christ; some of us must give all.

Who has taught us that we shall escape the tribulation of these perilous times, but an enemy and a deceiver desiring us unprepared to stand, to fight, to testify. The Master spoke at length concerning these times; we have not asked for understanding because we are afraid to have it. We had thought to escape these sorrows by believing a lie; ah, because the truth is too terrible to contemplate. There have been no times such as these in the door, no, nor ever shall be.

We will need the power of the Highest to overshadow us, to encompass and baptize us into his own Spirit, integrating, assimilating, absorbing us into One. We require this revelation: the reality of why He came. We mustn't presume to stand and to prevail in our own power. Only the Holy Spirit of the *resident-Christ* can speak and make war in the name of Christ with power and great glory.

We make room for GOD by casting the world out, and by surrendering lust and pride to a holy fire; and so it has aways been.

It is not over; I have not arrived. Of this I remind myself:

✳

But he that shall endure unto the end, the same shall be saved.
– **MATTHEW 24:13**

✳

It must be noted that the LORD Jesus Christ references *"the end"* (re. Matt. 24:12) in close proximity to *"the beginning of sorrows"* (re. Matt. 24:8).

This I have by the Word of GOD, definitively by the Holy Spirit of GOD, and the mind of Christ relative to this specific season: *"the beginning of sorrows"* has ensued some time ago. Moreover, who would split times (and hairs) in such a harrowing and prophetic era, except him and them) who desire you unprepared.

Frankly, my forefathers predominantly taught that we (Christians) would be spared this great tribulation even now pressing into our reality, that the rapture would occur before then. This is not what the Word of GOD (the LORD Jesus Christ) teaches. Those days are shortened for our sake (the elect), but we shall not escape them (re. Mt. 24:22).

This is not going to be popular. But Satan has infiltrated the pulpit, wanting us unprepared for unprecedented tribulation and persecution. But I ask you: My redemptive security comes at such a dear price, why should my resolve and allegiance to Christ not be tried by fire? Should I be allowed to circumvent the cross of Jesus Christ, and as a thief and a robber, be permitted to come up some other way?

Stark and unsparing the reality of that cross – that there is but one: and that the cross that Jesus bore, is my cross also. There is a great and terrible tribulation imminent; and, dear Christian, our refuge and our hiding place is in that cross. The same grace that saved my soul can keep it secure.

Precisely, these *Perilous Times* and trying circumstances seek my capitulation, instigating me to look for a convenient place to put down my cross. In a time of increasing faithlessness, our faithfulness is specifically tried by fire and unfavorable (and even desperate) circumstance, a comprehensively unstable economy and perverted (moral) social standard of unprece-dented darkness and progressive evil. How shall I put it.

What? I would keep the amazing grace with outstretched arms, and then fail at the trying of my faith. Indeed, and is not this appropriate time and the telling of the children of GOD by the assaying of that faith, and a remarkable oppor-tunity of increase? Or shall the testimony of the few, and the falling away of the many, not record the gospel ratio of the strait gate and narrow way? (re. Mt. 7:14)

Who, then, is preaching this daring, sound gospel message, this harrowing gospel of him who is a *consuming fire.*

✳

*Then said one unto him, LORD, are there few
that be saved? And he said unto them:*

*Strive to enter in at the strait gate: for many, I say unto
you, will seek to enter in, and shall not be able.*
– Luke 13:23-24

✳

This anonymous young man, hearing the LORD Jesus Christ teaching and preaching the kingdom of GOD, and (perhaps) considering the going (and the utter character conversion it would require), so arduous, that it inspired him to sponta-neously ask what each of us should be asking.

It can be said that this anonymous young man, (I call him young by the intonation of the Holy Spirit), represents the fallen nature and chronic need of all humanity. As (and if) you can receive it, he speaks for each of us, speaking out of the helplessness of our total depravity, referencing (or knowing and fearing) the pervasive exceeding sinfulness of sin. Although not many of us relish the revelation, here is hope for mankind.

Repentance and remission of sin is the gospel message – repentance the first gospel prerequisite of grace, if your will. We continue to make assumptions concerning the character and perfect will of GOD, outside the Word of GOD. By human reasoning and worldly counsel we make conclusions about GOD that are not scriptural. The Word of GOD only can be trusted to accurately speak for GOD. His name is Jesus.

The Word was with GOD in the beginning, and the Word *was GOD* in the beginning (re. John 1:1). We claim to know this.

The Word *was* GOD during creation, and the Word *was* GOD during the Exodus. The Word *was* GOD on Mount Sinai, at Jordan, and at Jericho. The Word *was* GOD on Mount Horeb, and the Word *was* GOD in Bethlehem of Judea. The Word *was* GOD at Jacob's well, and the Word *was* GOD at Calvary.

Jesus explicitly taught that: *"GOD is a Spirit, and they that worship him must worship him in Spirit and in Truth"* (re. John 4:24).

Succinctly and precisely, GOD is a Holy Spirit of a *Living Word.* His name is Jesus. He has always been GOD and he will always be GOD.

This is the revelation that GOD wants me to have (and that warrants such redundancy because of my hardness of heart). To understand and internally assimilate the Word of GOD, I must have the mind of this Holy Spirit – I must (form) the mind of Christ, the Spirit of the Father and the Spirit of the Son – the Spirit whom GOD is.

I must welcome and commune with the Holy Spirit of this *Living Word of GOD*. All else is ignorance, misdirection, and misinformation; and what some man has said about GOD.

※

*And the times of this ignorance GOD winked at; but
now commandeth all men every where to repent.*
– ACTS 17:30

※

GOD is essentially saying: Now that you know me, or that now that I have opened your understanding to grasp this information and knowledge that is readily available, I will overlook the previous miscalculations and assumptions you have cast upon my character and essence, and what you have decided I desire as worship – as you turn away (or repent) from the ways of your self-realization unto GOD-realization.

It can (broadly) but accurately be said of our forefathers and of contemporary Christianity:

※

Ye worship ye know not what.
– RE. JOHN 4:22

※

Continuing in the same consciousness of Christ: You predominantly worship what your forefathers have handed down to you – a self-celebratory form, seeking the honor one of another. You unconditionally accept what some man has said about GOD – without getting alone with the Word of GOD and forming the mind of Christ by his Holy Spirit for yourself.

The revelation of GOD is the selfless love of Christ sacrificed at Calvary and extended to all humanity. Concisely, GOD is Love, and the commandment is Love – and the preservation and continuity of that selfless love through the Christian community toward the lost, even the very worst of humanity. Everything not related to the identity and expenditure of the love of GOD for the lost is an erroneous notion of worship, and a vain religious form: the divisive self-inflating denominational opinions of men, earthly, carnal, antagonistic.

The Spirit and Truth of the Christian's life is that we are the selfless expenditures of GOD's love by association and suffering fellowship, a living sacrifice of grace freely offered the neediest in our neighborhood. All else is tinkling symbals and sounding brass (re. 1 Cor. 13:1), just making noise, the wasted breath of religious patter and denominational interests.

✳

But the hour cometh, and now is, when the true
worshippers shall worship the Father in Spirit and in
Truth: for the Father seeketh such to worship him.
– JOHN 4:23

✳

The spirit and truth of my life (who I really am when the preacher is not looking) ought to manifest as my being acquiescent and wholly aligned with the commandment of GOD's love for the world. Love has a name. Jesus Christ is the selfless love gift of GOD for the soul of the world.

Now the commandment of love is, concisely, to love GOD and to love my neighbor. This is also the commandment to which I acquiesce or surrender to, and become One with.

This is the commandment to which I repent: the commandment of GOD's comprehensive character and cumulative virtues – *perfect Love*. And no, I will not reach that perfection in this (natural) life, but in the life that Christ Jesus perpetually supplies: an ensuing dynamic progressive eternal sacrifice symbolized and embodied by a cross.

This is heady language, you say, an unreachable goal. Yes, and no. Here is the exemplification of that cross and the embodiment of that life which Jesus Christ freely gives.

＊

*I am crucified with Christ: nevertheless I live; yet not
I, but Christ liveth in me: and the life which I now
live in the flesh I live by the faith of the Son of GOD,
who loved me, and gave himself for me.*
– GALATIANS 2:20

＊

This is the Life that is going to [live] and prosper during perilous times, and there is nothing remotely religious about it. This is the *Living Christ*, both Father and Son by the Holy Ghost (or Holy Spirit) of GOD.

We must have this Holy Spirit whom GOD is; we must have the resident, indwelling, abiding Christ. This is GOD's provision, the redemptive Way and Truth and Life of GOD for fallen humanity.

I am trusting the resident Jesus to press to the front of my natural life this day, to purge my heart and my mind, to sanctify my thoughts before I speak, to give me wisdom and guidance before I act, grace for my behavior. Grace to aide and abet my absolute surrender to the sovereignty of GOD and his perfect will for me this day.

This is not religion; this is an internal raging, consuming fire, a dynamic transforming power, an enlightening intimate relationship. GOD shares his gift of eternal life with me, his character and essence; this is a singularly personal covenant relationship.

I cannot worship GOD aright without the resident Christ Jesus – he sanctifies my self-interests and aligns my will with his own; he shows me who GOD is, and often, shows me who I am not: purging the pride and lust of this natural life, cleansing me by the water of the Word and the blood of his cross. And this only makes me a Christian – from the inside out.

As Christian persecution manifests and proliferates in this country, as perilous times and great tribulation markedly and progressively increase, only them rooted and grounded in Christ shall stand, and few endure to the end. Those most vocal and demonstrative about their allegiance to the LORD Jesus Christ, those speaking out against the corruption of this world system and the rabid perversity of this country, those warning the populace of coming judgment, shall be targeted first.

We (Christians) must take up our cross and count it an honor to suffer with Christ Jesus, and so that we might also share his glory. To partake of the glory of his resurrection life, we must have first been made partakers of his death, and made One with his cross.

We must have repented from the insurrection of original sin, we must reject (and continue to war against) the insidious lust and pride of this natural life in its demand for ascendancy and dominance. We mustn't let ourselves go or fall into the complacency of religious routine or become dependent upon manmade ceremony. Worship in spirit and in truth is an intimate personal discipline, way before it is a corporate or public one.

We must capitulate to the commandment of love and submit ourselves as his living sacrifice in the world. This is to be the *spirit and truth* of our lives; for the Father seeketh such. This is true worship: to desire only what GOD wants, to be satisfied with my portion within the scope of my faith, to walk humbly among men and to forgive as I am forgiven.

Please understand, dearest reader and disciple of Christ, *"I am the man that hath seen affliction by the rod of his wrath"* (Jer. 3:1). And I do not take the Word of GOD by Jeremiah unto myself lightly, nor those of the Apostle Paul:

✳

From henceforth let no man trouble me: for I bear
in my body the marks of the LORD Jesus.
– GALATIANS 6:17

✳

And I must add, the scars of my own foolishness and sin.

These admonitions and cautions are always first mine, always my hand is out for grace and mercy, the efficacy of the blood of Jesus Christ upon my lips, upon my heart and my mind. Who is sufficient for these terrible things? Christ is my life or I am a vain endeavor; Christ is my righteousness or I have no hope in this world, or in the next one.

It is Christ's desire to awaken Christianity to the pressing reality of these perilous times and the terrible tribulation to come. The shepherd not preparing his sheep for the prophetic teachings of the LORD Jesus Christ and the progressive deterioration of society, and not forewarning and reminding them of the promised persecution of Christians, is remiss. The pastor teaching his flock that they will not have to endure this great tribulation is a heretic, a wolf and a witch doctor beguiling the naïve, placating them to sleep with a false sense of security. This is not the doctrine (or teaching) of Christ.

✳

> *GOD forbid that I should glory, save in the cross*
> *of our LORD Jesus Christ, by whom the world is*
> *crucified unto me, and I unto the world.*
> **– Galatians 6:14**

✳

We must live loosely to our accommodations and our conveniences; our possessions are indicative of grace and of the life more abundant, intended to show forth the goodness of GOD, a testimonial of his glory. Let us give Voice to the goodness of GOD without fear in the midst of a covetous and materialistic society. Let us give Voice to the LORD Jesus Christ as our Source, as our Savior and LORD, as Creator and Almighty GOD, as the only true GOD.

Dearest aspiring disciple of Christ, I must clarify something, or qualify my seeking, as it were. Alas, I have been indicted with legalism and fanaticism, of attempting to raise an untenable, unreachable and unsustainable standard. But the standard is not mine; it is the Gospel's standard, that of the Word of GOD, and one of sanctification from the world, and the perfecting of holiness in the reverent fear and honor of our Creator and GOD.

The further we follow the LORD Jesus Christ through this strait gate and upon this narrow way, the more strenuous and exacting the disciplines, the more piercing and terrible the mortifications upon the natural man, the more severe the accountability. Christian, the closer you get to GOD, the hotter the fire.

Moreover, as you love him, there is no grief quite like having disappointed the LORD. And his admonitions and stripes more penetrating, more caustic, or so I have found it.

✳

For unto whomsoever much is given, of
him shall be much required.
– LUKE 12:48

✳

GOD relentlessly, implacably, inescapably aligns me with both his character and his commandment – both of which are *perfect Love.* Not only to be made One with him in Christ

Jesus, but *"perfect in One"* (please see John 17:21:23). This is the LORD Jesus Christ's *high priestly prayer* for each and every son and daughter of GOD.

There is no stasis in the life of a Christian disciple, if so be, you are caught up in this exhilarating dynamic progressive spiritual phenomenon called being *born again.* Indeed, why should I think to live eternally when I will not submit to the Word of GOD, or agree to die to the lust and pride of this natural life; why should I think to share the glorious eternal life of the LORD Jesus Christ, but will not share his cross, his suffering, his death? Simply put, how shall I be *born again,* but first refuse to die?

Any other teaching is contrary to the doctrine of Christ. The Word of GOD is a sieve, and a crucible, a wine and an olive press, a furnace of affliction and a living refining fire. This is whom GOD is; I call him Father, and I call him Holy Spirit, but to be precise, his name is Jesus.

This only is the revelation of the Truth of our universe, and the next one, and the next one beyond that – that GOD manifested in the flesh for my sins. This only is the revelation that empowers and liberates – that makes men free, and free indeed. This only is the revelatory corridor that brings me peace with GOD, and it begins with the gospel of Jesus Christ and him crucified – and me crucified with him.

I am disillusioned and disenfranchised regarding the (denominational) religions of men. That is an oblique way of saying that I am set free from them. Neither the traditions of my forefathers nor ceremonial religious form can empower me against sin or keep me from temptation. Only the abiding

Christ of GOD by his Holy Spirit can liberate me from the appetites and lusts of the natural man, mortify the pride of life in me, and keep me unspotted and sanctified from the love and demands of this corrupt world system.

Only the resident Christ of GOD, who is *"both"* Father and Son by the Holy Spirit, and the accompanying revelation of the LORD Jesus Christ as GOD, can equip me to stand in these progressively perilous times and impending Great Tribulation. Only this can convert my irascible character and empower me to love as GOD loves. Once more, here is its exemplification and promise:

✳

Jesus answered and said unto him, If a man love me, he will keep my words: and my Father will love him, and WE will come unto him, and make OUR abode with him.
– JOHN 14:23

✳

The Christ of GOD (both Father and Son by the Holy Spirit) makes me a Christian from the inside out. Not only do I need to be saved, but just like the Apostle Peter, I must be *converted* (please see Luke 22:32).

The Apostle Peter boldly told the LORD, *"I am ready to go with thee, both into prison, and to death"* (re. Luke 22:33). With 20/20 hindsight, we know this is preliminary to Peter denying that he even knew the LORD three times. Nothing is quite so illuminating and telling of my character like having grossly missed it. As Friedrich Nietzsche says it, "What does not kill me makes me stronger."

What can we learn from the Apostle Peter's mortification of the natural man, the tempering of pride, and the excruciating and exacting conversion of his character?

※

Watch and pray, that ye enter not into temptation:
the spirit indeed is willing, but the flesh is weak.
— **Matthew 26:41**

※

Alas, we know this as the occasion of the LORD's own trial and prayer in the Garden of Gethsemane, and he had taken Peter, James, and John to accompany him, and told them:

※

My soul is exceeding sorrowful, even unto
death: tarry ye here, and watch with me.
— **Matthew 26:38**

※

All three of then fell asleep, but it seems that Peter was chosen to bear the brunt of the LORD's rebuke. The LORD addresses Peter alone on this occasion:

※

What, could ye not watch with me one hour?
— **Matthew 26:40**

※

We must have watched and prayed before the temptation (and/or testing, tribulation) occurs. Like the ten virgins who went forth to meet the Bridegroom, we must have oil in our vessels, along with our lamps. Hear me. The optimal time to procure oil is before darkness falls.

*

The night cometh, when no man can work.
– JOHN 9:4

*

In the case of the ten virgins, the Bridegroom came at midnight, and all ten had slumbered and slept. The Holy Spirit's point is that darkness fell way before midnight, and the opportune time to secure more oil is during the light of day.

Christian, there are times when grace and enlightenment seem scarce, and circumstances tenuous and exacting. And then there are times or seasons when grace appears near at hand, and abundant, when understanding and enlightenment are liberal and plentiful. But when the power of darkness falls, and these perilous times transition into the great tribulation, my faith and spiritual fitness will be relatively fixed. This will not be the optimal time to procure oil.

My fear (to which I give voice) evolves from the mind and heart of Christ by the Holy Spirit. The teaching and preaching that Christians will be raptured *"before"* this great tribulation has contributed to our complacency and *"laissez-faire"* Christianity. The word is French, and it literally means *"let do."* But I wonder how much of this liberty is spent tarrying with the LORD, watching and praying, and how much is spent in a wanton illicit love affair with the world?

Children, the Bridegroom is coming, and the door is going to be shut; the level of oil in my lamp, as it were, is going to be relatively fixed. The lukewarm and indolent will not stand in the evil day and power of Satan; those without oil will be cast into outer darkness. Those that have taught the Church that we will not have to endure (much, half, or all) of the Great Tribulation, and have contributed to our spiritual decline and unpreparedness, shall receive the greater condemnation.

Such is the worth and glory of this redemptive gospel, so precious the Word of GOD freely given, why should we not be partakers of its testing and refining fire? The Good News comes with a cross, the Bread and Wine of the covenant by breaking and crushing, the oil of anointing by the olive press of a Holy GOD.

By suffering association, by perilous times and great tribulation, by rebuke and spital and stripes and the fellowship of his cross, I am made partaker of his glory. Blessed be our LORD and Savior and Almighty Christ of GOD. Only Jesus can bring me peace and joy by the blood of his cross, and make me One with the Father.

Even so, come LORD Jesus. Selah.

– rdb

Book III

AND THEN

(A) Matthew

Immediately AFTER the tribulation of those days shall the sun be darkened, and the moon shall not give her light, and the stars shall fall from heaven, and the powers of the heavens shall be shaken.

AND THEN shall appear the sign of the Son of man in heaven: AND THEN shall all the tribes of the earth mourn, and they shall see the Son of man coming in the clouds of heaven with power and great glory.

And he shall send his angels with a great sound of a trumpet, and they will gather together his elect from the four winds, from one end of heaven to the other.

– Matthew 24:29-31

*

The word *"then"* as used twice in verse 30 of our primary text, and the word *"after"* as used in verse 29, are adjectives or adverbs used to establish the order of events in a period of time. I was only an average English student, but I venture to suggest that they are *adverbs*, as they denote action. They connect events that have already occurred to events that will follow them. As used here, they are very difficult to take out of context or misinterpret.

To misinterpret what the LORD Jesus Christ (the Word of GOD) is saying in these three concise scriptures, or alter the order of events that he has so precisely delineated, is the willful misconception of spiritual wickedness (or evil) in high religious places (the pulpit), and the wistful determinations of deluded minds.

That the *Church*, or the elect of GOD, is going to escape the Great Tribulation is popular teaching, but it is not the doctrine (or teaching) of Christ. To believe, or to even hope otherwise, is to be unprepared. This doctrine of devils is the anesthesia of contemporary Christianity, a very powerful religious narcotic that evokes a false sense of security.

Satan wants the masses deluded and unaware of the sign of the time, and so they predominantly are. Satan especially wants the Christian population inebriated with shiny things and covetous of social acceptance, complacent and care-free with our consciousness consumed with status, position, wealth – worldly things. And so we predominantly are.

If we could not buy or sell, we would be a people most miser-able. We are unaccustomed to need, we (broadly) live a life of surfeit and wantonness, indiscriminately buying and selling what does not satisfy. We have not experienced real paucity or scarcity; we give away what we will not eat and we will not wear and call it charity.

Our sense of entitlement knows no bounds; our elitist religious persona precludes us even considering tribulation, great or small. We are indoctrinated to believe we are too special for hardship or tragedy. Well? Someone must say what everyone is too afraid to say; that faced with starvation or thirst, or imminent violence, or the loss of our smart phone, we are going to capitulate to a mark (or a chip or a number) which allows us to buy and sell.

Faced with ostracism and exclusion, we are going to fold without a fight. It is unthinkable (preposterous really) to imagine ourselves banned or blacklisted, shunned from genteel society; nothing has been denied us, no accommodation or excess, no perversity or decadence.

We must yield ourselves (and our Christianity) to a rigorous unsparing assessment by the Holy Spirit. Can the religious effigy I present to the congregation on Sunday withstand persecution and tribulation on Monday? Indeed. We shall see if I am a soldier for Christ, or an imposter.

Religious observation and ceremonial form will be no help to me when these perilous times transmogrify into Great Tribulation. Only faith will stand in the evil day and power of darkness. My feigned Christian affect and self-righteous cloak shall be summarily dismissed, it is trial and tribulation which exposes my prevarication and dissimulation, rendering me naked in the light of a Holy fire. My religious accoutrements and Christian entourage will be no help when the powers of the heavens shall be shaken.

✳

Immediately AFTER the tribulation of those days shall the sun be darkened, and the moon shall not give her light, and the stars shall fall from heaven, and the powers of the heavens shall be shaken.
— **MATTHEW 24:29**

✳

This sounds like a *"nuclear winter"* to me, the heavens glutted with the debris and detritus of millions (or billions) of lives, the stark evidence of our implacable hatred for those different from ourselves.

It is *"after"* the tribulation of those days that the Son of man, the LORD Jesus Christ, shall appear in the clouds of heaven with power and great glory. Behold, it is written, and it is explicit. The LORD Jesus Christ (the Word of GOD) speaks it. Any misinterpretation is what I call a volitional deception. That is, I would rather be deceived than resign myself to the reality of this Great Tribulation.

There is a course of events which must occur before the rapture that the LORD Jesus Christ portentously calls:

✳

"Great Tribulation, such as was not since the beginning of the world to this time, no, nor ever shall be"
— **MATTHEW 24:21**

✳

This series of events shall encompass *"the beginning of sorrows"* through the *"Great Tribulation"* and extend unto the rapture of GOD's elect. The point must be emphasized: The Word of GOD (the LORD Jesus Christ) does not teach a *"pre-tribulation"* rapture or a *"mid-tribulation"* rapture, but teaches *"Immediately AFTER the tribulation of those days . . . AND THEN"* (please see Matt. 24:29-30) comes the rapture.

✻

Pointedly and concisely, and beyond
misinterpretation, the LORD says:

✻

But he that endures unto the end, the same shall be saved.
– MATTHEW 24:13

✻

Children, those days will be cut short for the elect's sake, yet the elect must endure them like the rest of the populace. This is part of our misconception and indoctrination by the wise men and witch doctors among our forefathers afforded place in the pulpit. That we can escape the Great Tribulation makes for a wonderful message and a very popular sermon; but it is the narcotic and anesthesia of devils wanting us unprepared for hardship. The greater unprepared I am for the hatred and betrayal and persecution by the masses, the greater my likelihood to capitulate to the mark of the beast and deny the LORD Jesus Christ.

(We) must especially be prepared for the more bitter betrayal of former brothers (and sisters) in Christ as mainstream Christians succumb to the disintegration of genteel society, and the startling revelation of our Christian love as an illusion, a chimera, insufficient religious rags.

Greater my inclination to acquiesce to the mark of the beast if my children and grandchildren are threatened, if my love of the world and her conveniences, amusements and entertainments, goods and services and shiny new technological toys are threatened. If my social status and wealth are threatened.

Stark the realization that the degree of separation between my "Christian" way of life and the way of the world is infinitesimal, indistinguishable. I have no strength and no faith to fall back upon because I have exercised no spiritual discipline, no sanctification, no separation from the world or what I have allowed myself.

Contemporary mainstream Christianity is woefully unprepared for hardship, lack, open persecution, the unbridled hatred of the masses and the betrayal of them they considered brethren. We are not taught to prepare for societal and civilized restraints to be lifted, for lawlessness and looting in our neighborhoods – that happens in those other neighborhoods. Ah, even as we have done nothing to alleviate the suffering and oppression (and persecution) of our neighbor, even so, we will be powerless to prevent our own.

This goes contrary to what (most of us) have been taught, and so our initial reaction is indignance and unbelief, anger and offense at the message. But I ask you, Christian: Who but a devil would want us unprepared for what the LORD Jesus Christ explicitly taught; that the elect would have to endure unto the end to be saved?

Granted, we do not want to believe the Church will have to go through the Great Tribulation any more than we want to believe in the eternal torment of hell (for ourselves); although many of us seem indifferent and resigned to the other fellow going there. Some of us wish him Godspeed.

What dad and what granddad handed down to us is more engrained, and of more value to us, than most of us would have imagined. Our readiness to defend this doctrine, and the level of our anger at it being challenged, testify to the degree of our indoctrination. Unfortunately, it is also an accurate indication of our profound ignorance of the scriptures, and our willingness to believe what some man has said, rather than search the Word of GOD with due diligence for ourselves.

Our faith must be challenged, so the depth of our unbelief is revealed: how chronic and how pervasive our malady, how infectious, how urgent and how lethal (and how eternal) our spiritual predicament. How profound our delusion.

Well? Shouldn't someone be asking these things? or rather, should we not be asking them of ourselves? If I truly believe in eternity, shouldn't I be preparing to spend it somewhere? Shouldn't I be laying up treasure in heaven?

Really. There are countless multitudes of mainstream Christians who would rather denounce me as a heretic and naysayer than even consider that they may have to endure the Great Tribulation to be saved.

It takes faith to believe in hell, just as it takes faith to believe in heaven. We have not exercised our spiritual acumen and discernment or engaged our faith to accept and believe the supernatural, the infinite, the inexplicable. We have not looked into these things with expectation of revelation, but are generally disassociated from the miraculous – the heavenly. We have not lived as if our citizenship is secured in heaven, but are enmeshed and ensnared with worldly concerns and illicit love affairs with carnal elements and persons.

Being born again of the water and of the Spirit is a supernatural phenomenon, a miracle – our supernatural transformation and assimilation into the love of GOD, aligned with his purposes in the earth: the saving of sinners by Grace. But we have (generally) been satisfied with a superficial facile religious form, a threadbare religious cloak of self-righteousness, a feigned piety. We have refused to die to lust and pride. Our religious affectation (of being born again), our presenting and posturing as if we have been raised to newness of life, is a self-promoting illusion – a willful self-deception.

We have not shown forth (or demonstrated) the miraculous phenomenon of being born again; we are generally unconverted, unchanged, impenitent. We have not submitted ourselves to the dynamic of the living Word of GOD. We have not exercised or nourished, or valued, the measure of faith afforded us by the grace and mercy of GOD. Ungrateful, unthankful, unholy.

This is the *Truth* that will get you ostracized, betrayed, even murdered by religious personages desperate and unwilling to change or relinquish their unholy love affair with the world. Hear me. The greater hypocrisy will be found within the hierarchy of formal religious organizations, zealous of status and position and power (and pride) – murderous and cunning in their defense.

The Word of GOD is not static, but cumulative: grace for grace, faith to faith – truth built upon truth, revelation upon revelation. The majority of us have ceased all forward momentum, ceased sowing and ceased gathering. These things are not said lightly, but out of the mind of Christ and the sorrow of his heart by association and suffering fellowship – free to all who will pay the fare thereof.

It is faith which makes the Word of GOD manifest. *"No Word from GOD shall be without power."* [The Worrell New Testament]

Faith is the catalyst (the food and the fuel) of the Word of GOD. *"According to your faith be it unto you"* is the kingdom maxim of the LORD Jesus Christ, the eternal Word of GOD.

The miracle of reformation begins inward, and then radiates outward. After I am *converted*, I may strengthen my brethren (re. Luke 22:32). Enough of us in unity, and we could see miracles of healings and deliverances, outpourings of the Holy Ghost and the salvation of souls.

It is my undivided interest and childlike expectation that arouses heaven and engenders a response: my watching and my praying and my willingness to put everything and everyone else on hold (as it were), while I tarry with the LORD Jesus Christ, the Living Word of GOD.

Let us keep this in the context of *"the beginning of sorrows"* unremittingly progressing into the *"Great Tribulation,"* and with the perspective that it takes faith to believe the negative as well as the positive. Otherwise, the Bible is a history tome, a heavy impenetrable document, and a dead letter. (Of course, it is our understanding, and our spiritual discernment that is dead.)

If I accept the beauty and majesty of heaven, I must also come to terms with the horror and reality of hell. What does my preparedness (or unpreparedness) to make it to heaven say about my faith? If I am selective in what I believe (and accept), how can my faith be full, comprehensive, real? If I say I believe in heaven, yet have made no qualifiable attempt to live according to every Word that proceeds out of the mouth of GOD, then my faith is superficial; without works (without my preparedness) my faith is dead. If such is my spiritual condition (and this is going to leave a bruise), then I am a liar, and the Truth is not in me.

The unconverted (and unsanctified) among Christianity is telling, blatant, embarrassing. Bad attitudes and behavior, engrained (character-deep) bigotry and prejudices, no love for one another, disdain or indifference toward whom we consider "lost." Moreover, if *"out of the abundance of the heart the mouth speaks,"* then how is it that Christians (relatively) talk about everything except the LORD Jesus Christ.

Without faith, I am going through the motions of some denominationally skewed religious form, trusting in ceremony, attendance, membership. *Without faith it is impossible to please GOD* (see Heb. 11:6).

Now, no Word from GOD shall be without power. According to my faith, that power is ignited and unleashed, meeting my faith with authority and might to change the circumstances within the orbit of influence that I occupy for the kingdom of GOD, and in the name of the LORD Jesus Christ. It is *"his"* power, after all.

＊

And Jesus came and spake unto them, saying, ALL Power is given unto me in heaven and in earth.
– **Matthew 28:18**

＊

Dearest reader, this exhortation on faith, and specifically faith in the Word of GOD, with all its accompanying admonitions, rebukes, indictments – is first mine. Welcome to my Bible study, where I humbly submit to the fastidious searching of the Holy Spirit and his illumination and exposure of my human condition, my bad attitudes, surreptitious bigotry, prejudice, pride, and elitist religious opinions – the revealing of (what I call) my *residual humanity.* You see, unlike many of my acquaintances, I am not quite convinced of my own (self) righteousness.

What some folks call legalism and morbid self-introspection, I call the spiritual disciplines of the Holy Spirit of the Living GOD laid out plainly in his Word to work sanctification and holiness into my Christian walk of faith. The growth of a living thing does not stop at inception. *Inception* (or conception) being the precise moment I repent of my sins and invite the LORD Jesus Christ into my heart and mind and soul.

With great sorrow, yes, I am suggesting that many of us (relatively) stopped growing spiritually right there. Faith not exercised, a static faith, is a dead faith; you can see it on many of our pinched parsimonious Sunday morning joyless faces.

Many of us summarily reject any suggestion that the Church (usually meaning our select denomination) will have to endure the Great Tribulation, adamantly (and often angrily) refusing to even consider it. That is for heretics and infidels of those other denominational persuasions, bare-faced sinners and the like. Never mind that the synoptic gospels (Matthew, Mark, and Luke) explicitly record the clear teaching of the LORD Jesus Christ that the elect must endure the Great Tribulation.

If I believe in the rapture but not the tribulation, my faith is selective, discriminatory, self-serving (and self-sparing). The word *synoptic* literally means *"with the same eye."* (I would say) it means to read with an unbiased expectation, with my will and my purpose aligned with GOD's own; or with a *single eye* as the LORD Jesus Christ taught it – in short, with no mixed motivation.

✳

The light of the body is the eye: if therefore thine eye
be single, thy whole body shall be full of light.
– Matthew 6:22

✳

This I learned the hard way. Why would GOD grant me more understanding and enlightenment (*greater Grace*), when I refuse to live and conform to the understanding he has already given? We wait on a *"Word"* from GOD, and often have not submitted to the last Word (or instruction) he gave.

Hence, we do not move from revelation to revelation; we get stuck and become defiant and/or complacent. The Word of

GOD is to be my daily portion. To complain or refuse to eat "what is on my plate" is not the way to endear myself to the Chef, as it were.

If I resist the Holy Spirit's enlightenment relative to a particular portion of the scriptures, I risk going no further with GOD – I am essentially ignoring what GOD is saying, (yes, *present tense*). The Word of GOD calls unbelief *"an evil heart of unbelief"* (see Heb. 3:12). Faith (in every Word that proceeds out of the mouth of GOD) is that critical. We have an entire generation of the children of Israel denied entry into the Promised Land as our example. That is, *"IF"* we really believe in Creation, the Exodus, and every jot and tittle of the Old Testament and the New.

So we see that they could not enter in because of unbelief.
— **HEBREWS 3:19**

As the children of Israel could not enter into the promised land because of unbelief, that same unbelief will prevent the preponderance of a worldly compromised Christianity entrance into heaven.

Strive to enter in at the strait gate: for many, I say unto you, will seek to enter in, and shall not be able.
— **LUKE 13:24**

An anonymous inquisitor had asked Jesus, *"LORD, are there few that be saved?* (see Luke 13:23). The scripture above is the LORD's portentous answer. This is the urgency and expediency of the Word of GOD, and the corresponding predicament of a compromised Christianity – and the broad way to hell. This is (what I call) the Gospel ratio of the *many* and the *few.*

We must believe that the Word of GOD is a *Living Word*, a perpetually presently speaking Word, an enlightening, transforming, character-converting Word of *Living Water and Spirit* – *"Ruach Elohim,"* the Breath of GOD.

Ah, relative to this *"entering in,"* please see Chapter 3 of the book, I AM (Jesus).

*

*I AM the Door: by me IF any man ENTER IN, he shall
be saved, and shall go in and out, and find pasture.*
– JOHN 10:9

*

Indeed, how can I *"enter in"* to the Word of GOD, if I seldom (or never) pick up my Bible? Now, *if* I do enter into the Word of GOD with purpose and sincerity, it will supernaturally begin to alter and transform my thinking, my speech, my behavior, my very character.

It will wash me and cleanse me and strip me of sin. It will sever (separate and sanctify) me from lust and pride and my illicit love affair with the world. And this is our predicament; *many* of us do not want to be separated from these things.

The alteration (and conversion) of my character requires submission and diligence – I must *enter in* to the Word of GOD, the LORD Jesus Christ, *the Door*, to be saved. Alas, so *many* of us stand at the Door and weep, or stand there and figuratively shake our fist.

We are indignant, petulant, self-indulgent and violently defensive, rejecting the very idea that there is so much spiritually dysfunctional about not only our thoughts and lifestyle, but our comprehensive character. Yes, this heavenly phenomenon called being *born again* is the radical expectation and exclusive purview of the Word of GOD; we must enter in to be saved.

We congregate on the wrong side of the Door. Whosoever has ears to hear, may they hear. We amass (and assemble) on the wrong side of the Door, where a religious *form* is embraced to ostensibly supplant our submission to this radical and militant (sin-rending) character conversion. *Many* of us have Church right there, on the portico, or the porch, at the very portal to the kingdom of GOD, obstinate and insulted at the suggestion that there is so much wrong with us (internally) – that there is so much *work* to do.

We insist that all we have to do is believe; (but faith without works is dead). We must *enter in* to the Word of GOD to be saved: we must live according to its precepts and commands, and submit to its miraculous transforming power. *No Word of GOD shall be without Power* (re. Luke 1:37, *Worrell New Testament*).

Faith is the incendiary catalyst that ignites the Word of GOD, releasing its power. For everything that the Word of GOD asks of me, there is an ample and eagerly available power to effect that change. The Word of GOD meets my faith and repentance with a (divine) and supernatural power – GOD's own Holy Spirit.

For decades, I stood at the Door and remonstrated, obfuscated, and procrastinated, self-indulgent and self-pitying. The power to change was readily available, the love of GOD seeking my highest good with great grace and tender overtures. The sad reality is that I did not want to change.

I was not the *Lone Ranger,* as we used to say. There were entire congregations and assemblies of us, if you have the ears to hear it. By astute observation and close scrutiny, I learned to emulate my elders: mature Christians, you understand. We tenaciously clung to the doctrine and ceremonial religious routine (or *form*) handed down to us by our forefathers. We had *Church* on the wrong side of the *Door.*

For Jesus to say, *"I AM the Door,"* sounded like some profound, esoteric, inexplicable, theoretical, archaic euphemism or metaphor: an abstract idealistic (but unrealistic) other-worldly statement. You know. We were not really expected to take his statement literally. Right?

A Christian who reads and studies his Bible is (sadly) an anomaly. But he or she has the Word of GOD upon their lips because the Word of GOD is abiding and overflowing their heart. The rest of us often call them *fanatics,* ignorantly dismissing their fervor, not understanding their fire.

Now, relative to the Great Tribulation, it takes faith to know that it is not only promised, but imminent. Unfortunately, this is the same reason the preponderance of us will not be prepared for its occurrence: *unbelief.* If we really believed that this horrible period of tribulation was coming, we would be determined to be more rooted and grounded in Christ each day. You would see us immersed in the Word of GOD.

We must be confronted; we must examine our own self. We must rise above being offended and take a studious and honest self-assessment. With such a superficial, one-dimensional faith, really just a ceremonial religious formality, many of us are going to fold when the fire is turned up. Our indifference, our complacency and compromise, will have eternal consequences.

＊

Immediately AFTER *the tribulation of those days shall the sun be darkened, and the moon shall not give her light, and the stars shall fall from heaven, and the powers of the heavens shall be shaken.*

AND THEN *shall appear the sign of the Son of man in heaven: and* THEN *shall all the tribes of the earth mourn, and they shall see the Son of man coming in the clouds of heaven with power and great glory.*
– **Matthew 24:29-30**

＊

Personally, I believe that the sun being darkened, and the moon not giving her light, is descriptive of a *nuclear winter*, following a nuclear war or holocaust. During that Great Tribulation, if we are not anchored by a genuine faith in a personal knowledge and revelation of the LORD Jesus Christ, we will capitulate to societal persecution and mob pressure, denying and disavowing the LORD.

Without faith, we attribute more significance or value to things temporal; it takes faith to believe in the miraculous, the supernatural, the eternal. This temporal life is indeed a marvelous gift and spectacular, intricate phenomenon, but with one glaring flaw: the insurrection of original sin handed down to us through Adam.

Ah, and then we worship and serve the creature more than the Creator (re. Rom. 1:25). This is idolatry: myself as god. Moreover, our affiliation and friendship and illicit love affair with the world is spiritual adultery (re. James 4:4).

This is not legalism; these are the commandments and expectations of the Word of GOD. His name is Jesus, and he will not take a harlot for his wife. If, when the LORD comes back, he finds me in bed with the merchants and witch doctors of this world, he will leave me there with them. These are the terms and conditions of sanctification and holiness, the joyful obedience of covenant love.

✳

*Wherefore come out from among them, and
be ye separate, saith the LORD, and touch not
the unclean thing; and I will receive you.*

*And will be a Father unto you, and ye shall be my
sons and daughters, saith the LORD Almighty.*
– 2 Corinthians 6:17-18

✳

Frankly, using myself as an example, I needed to be converted from (what I call) self-realization to GOD-realization. My first duty is not to myself, but to honor and worship GOD as Creator, Savior, LORD.

"Me first" is the world's philosophy, and mammon is the measure of success or coin of exchange, and myself driven by the reckless and mindless accumulation of things: to possess, to proliferate, to preen in the pride of this natural life and the acquisition of temporal trinkets and shiny things to represent my status (and superiority) among men – and to oppress other men to have them.

Indeed, as in the days of Noah, and as in the days of Lot, we are the prophetic replicas of those generations, practicing every perversity that comes to mind; incest, unbridled, indiscriminate fornication, pedophilia, homosexuality, same-sex marriage, and the killing (or murder) of the unborn. It should go without saying that a Christian is to separate themselves from these depravities and deviants, and as the opportunity arises, to speak out against such practices, condemning them.

Moreover, there are legitimate gatherings, mass amusements and entertainments, that a Christian has the liberty to attend, but which do not work the righteousness of GOD. In fact, they will dilute my faith and tarnish my testimony. The doctrine of sanctification commands that I *"come out from among them, and be ye separate, says the LORD"* (re. 2 Cor. 6:17). The following passage may be a bit lengthy for many of us, but an acute necessity for a few; whosoever has ears to hear, may they hear.

※

*Be ye not unequally yoked together with unbelievers: for
what fellowship hath righteousness with unrighteousness?
and what communion hath light with darkness?*

*And what concord hath Christ with Belial? or what
part hath he that believeth with an infidel?*

*And what agreement hath the temple of GOD with
idols? for ye are the temple of the living GOD; as GOD
hath said, I will dwell in them, and walk in them;
and I will be their GOD, and they shall be my people.*
— 2 CORINTHIANS 6:14-16

✳

Now, we are not to present as *"better"* than unbelievers, but
"different." We are to be separate in mind and heart, attitude
and behavior, with a distinct *"moral compass"* as they say,
and a different set of ethics – with a spiritual, eternal *modus
operandi*, rather than a temporal, fleshly one.

The Holy Spirit has shown me (over the years) that the phrase
or command, *"Touch not the unclean thing"* of 2 Corinthians
6:17, is an admonition for Christians not to partner or form a
covenant affiliation with those who endorse (and are allegiant
to, slaves really) of this world system's general morality and
what it interprets as wealth or success, or what has value.
Concisely, we are not to have the same idols, or gods. We
are not to spend our lives, our time and attention and substance, pursuing and worshipping temporal (fleshly) things.
We are not to lay up treasure on earth, but to mind heavenly,
eternal things, to walk by faith in (what I call) a perpetual
"Christ-consciousness."

Let us clarify something. We are to associate with sinners, even love them in Christ Jesus – how else will we witness to them but to offer them the love of GOD in Christ? But we are to establish no contract or covenant with them, no partnership, no endorsement of what this world system presents as having the preeminence. We are not to worship or bow down to their gods.

GOD has always put a difference, in every era of time, between his people (or elect) and the peoples of the nations around them. We have Israel for our example and pattern; and contemporary Christianity is supposed to be the prophetic parallel of that pattern. And any Christian with the eyes to see, already knows, if they will admit it to themselves, that there is little or no degree of separation between us and unbelievers.

You cannot tell us apart in thought, speech, or usually behavior. Out of the abundance of our *Christian* heart, we talk about what the world talks about. Consider this; do not summarily dismiss it.

❋

> *Take heed to thyself, lest thou make a covenant*
> *with the inhabitants of the land whither thou*
> *goest, lest it be for a snare in the midst of thee.*
> – EXODUS 34:12

❋

It is one thing to utilize an object, and an altogether different thing to covet that object, to lust after it, or to envy your neighbor for having one. Moreover, is my time and attention and resources (or money), or a disproportionate or exorbitant use of them, spent upon an object (or person) which renders that relationship as having covenant implications? I can make a god (little *"g"*) out of almost any(thing,) activity, or person.

Now, you would have to recognize and accept that you are primarily a spiritual being, *"before"* you are a physical one, to know this is true. And we might just as well put the rest of it out there. This soul that I am the caretaker of, is eventually going to have an eternal disposition of one or two places: heaven or hell (or, a lake of fire, to be precise).

Children, the question begs to be asked, acute and terrible, painstakingly personal – what do we really believe? Our faith determines not only our portion, but our position (or place) in the kingdom of GOD.

✳

The just shall live by faith.
– SEE ROMANS 1:17, HABAKKUK 2:4, GALATIANS 3:11,
HEBREWS 10:38

✳

Living by faith in every Word that proceeds out of the mouth of GOD shall indubitably distinguish me from the people of the world (or unbelievers) around me. The Word of GOD, coupled with my faith in what GOD says, methodically and miraculously transforms my thoughts and behavior, irrepressibly converts my very character, and inevitably separates (or sanctifies) me from the unbelievers around me. Here is what Jesus says (present tense) about his disciples, and his prayer for them:

✳

They are not of the world, even as I am not of the world.

Sanctify (or separate) *them through*
thy Truth: thy Word is Truth.
– John 17:16-17

✳

(Broadly), contemporary Christianity's attraction, infatuation, and illicit love affair with the world, and the *things* of the world, our lusting to be like the Joneses, and reckless pursuit to have what the Joneses have, is a pernicious and lethal *"snare"* in the midst of us (re. Ex. 34:12). And it is progressive. Concisely, it's a trap. I must take the time and the space to list the Hebrew/Greek interpretation for the word *"snare"* as used in Exodus 34:12.

{A *"noose"* for catching animals (literal or figurative); by implication, a *"hook"* (for the nose) – to be *"ensnared,"* a *"gin,"* or a *"trap."*

The proper understanding of this Hebrew word is the *"lure"* or *"bait"* placed in a hunter's trap. It also means a *"moral pitfall,"* and anything that lures one to ruin and disaster.} [*Hebrew/ Greek Key Word Study Bible, AMG Publishers*]

✳

The hunter is Satan, a clever and cunning predator, and he is a determined, ruthless collector of souls.

✳

Be sober, be vigilant; because your adversary the devil, as a roaring lion, walketh about, seeking whom he may devour.
– 1 PETER 5:8

✳

Again, it takes faith to believe and accept that Satan is very much real and earnestly seeking souls to devour, *"going to and fro in the earth, and walking up and down in it"* (see Job 2:2).

It takes faith to acknowledge and accept that Satan is *"the god of this world who has blinded the minds of them that believe not"* (see 2 Cor. 4:4).

It takes faith to accept and internally assimilate that Satan is *"the prince of the power of the air, the spirit that now worketh in the children of disobedience"* (see Eph. 2:2).

The bait is the *"things of this world"* and their allure which engenders desire (or lust) and covetousness within us. It can be status or fame, money, success, fashion, or the latest technological toy. These things awaken, feed, and aid and abet the pride of life within us, eliciting arrogance, and a sense of entitlement and superiority. And the LORD hates a proud look (re. Prov. 6:16-17).

The true spirit and meaning of my life is not about what I have, but about what I do. And what I do with what I have. We miss the reality (and the freedom) of life, primarily because we prefer the illusion of liberty.

Too many of us are slaves to what we possess. There is life more abundant in Christ Jesus, freedom, and freedom indeed, but we prefer the facsimile and the form that allows our excess and wantonness, and that which ministers to the pride of our life. What we often consider our privilege and entitlement, our liberties and rights, too often has us mercilessly ensnared and enslaved.

Too many of us *"walk according to the course of this world"* (re. Eph. 2:2). We compromise Christian ethics and values for (what we consider) personal liberties. What we allow (and tolerate) shifts right along with ever-increasing societal permissions and perversities. Not much troubles our conscience any longer.

We *tsk tsk* and feign indignance and shock at the latest (trending) promiscuity, too often eager to sample the newest outrage that society is willing to not only tolerate, but promote. The god of this world has infiltrated and polluted Christianity, and we have yielded (without a fight) *en masse* to his evil so we can partake of what the world is consuming and perpetrating.

The Christian infrastructure of righteousness, sanctification, holiness, is systematically being weakened and dismantled from the inside-out.

This is a hard word, yet this is the mandate laid against my heart and soul: that I cry aloud, and spare not (re. Is. 58:1). Children, there are no hybrid Christians in the kingdom of GOD; that is, persons with a consciousness and loyalty divided between the world and the LORD Jesus Christ. Sunday is too often a token, empty gesture, more to salve our conscience than to serve GOD. The remainder of the week we vigorously serve ourselves – knowing not (or acknowledging not) that we are actually serving Satan, subservient (or slaves) to the *"course"* of this world. On the broad way to destruction right along with them.

We may insist that this is not the case, but our denial is a con-voluted self-serving (pernicious) delusion, the poor diagnosis (and prognosis) of a fatal malady. Volitionally (or willingly) self-deceived, we convince ourselves that religious ceremony shall suffice to secure our soul, routinely, mechanically, going through the motions of a superficial Christianity: our hearts and minds and souls progressively merged and enmeshed with the course of this world, our consciousness blinded.

As such, we shall never stand in the evil-day (and power of darkness) of this imminent Great Tribulation. We are not mentally, physically, or spiritually prepared for inordinate hardship; we are soft and self-indulgent.

Concisely, a compromised Christian has no power. A Spirit, who is a Holy Spirit, will not sign off on, or cohabitate with, a soul that has sided with this world so that he/or she can continue to lust after its goods and services, ministering to the flesh.

To think that we are going to escape the Great Tribulation because of privilege and entitlement, or pedigree, (or as GOD's elect), does not line up with the Word of GOD. The rapture comes AFTER the tribulation of those days; it is written.

It is the doctrine (or teaching) of Christ, of GOD. Anything else is conjecture and presumption; frankly, a wistful voli-tional self-delusion, a willful ignorance – avoidance, denial, a rejection of the Word of GOD in favor of fables and dissim-ulation, misdirection.

This is a generational ignorance, a neglect of the Word of GOD, accepting what some man has said rather than developing a personal, intimate relationship with the Word of GOD (the LORD Jesus Christ) for myself.

My presumption to escape the Great Tribulation came from the pulpit. That is correct, preachers perpetuated that pipe-dream, that castle in the air – that mass delusion and bare-faced lie out of hell. Someone must confront and expose that dissimulation, that damnable doctrine. The unprepared will be swept away into eternal perdition. Selah.

*

(B) MARK

*AND THEN shall they see the Son of man coming
in the clouds with great power and glory.*

*AND THEN shall he send his angels, and shall gather
together his elect from the four winds, from the uttermost
part of the earth to the uttermost part of heaven.*
– MARK 13:26-27

*

The gospel according to Mark is concise and acute. Some Biblical scholars (many of them simply history students, as I say) immediately diminish and dismiss its significance by accentuating the fact that approximately ninety percent of its bulk is also recorded in Matthew and Luke.

This does not make the Word of GOD a redundant document. Rather, it exposes our general ignorance and hardness of heart, and the embarrassing fact that we do not have *"ears to hear."*

It is important to note that the scriptures above were penned by John Mark, but they are spoken by the LORD Jesus Christ. Am I still listening to what some man has said about GOD; is my faith predominantly in the preacher?

✳

And he said unto them, Take heed what ye hear: with what measure ye mete, it shall be measured to you: and unto you that hear shall more be given.
– Mark 4:24

✳

My investment in the Word of GOD is not measured according to hours and minutes or finite time, but by my love for the LORD Jesus Christ: by my sincerity and willingness to conform to its commands, by my pureness of heart and radically transformed mind. Living relationships are measured by levels of intimacy and trust, by fidelity, and by the merging of purpose, of virtue, of character and essence. The Word of GOD is a Living entity; his name is Jesus. Am I listening, or simply reading?

As the citizens of Sychar said to the Samaritan woman at Jacob's well:

＊

Now we believe, not because of thy sayings: for we have heard him ourselves, and know that this is indeed the Christ, the Saviour of the world.
– JOHN 4:42

＊

Now, John Mark is not copying or plagiarizing what Matthew or Luke either wrote or said; John Mark is recording what he personally *"heard."* He was not confused as to whose gospel this actually is. He starts his personal account as follows:

＊

The beginning of the gospel of Jesus Christ, the Son of GOD.
– MARK 1:1

＊

The gospel of Jesus Christ is cumulative and complimentary, line upon line, precept upon precept (re. Is. 28:10): grace for grace, truth upon truth, faith unto faith, the progressive revelation of the Living GOD – the revelation of himself, from an inexplicable divine perspective.

Ask, seek, knock is the methodology of the Word of GOD; every Christian knows this. But are we invested, motivated, receptive, submissive, compliant or obedient? Do we really want to know, so that we may really live it?

＊

Whom shall he teach knowledge? and whom shall he make to understand doctrine? them that are weaned from the milk, and drawn from the breasts.
– Isaiah 27:9

❋

Using myself as an example, I grew weary of wise men and witch doctors censoring and editing the Word of GOD, arrogantly and presumptuously endeavoring to teach me about GOD, only to later discover that much of their doctrine was self-serving denominationally-skewed conjecture and supposition – much of it blatantly erroneous. I grew disillusioned and disenfranchised of organized religion and the unqualified and inept vouchsafing of pretenders and deceivers spoon-feeding me biased doctrine. GOD was drawing me from the breasts of religious denominational enclaves of backroom bigots and clandestine haters, and from sour milk.

Our innate hesitancy and chronic neglect to read, assimilate, and apply the Word of GOD to our lifestyle is because it is confrontational and mortifying to our fallen nature (or to our flesh) – as it is intended to be. As I have written: When I look into the Word of GOD, the Word of GOD looks into me. From an acute (and agonizing) personal perspective, the revelation of GOD is the simultaneous revelation of the innermost me, if I will accept it. Or as the Word of GOD puts it, if I will *"hear"* it.

The Holy scriptures are GOD's gospel, everything he wants us to know about his essence and character revealed in Christ Jesus: a Healer and a Deliverer and a Savior – the Almighty. Christian, GOD wants to speak these Living Words into your heart and mind and soul in a marvelously individual way, just as he did for his disciples in the Bible. He speaks them *Now*; their context is immediate and comprehensive.

There is no boredom or stasis, and certainly no redundancy, to an intimate relationship with the Living GOD. He created a vast but intricate universe for us to behold, the marvel, and miracle, of our own bodies to mystify and awe.

Conclusions of redundancy reside within my own closed mind, rendering me a prisoner of a negative, proud consciousness, servant of an obtuse impenetrable heart. We resist the Word of GOD because it commands the sacrifice of change (or repentance) from our implacable character.

But if I can take the burn, and the cutting and the crushing, the Word of GOD will set me free from the tyranny of myself: from the bondage of sin and self-realization, from my being a pitiful slave to this merciless world system, a toy (and a tool) of Satan. The Word of GOD will liberate me from the base servitude of my own aberrant appetites.

The Word of GOD (the LORD Jesus Christ) is passionate for a private, intimate conversation with me (and with you), those Living Words permeating the heart and soul and mind, much like water and oxygen are carried on red blood cells to every organ and limb in our body (and to each individual cell) for intricate and miraculous life processes. GOD does not simply want me to stop a couple of obvious bad behaviors and then go take my place on the church pew; GOD wants to transform my thoughts and alter my attitudes, and convert my very character.

Contemporary Christianity (predominantly) does not ingest the Word of GOD, we ingest other things: sexually explicit television and advertising, sordid internet sites, social media exhibitionism and sundry self-indulgences, amusements, entertainments, distractions. (I know) most of us Christians have the Bible on our smart phone, or android, with its own app. But (to me) storing the Word of GOD on the same hand-held technological device by which I couple and fornicate with the world, well . . . it just doesn't feel chaste.

This is all indicative (or symptomatic) of the *"place"* we give the Word of GOD in our lives. Few of us open our souls that he (the Word of GOD) might delve into our secret places. And then on Sunday we allow the preacher to feed us bits and pieces that are often denominationally skewed (or favored), and sometimes that are grossly inaccurate. Because we will not read and study, question and meditate upon (and wait upon) the Word of GOD for ourselves. Frankly, this is an embarrassing but accurate reflection of my true dedication and love for the LORD Jesus Christ, (or not).

The *true* author of the gospel records of Matthew, Mark, Luke, and John is the Holy Spirit whom GOD is. Remember, *"GOD is a Spirit"* (re. John 4:24); the LORD Jesus Christ says it concisely and explicitly. Moreover:

✳

All scripture is given by inspiration of GOD,
and is profitable for doctrine, for reproof, for
correction, for instruction in righteousness.
– 2 Timothy 3:16

✳

For further clarification, we allow the Word of GOD to speak for himself; for, as an astute and comprehensive understanding, I must have in residence the same Holy Spirit who breathed the Word of GOD upon parchment and paper.

＊

Knowing this first, that no prophecy of the scripture is of any private interpretation.

For the prophecy came not in old time by the will of man: but holy men of GOD spake as they were moved by the Holy Ghost.
– 2 Peter 1:20-21

＊

GOD, who at sundry times and in diverse manners spake in time past unto the fathers by the prophets.

Hath in these last days spoken unto us by his Son, whom he hath appointed heir of all things, by whom also he made the world.
– Hebrews 1:1-2

＊

GOD speaks best for himself. The Bible reaffirms and qualifies itself at every turn, full circle, so to speak. The Word of GOD delights to speak into my circumstances, echoing, reverberating, filling my heart and mind and soul with health and peace and joy, with what is pure and true and holy – displacing and dethroning self and pride, altering attitudes and eradicating prejudices, systematically converting my character.

If I am not hearing from GOD, then at some critical juncture, I stopped listening, stopped following. The Word of

GOD is to be received, assimilated, and put to practical application to methodically transform me from the inside-out. If I am not hearing from GOD, most likely there is some attitude, or aberration, some lust or some sin, some resentment or unforgiveness, that I refuse to surrender to the flame. Until I utilize the last thing GOD said, I may well not be granted the next thing; I may very well sit in the sorrow and silence of my soul for a season.

The Word of GOD is indeed confrontational, character-conforming – as it is intended to be. Children, GOD loves us too much to leave us as he found us. And he realized that some of his commands and expectations in the scriptures are of the genre of *dark and hard sayings, things terrible, and hard to understand.*

※

And blessed is he, whosoever shall not be offended in me.
– **Matthew 11:6**

※

John the Baptist, enduring the hardship and isolation of prison, had questions – even after having baptized Jesus and declaring him *The Lamb of GOD* (re. Mt. 11:3, John 1:29). Thomas and Philip and Judas (not Iscariot), even after spending three years in close proximity to the LORD, seeing the miracles that Jesus performed and hearing his teaching, still had questions – chiefly, comprehending, accepting, and internalizing the deity of the LORD Jesus Christ. And so it is with us. I despair of the Christian who has no questions.

Relative to my sincerity and godly motivation, the Word of GOD that I read and study and meditate upon, is accompanied with a *Living Spirit* to give me understanding. He who has ears to hear, let him hear.

Once more, here is a kingdom principle that the LORD Jesus Christ spake (and still speaks), faithfully recorded by John Mark, who was obviously listening with godly intent. This militantly transformed my experience, encounter, and intimacy with the Word of GOD.

＊

And he said unto them, Take heed what you hear:
with what measure ye mete, it shall be measured to
you: and unto you that hear shall more be given.
– MARK 4:24

＊

This is blunt, and perhaps even crass: But when talking to another person, and having needed to repeat ourselves several times, and we conclude that this (hypothetical) person has not heard a thing we have said, then we no longer waste our breath, as they say, trying to reach them.

Much of this has been covered or touched upon, but the Spirit still speaks, and the imperative that we have this Word of GOD (and that he has us), justifies my own redundancy. According to the Hebrew/Greek dictionary, the word *"hear"* encompasses the following: *to grasp or comprehend; by implication, to give heed to, to obey; in a forensic sense, to hear as a judge or magistrate, i.e. to try, or examine judicially.*

By faith we absorb the Word of GOD, by questioning, by lingering over its mysteries and revelation, by tarrying for the LORD (and with the LORD), for answers, for understanding – by spending quality time with the LORD Jesus Christ, *The Word of GOD.* We approach a holy, living entity with reverence and expectation, waiting patiently for the LORD: for sustenance and healing, for revelation and power, for our portion day-to-day, and for eternal life.

By faith we converse and interact with the Word of GOD, with gratitude and worship befitting the Creator of the heavens and the earth, and the manifest *Breath of Life* which makes us living souls – *Ruach Elohim* (re. Gen. 2:7). It pleased GOD that his fullness dwell and be exhibited (and embodied) in and by his Son, the *Living Word.* Using finite terms, the Word of GOD is his DNA, as it were, his genetic code and composition, his essence and comprehensive character, his very identity. His name is *Jesus.*

By faith we imbibe, ingest, (and digest) the Word of GOD. He is the bread and wine of the sacrament, and our *living sacrifice.* Or, as the LORD Jesus Christ defined the living, radical phenomenon of the transforming and life-altering and life-giving power of the Word of GOD:

✳

> *It is the Spirit that quickeneth* (or gives life); *the flesh profiteth nothing: the Words that I speak unto you, they are Spirit, and they are Life.*
> **– John 6:63**

✳

If we read the Word of GOD as an historical tome, or read without expectation or faith that it is indeed a *living entity*, we are simply perusing another book. Our lack of faith renders it common, flat-lined, one-dimensional, finite and linear, a dead document. Of course, it is my understanding that is dead. As I have written: To the dead all things are dead.

Faith is the divine catalyst of the Word of GOD – the fire starter, if you will. (I like to say), faith incites all of heaven to their feet. Trust him alone, and see if it is not so.

Now, as concerns the gospel of Jesus Christ as recorded by John Mark, he was not quoting or paraphrasing either Matthew or Luke, or John. Mark records his own encounter: adverse orchestrated circumstances and their miraculous resolution. Mark records his own singular experience with the Word of GOD, the LORD Jesus Christ. He understood the urgency and imperative to *"hear"* the Word of GOD, to give the Word an audience, a place reserved.

Hear me. Thank GOD (*no comma*) he came himself in Christ Jesus to walk among men: to heal, to deliver, and to save. This is Grace.

Now, the Spirit that was upon John Mark as he penned this gospel is the very same Spirit that was upon Matthew and Luke as they were moved by the Holy Spirit of GOD in Christ. These men did not write down (or plagiarize) someone else's testimony; these men recorded what they saw, and what they heard.

The gospels Matthew, Mark, and Luke are called the *"synoptic"* gospels; the term really means to *"take a common view."* This apparently is some obscure wise man's term, a witch doctor's perspective. Whosoever views these gospel accounts as common and redundant has no opinion and no argument; his conclusions do not rise above the physical to the spiritual. He is lost and undone, not to honor the Holy Ghost upon these men, and give him glory and thanksgiving for his Word.

To view these gospels as common, you might just as well read a history book. Children, to take a common view, and treat the Word of GOD as a finite or ordinary document, is to reveal the lack of one's faith. I call it a flat-lined and one-dimensional perspective – that to the dead, all things are dead. He who has ears to hear, let him hear.

This Word of GOD, the Holy Spirit of this *Living Word,* fills and rules the universe. His presence stands down chaos and disorder. The universe is minutely and miraculously balanced upon the Word of GOD. His is the Breath of Life within our lungs even now.

Please do not misunderstand me, you know that I am a sinner saved by grace. Yet, I hear as John Mark heard, by the same Spirit. Christian, this is the intimacy GOD desires to have with all of his children.

At this point, I must share something singular to the gospel according to Mark – actually the gospel of the Holy Spirit, who allowed Mark, or conscripted him, rather, to record the thoughts and feelings and the character of GOD in and by Christ Jesus.

Matthew, Mark, and Luke appear similar, kind of like three brothers look alike – yet each brother is a complex individual beneath their similarities.

Exclusive to the gospel of Mark, according to my humble research, is a scripture or statement quoting something that Moses by the Spirit and Voice of GOD, instructed the children of Israel in the wilderness, as recorded in Deuteronomy 6:4. Please, hear me. It is essentially GOD quoting himself, provided the Holy Spirit has opened our understanding to know who Jesus is.

I will list the scripture from Deuteronomy 6:4, and then list the conversation in Mark which gives the context and circumstances of Jesus quoting Moses (as it were, or from a finite perspective). Amazing.

✳

Hear, O Israel: The LORD our GOD is One LORD.
– Deuteronomy 6:4

✳

One of the scribes asked the LORD Jesus, "*Which is the first commandment of all?*" (see Mark 12:28). The following is the entire answer the LORD Jesus Christ gives him. The revelation here is so vital and so marvelous that I am moved by the Spirit of GOD to submerge myself (and surrender myself), abandon myself to the Word of GOD. This exposition, or one like it, is recorded in every book I write for the LORD, perhaps twice in some.

✳

And Jesus answered him, The first of all the commandments is, Hear, O Israel; The LORD our GOD is One LORD.

And thou shalt love the LORD thy GOD with all thy heart, and with all thy soul, and with all thy mind, and with all thy strength: this is the first commandment.

And the second is like, namely this, Thou shalt love thy neighbor as thyself. There is none other commandment greater than these.
– MARK 12:29-31

✳

Now, the first part of Jesus' answer to this scribe, as well as to the multitude which had gathered, is what I call the *"prelude"* or *"preamble"* to the commandment. Though not *technically* a part of the commandment; it is indivisible from the commandment. It is a declaration of fact descriptive and pivotal of GOD's identity. It stands alone here in Mark, as it does in Deuteronomy – a direct quote. In reality, this is GOD quoting himself, the Word of GOD, Old Testament and New Testament. Indeed. The Word of GOD speaks best for himself.

Jesus was always teaching, and preaching. Here is the revelation that I want to share with those that have ears to hear it. When asked which is the first commandment of all, he prefaced the commandment with an astounding declaration relative to GOD's essence or identity. Uh, for those of us who presume to attach a numerical value or integer upon the GOD that created and sustains the universe, and, I am convinced, the multiple universes beyond this one.

Let's stop referring to GOD as a *person,* unwittingly diminishing the absolute authority and autonomy of the Almighty. *"GOD is a Spirit"* (re. John 4:24). And he is *One* in both essence and purpose.

It is GOD, the Living Word of GOD, the LORD Jesus Christ, who places the identity (character and essence) of GOD, before the commandment. We have not apprehended the significance of this revelation; we have honored it no more important than the semantics of a secular book.

Moreover, *"Hear, O Israel"* prophetically equates to *"Hear, O Christianity."* And we have discussed the word *"Hear"* relative to the Word of GOD, that it implies internalization and assimilation into my heart and mind and soul, application to my thought, speech, behavior, and comprehensive lifestyle.

❋

Be ye doers of the Word, and not hearers
only, deceiving your own selves.
– JAMES 1:22

❋

This is imperative. The LORD Jesus Christ is effectively saying (if I may) that before we endeavor to keep the commandment, or even attempt to love GOD and love our neighbor, that we need to *"Hear"* something profound and revelatory concerning the essence and identity of GOD.

It has been my experience, that the preponderance of Christianity goes directly to the teaching and preaching of the commandment in verses 30 and 31, totally missing the significance of the revelatory preamble in verse 29 of our current text – having *heard* nothing.

This in foundational, crucial. This revelation is to be accepted and internalized, incorporated into my relationship with GOD.

✳

One LORD, One Faith, One Baptism.
– Ephesians 4:5

✳

This is not the time or place to elaborate in depth, but the Holy Spirit incites me to say, that there is *One Baptism* that will tell: One Baptism with power, and it is not water baptism, it is Spirit baptism. But that is a book for another day.

GOD intends that we build upon this revelation: *"The LORD our GOD is One LORD."* Please, let us stop referring to GOD as *three* persons. He is Father and Son by the Holy Spirit, and he is One LORD and One GOD.

As the Word of GOD (the LORD Jesus Christ) states it:

✳

I and my Father are One.
– John 10:30

✳

Succinctly, GOD is not a trinity of three persons with three different offices and three different sets of duties. He is One LORD and One GOD, One Holy Spirit, and he is of One mind and One will. His Word holds the universe in place, compels the sun to shine, and dictates the seasons. Dear children, he is the One Breath in our lungs.

Before we do any other thing, or begin to practice religion, or indulge in self-serving and self-promoting church ceremony – before I boast of how much I love GOD and love my neighbor, or before I build a bigger edifice (or idol) to contain my vanity and pride, GOD wants me to *hear* something: to sit in silence and awe, to pray for enlightenment, understanding, wisdom. And for Grace.

It is GOD who puts this revelation of his essence and identity *"before"* the commandment. GOD wants us to *know* him *"before"* we endeavor to love him, to have as comprehensive an understanding of his character as possible, *"before"* worshipping and loving him. Otherwise, our worship can be included in the Word (of indictment) that the LORD Jesus Christ gave the Samaritan woman at Jacob's well: *"Ye worship ye know not what"* (see John 4:22).

GOD has no duties or responsibilities specific and exclusive to one person of the Trinity. Doing so diminishes the omnipotence and autonomy and deity of GOD by two-thirds. Any reference to GOD as a person is a foundational error giving my flesh a pass, attenuating my responsibility. We then build upon this fundamental error.

There is no schism in the perfect unity of One. The Father and the Son are indivisible by the Holy Spirit whom God is. Jesus has told us so, but many of us have not *"heard"* him.

For my understanding to be opened to receive and absorb the holy scriptures, I must have respect to the Word of GOD – a sincere and genuine faith reaching for God, to know him, that I might better serve him and worship him in spirit and in truth. When I am prepared to "*act*" upon this Word of GOD, to integrate this Living Word into my own lifestyle, GOD will grant me "*ears to hear*" and the grace to meet the expectations and commands of this *Truth*, a conqueror in Christ, an overcomer.

We (broadly) have no respect unto GOD, no interest surveying the Word of GOD to find him, to study and meditate upon the Word of GOD, to establish and maintain an intimate relationship with him. We have little or no faith; frankly, we generally do not know who Jesus is.

Here is one exploit of Jesus many of us have not considered – one identifying and quantifying characteristic:

✳

By the Word of the LORD were the heavens made, and all the host of them by the breath of his mouth.
– Psalm 33:6

✳

This is why I must know who the Word of GOD is: that I might worship him and acknowledge him as GOD my Creator. That I might know his name, and prepare him a habitation.

It pleases (and honors) the Father to be represented by his Son – who is the heir of all things, and of all authority.

✳

For it pleased the Father that in him should all fulness dwell.
– Colossians 1:15

✳

In whom are hid all the treasures of wisdom and knowledge.
– COLOSSIANS 2:3

✳

For in him dwelleth all the fulness of the Godhead bodily.

And ye are complete in him, which is the
head of all principality and power.
– COLOSSIANS 2:9-10

✳

(Personally), I call GOD, Father, and I call him Holy Spirit;
but to be precise, his *name* is Jesus.

✳

And she shall bring forth a son and thou shalt call his
name JESUS: for he shall save his people from their sins.
– MATTHEW 1:21

✳

Neither is there salvation in any other: for
there is none other name under heaven given
among men, whereby we must be saved.
– ACTS 4:12

✳

Again, personally, I have studied at length every *"I AM"* statement made by the LORD Jesus Christ as recorded in the gospel of John. Together, they comprehensively represent and
constitute the virtues, power, and divinity that only GOD
our Creator could possess. The LORD Jesus Christ repeatedly

said that he (himself) possessed the supernatural qualities and characteristics and power that only GOD, our Creator by definition, could possess.

The LORD Jesus Christ repeatedly affirmed that he was/and is GOD, without saying it directly. He wants his own heirs, his children, to seek out the hidden wisdoms of GOD: to plumb his depths, to communicate with his essence and mine this wisdom and knowledge like gold, and like silver, to examine, and concur, with the characteristics only GOD could possess.

I must know who Jesus is (for myself) in order to be saved. The preacher or televangelist knowing him, or the old timer at the end of the pew knowing him, is not going to help me when I am face-to-face with him, unable to look upon his countenance with faith and loving confidence, and dreadfully comprehend that I do not know him at all.

There is revelation available for every Christian, of the LORD Jesus Christ using the name of GOD, (*I AM*), that GOD gave Moses (re. Ex. 3:14), to repeatedly refer to himself. The Pharisees graphically understood exactly who Jesus of Nazareth was openly and explicitly claiming (and affirming) himself to be. Many times they sought to arrest him or stone him for what they perceived (and presumed) to be blasphemy.

There is a divine revelation of Jesus as GOD that transcends a perfunctory curiosity and superficial relationship with the Word of GOD. Within the folds and intricacies and hidden wisdom of this progressive living revelation the Father awaits his children – the fastidious, intrepid seekers of GOD.

The mystery of the Christ, the Father and the Son indivisible by the Holy Spirit, awaits those that love and obey the Word of GOD.

(I realize) that I am not just suggesting that I must have this revelation to be saved, but that I am declaring it. Please hear me, for we are at the nexus and marrow of the revelation of GOD in his Christ.

❋

I said therefore unto you, that ye shall die in your sins: for if ye believe not that I AM (He), ye shall die in your sins.
– JOHN 8:24

❋

(If I may paraphrase for the LORD) out of the mind of Christ, as it were, and as you can receive it; from another perspective to help us understand and apprehend, the LORD Jesus Christ is fundamentally saying: "If you do not believe that *'I and my Father are One'* (John 10:30), *'ye shall die in your sins"* (re. John 8:24).

In this specific conversation recorded in the 8th chapter of John, Jesus is addressing the Pharisees. They are the singular religious enclave of their era who prided themselves (and presumed themselves) as knowing the most about GOD and about the Law. (It seems) from a contemporary perspective, that each ensuing religious denomination presumes this elitist doctrinal inerrancy of themselves. Until this day. Just saying.

Jesus says something astounding to the Pharisees concerning the Father that he would later say to Phillip and his disciples in what we call the Upper Room Discourse.

＊

Then said they (the Pharisees) *unto him, Where is thy Father? Jesus answered, Ye neither know me, nor my Father: if ye had known me, ye should have known my Father also.*
– JOHN 8:19

＊

The Father dwells within the intricacies and catacombs of Christ, within the progressive living revelation of the Father and Son as One LORD – hidden from the wise and prudent, but revealed unto babes: unto the guileless and the impartial, the innocent and the accepting, the humble and the eager. Them without prejudice or judgement, without learned bigotry and handed down hatred.

We know who Jesus is "historically." This is not the same as knowing him personally and intimately, having him dwell (and abide) within us as the Holy Spirit reveals him to our spirit- man or spirit-woman. Neither is believing on Jesus the same as following him – that is, reading and applying his Word to our lifestyles, conversing with him, searching out his hidden wisdom, his characteristics, his essence.

I have written this many times, but it's urgency and necessity commands repetition: If I declare that I love Jesus, a corresponding love for my own Bible will corroborate my testimony. If there is a discrepancy, then a thorough self-assessment is in order. An objective examination may reveal a gaping unbalance, and save my soul. The most dreadful words in all of eternity will be: *"I never knew you: depart from me, ye that work iniquity"* (see Matt. 7:23).

The revelation of GOD (I find) is incremental, progressive, conditional. All of my writing endeavors to express this divine enigma, this mysterious and awe-inspiring revelation of the Father and the Son as One LORD by the Holy Spirit. It behooves every Christian to ask of themselves: Where am I on the revelatory continuum of getting to know GOD? Do I really know who Jesus is? Welcome to my Bible study.

The Father is in Christ Jesus the Son; and Christ Jesus the Son is in the Father as One LORD. This is the doctrine of Christ, and the LORD Jesus Christ expresses this revelatory Truth as follows:

*

All things are delivered to me of my Father: and no man knoweth who the Son is, but the Father; and who the Father is, but the Son, and he to whom the Son will reveal him.
– LUKE 10:21

*

To really know who Jesus the Christ is, intimately and personally, I must realize him as One with the Father by the Holy Spirit. It is the LORD Jesus Christ who reveals this mystery and divine wisdom unto me. Truly, I have no adequate finite words to express this magnificent revelation, except to simply say: It takes GOD to show me GOD.

This revelation will not come to us sitting anesthetized and dumfounded in the corner of the pew, by osmosis (as it were) listening to the preacher, but alone with GOD in our prayer room. We must *"want"* to know, beyond our entertainment and our luxury. We are not given the time; we must take the time.

We presume upon a familiarity with GOD that too often does not exist. We presume upon an intimate relationship with GOD outside the Word of GOD. That is, we have not spent the quality time reading and studying and meditating upon the Word of GOD to corroborate our presumption. We then rest upon this wistful conjecture supposing our soul is secure in a superficial knowledge of GOD. But do we *"know"* him?

No man or woman comes unto the Father except by the LORD Jesus Christ, (see John 14:6). The Father resides deep within the character and innermost catacombs of Christ. Only when I know who Jesus is will I realize, and be reconciled with, the Father.

※

If ye had known me, ye should have known my Father also: and from henceforth ye know him, and have seen him.
– John 14:7

※

Succinctly and unapologetically put, when I know that Jesus is GOD, then, I can attest to knowing him. When I realize and internalize that the Father and Jesus Christ the Son are One LORD and One GOD by One Holy Spirit, then, I can testify to knowing who Jesus is. This is the Doctrine of Christ, and John the Beloved adds a dire foreboding to those that have not realized this revelatory truth and entered into this knowledge.

✻

Whosoever transgresseth, and abideth not in the Doctrine of Christ, hath not GOD. He that abideth in the Doctrine of Christ, he hath both the Father and the Son.
– 2 JOHN, VERSE 9

✻

We dismiss this teaching (or doctrine) at our own peril. To effectively know Jesus Christ, we must realize that he is One with the Father by the Holy Ghost – that Jesus is GOD.

✻

I said therefore unto you, that ye shall die in your sins: for if ye believe not that I AM (He), ye shall die in your sins.
– JOHN 8:24

✻

As it is written in the gospel according to Mark, and spoken by the Lord Jesus Christ: *"Hear, O Israel; The LORD our GOD is One LORD"* (see Mark 12:29). And his name is Jesus.

The Holy Spirit obviously deemed it critical that I pen this lengthy exposition. To know that Jesus Christ was/and is GOD – this only, is to *"know"* him.

✻

The gospel of Jesus Christ according to Mark, as the Spirit of GOD moved upon him, concurs with (and complements) both Matthew and Luke. Mark records Jesus as saying the following about the perilous times of these end days:

✻

For in those days shall be affliction, such as was
not from the beginning of the creation which
GOD created unto this time, neither shall be.
– **MARK 13:19**

✳

Mark's record of Jesus citing the timeline of these end days agrees with both Matthew and Luke. Frankly, it cannot be misinterpreted. Wishing it were different, or teaching and preaching it differently, will not change it. The Word of GOD which prefaced the beginning of Book III warrants repetition, but let us include the context of these scriptures relative to the Great Tribulation.

✳

But in those days, AFTER THAT TRIBULATION, the sun
shall be darkened, and the moon shall not give her light.

All the stars of heaven shall fall, and the powers
that are in heaven shall be shaken.

AND THEN shall they see the Son of man coming
in the clouds with great power and glory.

AND THEN shall he send his angels, and shall gather
together his elect from the four winds, from the uttermost
part of the earth to the uttermost part of heaven.
– **MARK 13:24-27**

✳

The general order of these events cannot be misconstrued; the rapture (or the gathering of the elect) shall occur AFTER THAT TRIBULATION. Teachers and preachers (and writers) asserting and attesting otherwise shall bear the greater condemnation for their students, parishioners, and readers being unprepared for the exceeding hardship of the Great Tribulation, as GOD sees fit.

The preponderance of contemporary Christianity is unprepared for hardship, persecution, tribulation. (Broadly) we have not suffered with the LORD or taken up our cross, yet we presume upon his grace, expecting sweet meats and amenities, luxuries, delicacies – excess.

We have not suffered with the LORD that we might share his glory. If we suffer no persecution for being a Christian, the world is unaware that we are one. (Generally) we have not taken a stand for the Word of GOD. We are the silent assembly, unsanctified, unholy - sustained at Satan's table, partakers with infidels and fornicators. We are (basically) the world's whore, courting favor for goods and services, and the next perversity.

Think about it. There is no witness in our mouth chiefly because there is no *Witness* residing in our heart and soul. It is cluttered with other things. We have no vision for the Kingdom of GOD – we have television. We talk about what the world talks about, we partake of the same entertainments and amusements, we worship their gold and silver, and covet their electronic devices.

We eat and drink and fornicate with infidels; there is little (or no) degree of separation between the children of GOD and the children of Belial. It is better that I be offended, and amend my ways, than arrogantly persist living for myself, denying and rejecting the Word of GOD, rushing headlong into eternal perdition and hell fire, irredeemably lost.

A genuine faith in the Word of GOD manifests as spiritual preparedness, progressive sanctification, the perfecting of holiness in the reverent fear of GOD. If we do not believe the Word of GOD as written by the three witnesses of Matthew, Mark, and Luke, we would not receive the testimony of a hundred.

To believe is to deny one's self, and to henceforth live unto GOD. I call it *self-realization* versus *GOD - realization*. To live unto myself is the blatant insurrection of original sin, putting the creature before the Creator.

That we might retain our autonomy and worldly status, and in the interest of preserving our aberrant appetites, we have religious *form* to supplant a genuine faith – saving our lives for ourselves. We are essentially the self-deluded, vainly hoping that a superficial religious ceremony shall suffice to substantiate our claim to Christianity. We are religious effigies, a mere shadow of whom we should be.

(Generally) we have not heard the Voice of these synoptic gospels, or that of the gospel according to John, for that matter. We bask in Grace, and hide from Truth. Our dilemma is, we do not want to change – to repent and yield to a radical transformation, to be miraculously converted at the very core of our character.

We have not allowed the Word of GOD access to our wood, hay, and stubble, as it were. We have not heard the prophetic portend and reality of this imminent Great Tribulation. Hear me. When the time comes that we cannot buy or sell without a mark in our hand or in our forehead, innumerable multitudes of fair-weather Christians will line up (indistinguishable) from the denizens of the world with whom they have worked and played and fornicated.

The Great Tribulation will be a profitable era for Satan's recruitment for hell, one-dimensional Christians mingled with a staggering multitude of infidels and homosexuals. Well? Someone has to say it. Same sex marriage is a non-stop ticket to hell, and one of the primary reasons that GOD's hand of judgment is upon this country even now – that, and the merciless murder of the unborn.

America is intoxicated and obsessed with herself, with Hollywood and professional sports, with secular music and social media madness, self-indulgent and spiritually sleeping. The gospel of Mark records the LORD Jesus addressing this condition.

❊

*Watch ye therefore: for ye know not when the
master of the house cometh, at even, or at midnight,
or at the cockcrowing, or in the morning.*

Lest coming suddenly he find you sleeping.

And what I say unto you I say unto all, Watch.
– MARK 13:35-37

❊

The cares of this life, coupled with the entertainments and pleasures of this world (temporal things), have severed us and desensitized us to our spiritual welfare and subsequent eternal destination. Self-image and self-interests never cease to strive for ascendancy, for domination. We conveniently (or selectively) forget that we are active combatants in a terrifyingly real spiritual warfare.

Both figuratively and literally there are giants in the promised land, and they are not going anywhere of their own accord. They must be fought and overcome. I speak of generational dysfunction and personality disorders, ingrained character flaws – a perennial warfare, as it were. Indeed. Some of us have to fight harder than others.

The LORD Jesus Christ understands the human condition as only our Creator can. He also notes our spiritual lassitude and carelessness, our thoughtlessness, the hard -hearted resistance of the natural man to submit to the Word of GOD.

Many of us, professing Christians, have not developed a love for the Word of GOD. We claim the blood of Jesus for the forgiveness of sins and casually take the name of Christ unto ourselves, but have spent no quality time and energy to develop a personal (intimate) relationship with the Word of GOD. (Bluntly), we do not *"know"* the LORD Jesus Christ like that.

Many of us are going to be gravely disappointed and very, very angry to find ourselves in the midst of this coming Great Tribulation. If we have no resolve to know the Word of GOD, no motivation to watch and pray, how will we fare when we cannot buy or sell without the devil's mark?

Our religion has not prepared us for hardship, has not fundamentally altered our attitude or mortified our love for this world and worldly things – has not dramatically *"converted"* our character. Only the Word of GOD, the Holy Spirit of a living Word, can change a heart and mind and secure a soul. Who, then, has the ceremony been for?

We presumptuously think that church attendance and a superficial self-celebratory ceremony substantiates our claim to Christianity. But when we continue to live unto self-interest and worldly things, there is no Christ in our Christianity. And no power.

The Holy Spirit of this living Word (Jesus, by name) will not collaborate or partner with those that live unto themselves in the pursuit of worldly things, driven by the pride of this natural life, and the insatiable appetite of me, me, me. We are anesthetized and figuratively drunk or inebriated on self-realization and temporal concerns, distracted, asleep.

(Before moving on), the gospel of Jesus Christ as recorded by Luke concurs with Matthew and Mark; that is, Jesus' second coming, and the rapture, will occur after the Great Tribulation. All three of these synoptic gospels, as we call them, both agree and complement one another. Each of them also contain(s) knowledge and wisdom supplemental to one another.

It is the hungry and the thirsty and the intrepid of the LORD's disciples, who plumb the depths of the Word of GOD to lay hold upon wisdom and revelation. Dearest reader, GOD has never ceased speaking to them with ears to hear, to the seekers (and knockers) of GOD; he has never ceased revealing himself within the mysteries of Christ.

Our greatest deficiency is allowing the preacher to read and interpret the Word of GOD for us. To be saved, to be prepared for these end times (and the day of the LORD), we must be *"in"* the Word of GOD, and the Word of GOD "*in*" us. I despair of a second-hand diet, and of our selective whimsical appetite for things spiritual.

Do not take your rest or base your souls confidence of salvation upon ceremonial religious form. Religion cannot convert my character or birth me anew; only the Spirit of GOD can transform my thinking and regenerate my heart, or alter my life mission from self-realization to GOD realization.

On a physical parallel, we often eat the same meal or dish on a regular basis; moreover, we eat every day. The same repetition occurs on a spiritual continuum. We eat daily to grow and sustain both our physical and spiritual essence. Yet many of us have read our Bible once and assume this suffices to "*know*" the Lord Jesus Christ; this is giving the Word of GOD no more honor than a library book.

My pastor serves up the Word of GOD on Saturday or Sunday, and perchance he does an excellent job of it, but this one meal (as it were) does not sustain me the rest of the week. One meal a week results in spiritual malnourishment, anemia, lassitude, impotence. Frankly, many of us eat worldly things rather than spiritual; and except when in a church service - we eat at the devil's table.

Christian, if you do not know that the Word of GOD is *Living*, that it is spiritual meat and drink, then I despair of you having "life" in you. Jesus was teaching on himself being the "*Bread of Life.* The following Word of GOD ought to be a staple in every Christian's diet. Its revelatory importance warrants it repetitions.

✳

*Then Jesus said unto them, Verily, verily, I say unto
you, Except ye eat the flesh of the Son of man, and
drink his blood, ye have no life in you.*
– JOHN 6:53

✳

[The following is a general statement.] The synoptic gospels
record the things Jesus said; the gospel according to John
reveals who Jesus is.

It is my assertion that of all the disciples, John knew Jesus
best – and the Word of GOD corroborates, (or bears witness
to it). I speak primarily of his deity.

[This would be an impossibly lengthy exposition here and
now; I refer you to the two books which preceded this
one: *I AM (Jesus)*, and *I AM (He) / addendum to I AM (Jesus)*, a
collective 1100 pages].

The flesh and the blood of Jesus Christ is the *"sacrament"* of
GOD, the same flesh that was torn and the same blood that
was shed at Calvary. Jesus Christ is the epicenter of salvation:
faith that he is the all sufficient sacrifice of GOD. I deny myself, and take up this cross daily. My natural man is crucified
with Christ, that henceforth I should live unto GOD.

Here I am reconciled to GOD in Christ; here my regeneration
not only begins, but daily manifests: radically transforming
my heart and mind, perpetually converting my very character. My life not only begins at that forbidding cross, but also
continues. I am being born again *Now.*

The self-denial is excruciatingly real; the austerity is acute.
The death throes, the mortification of my natural man,

is unavoidably painful. This is the diet of the disciples of Jesus Christ.

This is not so much preached (I would think), due to its unpopularity. Yet the Holy Spirit shows me that this is the flesh and blood of the Son of man: that I daily partake of that cross, not only becoming intimately acquainted with Jesus Christ, but being made progressively One with that old rugged cross. Children, this is the gospel. This is the LORD's supper; this is the LORD's table.

To partake of the Lord's eternal life, I must also partake of his death, his cross. This is asceticism (or self-denial) at its finest: to daily identify with the cross of Jesus Christ, laying down my life for my friend.

We Christians must realize and assimilate into our lifestyles that God is making us One with the flesh and blood of Christ, One with his cross, One with his sacrifice, One with his love. We are by extension and embodiment the expenditures of GOD's grace in the world, to represent his love, mercy, forgiveness; in short, his virtues. What would Jesus do?

Except we identify with the cross of Jesus Christ, to partake of his flesh and his blood, and submit to being an extension of his love for the world in Christ Jesus, there is no Life in us. Figuratively (but also in reality) we must ingest the Word of GOD, and submit to his Spirit's mortification of our natural man. This is not the sweetmeats and delicacies that we are accustomed to; this is the gospel of Jesus Christ and him crucified.

This cross must be preached in all its horror and austerity, and in all its redemptive power. This cross is the vortex and nucleus of Eternal Life: where the Lamb of God is slain, the most Holy place of GOD.

✳

*And there I will meet with thee, and I will commune
with thee from above the mercy seat, from between
the two cherubims which are upon the ark of the
testimony, of all things which I will give thee in
commandment unto the children of Israel.*
– Exodus 25:22

✳

What GOD did for Moses, that is, the Way that GOD made for Moses to meet with him and commune with him, is the type and shadow of the Way that the LORD Jesus Christ makes for every Christian in the New Testament.

✳

*Having therefore, brethren, boldness to enter
into the holiest by the blood of Jesus.*

*By a new and living Way, which he hath consecrated
for us, through the veil, that is to say, his flesh.*
– Hebrews 10:19-20

✳

We meet with GOD (and commune with him) no other place but in Christ Jesus at the mercy seat. The blood of Jesus gives us authority and confidence to draw near unto God with boldness of access. The flesh of the LORD Jesus Christ represents the veil into the most Holy place that was rent from the top to the bottom.

We are made One with GOD in Christ at the mercy seat – not faultless, but blameless. The LORD Jesus Christ is our High Priest now, and it is his blood upon the altar. This is (what I call) the most Holy place of perpetual atonement. To be in this place (by faith) is to be "*in*" Christ.

The following is covered in detail in other writings, but warrants repetition. And the Holy Spirit exacts it of me here.

✳

I am the Door: by me if any man ENTER IN, he shall be saved, and shall go in and out, and find pasture.
– John 10:9

✳

There is no reconciliation with GOD outside the LORD Jesus Christ, the Living Word of GOD. My ceremonial religion is in vain if I do not ENTER IN to the LORD Jesus Christ – (again), the Living Word of GOD.

To *enter in* to the Word of God is to read and hear and meditate with purpose, and with a submissive intent to obedience. The Word of GOD requires of me, and extracts from me, my bad attitudes and prejudices, my envy and lust, my love for the world. You get the idea.

The Word of GOD is caustic, an astringent to my natural man – its Intent is to totally transform my heart and mind and to radically convert my character. The extrication of my personality disorders, and the eradication of bias and greed and jealousy (et. al.), is an excruciating (daily) procedure. The Word of GOD wrests my autonomy, my insistence to be my own god, from my white knuckled fists – Jesus, fully intending to be my first love.

To save our lives for ourselves, and to spare ourselves the acute (and painful) transformation of our desires, and the bare exposure of our inner man's perversities, the preponderance of contemporary Christianity has *church* on the wrong side of the Door. On the porch, if you will.

To *enter in* to the Word of GOD is to tarry with Jesus in the Garden of Gethsemane, follow him to Pilate's Hall, and on to Golgotha (or Calvary). My natural man must be crucified with him there, and for this to be a theoretical or figurative process, the austerity and the death throes are excruciatingly real.

The self-denial is real. The surrender of my love of the world for a godly lifestyle is real. The character conversion is fastidious and exacting, agonizingly real. It is called being *"born again."*

Genuine faith is dynamic: it enters into the Door, it obediently follows, it is forever reaching for the revelatory Word of GOD – restless to know Jesus better.

These are not ramblings and redundancies; these are the heart and mind of Christ revealed. Out of the heart of the Holy Spirit, I write what I hear to honor the LORD Jesus Christ. Simply put, as you can receive it, I write for GOD from inside the Door.

✳

(C) Luke

*And there shall be signs in the sun, and in the moon,
and in the stars; and upon the earth distress of nations,
with perplexity; the seas and the waves roaring.*

*Men's hearts failing them for fear, and for looking
after those things which are coming on the earth:
for the powers of heaven shall be shaken.*

*AND THEN shall they see the Son of man coming
in a cloud with power and great glory.*
– Luke 21:25-27

✳

The gospel of Jesus Christ according to Luke complements (and helps complete) the comprehensive chronology of the LORD's return. It is from within the Word of GOD (the LORD Jesus Christ, the Door) that the revelation of GOD in his Christ progresses. To *many*, these words are superfluous repetition and redundancy; and to a *few*, these words are Spirit, and they are Life. As I have written: To the dead all things are dead.

From outside the Word of GOD, (from the portico, if you will), wise men and witch doctors dissect the Word of GOD as a textbook or self help guide, spinning doctrine diminished and polluted with worldly wisdom and the counsel of infidels. Denominations and disunity are spawned from the worldly compromised minds of these scholars. Frankly, they occlude the portal to the kingdom of heaven, *"not entering in themselves, and hindering those that would"* (see Matt. 23:13).

GOD speaks from the bowels and catacombs of Christ, revelatory wisdom and Words of Life. GOD speaks best for himself. Pharisees and pretenders congregate at the Door and pontificate, vying for position, complicating the simplicity that is in Christ. It is only sinners saved by grace who seamlessly enter into Truth: babes and sucklings and the unseemly. The wise and the prudent prop up (or honor) only themselves and one another, enmeshed or ensnared within the morass and maelstrom of their unregenerate religious minds, indentured servants of arrogance and pride.

We will be without excuse for not believing the synoptic records of Matthew, Mark, and Luke. Have we considered that GOD has had to repeat himself due to the hardness of our heart, or that we are slow to hear? The pride of this natural life and our love (and lust) for the things of this world are not easily mortified, arrogant and capricious characters not easily converted.

We must be repeatedly exposed to the Holy Spirit of this Living Word, totally immersed and assimilated into Jesus.

❋

Seeing ye have purified your souls in obeying the truth through the Spirit unto unfeigned love of the brethren, see that ye love one another with a pure heart fervently.

Being born again, not of corruptible seed, but of incorruptible, by the Word of GOD, which liveth and abideth forever.
– I PETER 1:22-23

❋

This Word of GOD that we are reluctant to read and meditate upon, or that we read once and done, that we resist and rebel against, is our spiritual Breath of Life and very heartbeat. We will not be born again without it. Yet many of us relegate it to 30 or 40 minutes once a week as part of our ritualistic religious ceremony, with the singing (and the band), and the announcements, and don't forget the offering, having the preeminence. We leave with a sense of having worshipped well, pleased with ourselves; we then return to our lives unchanged, unrepentant, and unconverted.

I belabor the point into redundancy because the preponderance of us are lost and undone, anesthetized, hypnotized by the lust of this natural life, mesmerized by illusion, pitiable slaves to our illicit love affair with the world. The Word of GOD that could have radically and miraculously converted our character was not allowed access, but rejected, given an insignificant place in a self-inflating, self-serving religious form, and then put on a shelf or in a corner the remainder of the week.

Perilous times are progressing, proliferating. (Broadly), We look unto government as our source and as our security, instead of submitting ourselves to GOD, to the Holy Spirit of a living, dynamic and incendiary, eternal Word. His name is Jesus.

✳

I said therefore unto you, that ye shall die in your sins: for if ye believe not that I AM (He), ye shall die in your sins.
– JOHN 8:24

✳

My source, my genesis and my revelation, is that eternal spark in the image and likeness of GOD that makes me a living soul, the kingdom of GOD evolving within me – the resident Christ, the Holy Ghost making me One with GOD by faith in Jesus Christ. His Word is my meat and drink, this is the sacrament of GOD, the Host, if you will, or if I may express it like that.

My hope is that eternal spark which hardwires me to GOD, and his Spirit bearing witness to my faith in the blood and body of the LORD Jesus Christ. This perpetual divine phenomenon of being born again, I sometimes call my "becoming." It is the *perpetual present tense*, incalculable Word of GOD, it is Jesus, who sustains and perfects this transformation. He (only) is the perfect one; He is the Holy One – the heavens are his throne, and the earth is his footstool.

This is GOD's phenomenon, the mystery and good pleasure of his own will, to choose babes and suckling and the unseemly. I boast only of grace, of the cross of Jesus Christ and him crucified; my portion is mercy. All glory and honor and praise to our LORD and Savior Jesus Christ.

＊

The gospel of Jesus Christ by Luke records the LORD using the phrase, *"distress of nations, with perplexity"* (re. Luke 21:25). As perilous times progress and worsen, the resources of nations shall be taxed thin, civil unrest and lawlessness will proliferate. Many people will be plagued with uncertainty and fear; indeed, desperate with fear and rising anxiety, many people will become increasingly unstable and unpredictable.

Legislators and government bureaucrats will be viewed by many as having failed the populace; any martial law implemented shall be responded to as a betrayal. Mindless (rabid) pillaging and plundering shall ensue, men increasingly confused and indecisive, prone to spontaneous violence, senseless destruction.

(To me), the words *"the sea and the waves roaring"* are both figurative and literal. The unpredictability and dissolution of the climate shall accelerate. The extremes and violence of the weather shall be unprecedented, capricious and inconsistent, volatile and deadly.

I share a quote from the United Nations Secretary General, Antonio Guterres: Mr. Guterres warned that *war, famine and climate change are setting the stage for a winter of global discontent. "We are in rough seas" Guterres said. A cost-of-living crisis is raging.*

Trust is crumbling. Our planet is burning - with the most vulnerable suffering the most.

✳

We are gridlocked in a colossal global dysfunction, our own worst enemies. As chaos supplants order, many will become paralyzed with fear, obsessed with the deterioration of established (and genteel) society. Yet this civil society will continue to fracture and progressively unravel along with the hope of billions who have become dependent and enslaved, viewing the world as their source of peace and joy. Not prepared for affliction and tragedy, many will react with an insane rage and consuming bitterness.

As the implosion of civilized society escalates, the hope of many will be shattered; and hearts will fail when all hope is lost. Raw terror shall reign for a season; to put it delicately would be to deceive you. This is *the Day of the LORD.*

✳

AND THEN shall they see the Son of man coming
in a cloud with power and great glory.
– LUKE 21:27

✳

The *"Living"* Word of GOD corroborates and qualifies himself . . . all by himself. He keeps his own books and itinerary, his own counsel and divine purpose, his own good pleasure and autonomy.

The Lord keeps his own time – he is the GOD of Infinity and the GOD of Now, Alpha and Omega, *"a very present help in time of trouble, and he* "knoweth" *them that trust in him* (re. Ps.46:1).

The Word of GOD establishes and (emphasizes) that the Rapture shall occur *"after"* the Great Tribulation. The *"Day of the LORD"* is not a 24-hour day, as our finite minds understand it. The Word of GOD by the Apostle Peter speaks of the heavens and the earth being kept in store, reserved unto fire against the day of judgment and perdition of ungodly men (see 2 Peter 3:7). Regarding that day of judgment relative to GOD's concept of time, he goes on to specify the following:

✳

But, beloved, be not ignorant of this one thing,
that one day is with the LORD as a thousand
years, and one thousand years as one day.
– 2 PETER 3:8

✳

We will (hopefully) return to Peter's second epistle and review what the Holy Spirit compelled him to record concerning this *Day of Judgment,* and what may be called the culmination of this Great Tribulation (which has already begun) and the second coming of Christ.

To note, *"the day of the LORD"* represents an era or an unspecified and unlimited (sovereign) period of time, as we understand it in a finite sense. The will of GOD concerning times and seasons resides within the heart and mind and unsearchable counsel of the Ancient of Days (see Daniel 7:9, 13, 22).

The patriarch Job speaks of the unlimited, unquestionable autonomy and sovereignty of GOD:

✻

But he is in One mind, and who can turn him? And what his soul desireth, even that he doeth.
– JOB 23:13

✻

There are many scriptural references describing what the Word of GOD says in relation to *"the Day of the LORD."* I am moved to list only three occasions at this time, as I beseech the Holy Spirit for greater grace, and for ears to hear: Thus sayeth the LORD:

✻

Shall not the Day of the LORD be darkness, and not light? even very dark and no brightness in it?
– AMOS 5:20

✻

*That day is a day of wrath, a day of trouble and distress,
a day of wasteness and desolation, a day of darkness
and gloominess, a day of clouds and thick darkness.*

*A day of trumpet and alarm against the fenced
cities, and against the high towers.*

*And I will bring distress upon men, that they shall
walk like blind men, because they have sinned
against the LORD: and their blood shall be poured
out as dust, and their flesh as the dung.*

*Neither their silver nor their gold shall be able to deliver them
in the Day of the Lord's wrath; but the whole land shall be
devoured by the fire of his jealousy: for he shall make even
a speedy riddance of all of them that dwell in the land.*
– Zephaniah 1:14-18

*

*Behold, the Day of the LORD cometh, cruel both
with wrath and fierce anger, to lay the land desolate:
and he shall destroy the sinners thereof out of it.*

*For the stars of heaven and the constellations thereof shall
not give their light: the sun shall be darkened in his going
forth, and the moon shall not cause her light to shine.*

*And I will punish the world for their evil, and the wicked for
their iniquity; And I will cause the arrogancy of the proud
to cease, and will lay low the haughtiness of the terrible.*
– Isaiah 12:9-12

*

(Relatively), the Day of the LORD will likely culminate or coincide with the second coming of Christ and the rapture of the elect. And remember, it is for the elect's sake that those days will be shortened, else there would be no flesh saved (see Matt. 24:22). No man can predict the timing and disposition, or the exact order of such terrible and glorious prophetic fulfillment.

✳

It is not for you to know the times or the seasons,
which the Father hath put in his own power.
– ACTS 1:7

✳

(I believe) that the Day of the LORD is expressive of the time span of the Great Tribulation, and beyond. The LORD Jesus Christ shall have the last word (as it were), concerning the timing, disposition, and destruction of the earth with fire.

For those of us who would wait until the last possible moment to make a decision to live for the honor and glory of GOD in Christ, the grace that would have encouraged, comforted, and strengthened us in the midst of the most important decision of our life, will be scarce.

✳

Seek the LORD while he may be found,
call ye upon him while he is near.
– ISAIAH 55:6

✳

When the whole world seems to be coming down around my ears and upon my head, and I am distracted and alarmed as civilized society implodes and disintegrates, will not be the ideal time to make covenant decisions. During these Perilous Times, we know that there will be strong delusion in the earth: overt, unprecedented evil, civil unrest, no law and order, scarcity of the basics of survival, and insecurity about their continued availability.

When the food supply chain is abruptly broken, and with no repair in sight, or when I am without heat in the middle of the winter, or even fighting off home invasion, my consciousness will be consumed with the basics of survival. The Grace of GOD's presence shall still be there, but I will be less amenable or fit to lay hands upon it.

Perilous Times shall continue to perpetuate and escalate, while many wait in vain for conditions to get better, looking unto governments for resolution. The beginning of sorrows are painstakingly transitioning into desperation, *"distress of nations, with perplexity"* (re. Luke 21:25).

(I am aware) that this manuscript is confrontational, even insulting if examined in the wrong perspective. It is intended to engage, challenge, and exhort all of us unto change (repentance, conversion). Me first. There is Grace and Truth here sufficient for a wake-up call.

✳

And blessed is he, whosoever shall not be offended in me.
– Matthew 11:6

✳

What would you have me say? and me remain loyal to the Word of GOD and the mandate of the Holy Spirit laid against my soul?

As mentioned, *perilous times* will continue to progress and worsen as the second coming of Christ draws near, grace will become precious, difficult to lay hands on as the end of the age and the utter destruction and implosion of the earth comes to a close. But for now, mercy and grace, strength and comforts abound; this is an especially auspicious time to call upon the LORD.

✸

(For he saith, I have heard thee in a time accepted, and in the day of salvation have I succoured thee: behold, now is the accepted time, behold, now is the day of salvation.)
– 2 Corinthians 6:2

✸

For years I thought, presumed actually, that the grace of GOD was unlimited and abundant and would always be available. In fact, I arrogantly (and with a self-serving sense of entitlement) presumed that the grace of GOD would be at my fingertips, as it were, and that when I really needed the LORD, all I had to do was call upon the name of Jesus, and he would immediately be there to rescue me from my latest self-indulgent, self-inflicted tragedy.

After repeated episodes of shamelessly taking advantage of the grace of God over and over, really, habitually taking the LORD Jesus Christ for granted, and . . . well, and to be painstakingly honest, treating him as my personal servant, GOD had to distance himself from my duplicity and pride and from my perpetually sinking back into the same old sin: my depraved and sensual excess and collaboration and love for the world. Each time I backslid (and I might as well call it by name), the grace and mercy of GOD grew increasingly difficult to lay hands upon, and in my shame and self-induced failure, to once again wrap the goodness of GOD around myself like a familiar cloak, warm and comforting.

I was gradually but progressively (and inexorably) being required to bear the weight of my own sin for a season, my own sorrow, shame and hurt. This was/and is the LORD's correction, as I personally was made to understand it. The stripes were essentially self-induced; I was allowed to taste the wages of sin that I might better comprehend the price and riches of Calvary – the cost of my redemption and deliverance, the wealth and the glory of resurrection life.

For clarification sake, I cannot speak about anyone but myself; I do not presume to know the measure of grace and truth, and faith, upon another's walk or life. And in wisdom, the Holy Ghost keeps this information from me. It is of contemporary Christianity (and myself first), and primarily in this country, that the Holy Ghost shares with me his assessment, sorrow and anxiety at our spiritual dysfunction. The heart and the mind of Christ comes with an old rugged cross, stripes, wounds, spittle.

As you have ears to hear it, and as you can trust the LORD to utilize an unseemly and unlikely instrument as myself, this book, this insult and terrible portend, originates from the thoughts and feelings of the LORD Jesus Christ. I take nothing upon myself, but by the violence of my faith, I ever seek the kingdom of GOD, and the honor of my LORD and Savior, my Creator and GOD, the LORD Jesus Christ.

What shall I say then, without being unfaithful to my Master? me, an unprofitable servant, a babe, a steward of words and unspeakable revelation, the imminent perdition of pretenders and prostitutes, harlots – the world's whores. My own crushing, the Crucible of Truth I have pursued, elicits my tears, commands my crying aloud. Christian, you would not want my calling, the destruction I have seen - the immobilization and utter silencing of Babylon, the terrible silencing of America.

Tragedy upon tragedy shall ensue and proliferate until the time of Jacob's trouble is full; no earlier tribulation, war or famine, shall compare.

✳

AND THEN shall they see the Son of man coming in a cloud with power and great glory.
– LUKE 21:27

✳

We must speak more of this Day of the LORD and its impact upon the heavens and the earth, and of the concurrent (or parallel) second coming of Christ according to the times and seasons the Father has put in his own power, (re. Acts 1:7). While the Holy scriptures repeatedly emphasize that the rapture will occur AFTER the Great Tribulation, beyond the surety of this Word of GOD, the order of times and seasons according to the wisdom of men, is predominantly speculation. Christian, trust fully in the Word of GOD only, and consider what the preacher says with a grain of salt, as they say. No disrespect intended, but we must know what God says.

※

*But the Day of the LORD will come as a thief in the night;
in the which the heavens shall pass away with a great noise,
and the elements shall melt with fervent heat, the earth
also and the works that are therein shall be burned up.*
– 2 PETER 3:10

※

(If this even applies), when a thief cases your house or business as a potential target, the time of his breaking and entering is at his own discretion. It is designed to catch you asleep or preoccupied, negligent of security features and duties – intoxicated by excess and self-indulgence, sleeping heavily, or passed out, as they say.

We might just as well follow the same theme; these are, of course the words of the Living GOD, having humbled himself as a sacrifice for the worst of humanity, the least of these - leaving us just not an example, but the reality and exemplification of love. How many of us (I wonder) shall the love of GOD for our neighbor find us abysmally lacking? or so immersed and consumed with work and the single minded accumulation of wealth, the rabid acquisition of temporal things, or the preening and mean spirited positioning for status or titles, soliciting and prostituting ourselves for the superficial honor one of another. Not just spiritually asleep, or even lukewarm, but fundamentally dead. Someone has to say it just like that.

Still considering our current text of 2 Peter 3:10, let us review the remainder of its horrible prophetic portend; whether this is (in a sense) the finality of the Day of the LORD, only GOD knows. The following immutable phrases are the Word of GOD by the Apostle Peter as he was moved by the Holy Ghost.

✳

The heavens shall pass away with a great noise, and the elements shall melt with fervent heat, the earth also and the works that are therein shall be burned up.
2 PETER 3:10

✳

Now, to qualify, I am not a physicist or a scientist, or anything of that sort; I am a sinner saved by grace. But the above sounds like a nuclear Holocaust. Whether GOD is going to allow humanity to utterly destroy one another, or whether he will destroy the earth personally (as it were), perhaps like Sodom and Gomorrah on a larger, absolute scale, the ultimate results will be the same.

The apostle Peter does go on to say that we (Christians), according to GOD's promise, look for new heavens and a new earth (see 2 Peter 3:13). But before he writes this, the Holy Ghost moves him to repeat and explicitly emphasize the total destruction of not only the earth, but declares that the *"heavens"* will be on fire.

✳

*Seeing them that all these things shall be
"dissolved", what manner of persons ought ye to
be in all holy conversation and godliness.*

*Looking for and hasting unto the coming of the Day of
GOD, wherein the heavens being on fire shall be "dissolved,"
and the elements shall "melt" with fervent heat?*
– 2 Peter 3:11-12

✳

All the worldly things that we lust for and strive for, to hoard and accumulate, to upgrade – the shiny things and electronic toys that glut our consciousness until there is no room for the Word of GOD, all these things shall be dissolved. The elements of our greatest architectural achievements, our luxury automobiles and yachts, the gold and silver we covet, shall "*melt with fervent heat.*"

How many of us (I wonder) live loosely to material possessions because our consciousness and love are in Christ Jesus, our citizenship and treasure in heaven.

It takes faith to believe in eternity, just as it takes faith to believe in the horror that is coming upon the earth, it's total dissolution, its absolute destruction. For many of us, our thoughts do not rise above what is finite or transient – wood, hay, and stubble.

We work 40 or 50 years preparing for retirement, laying up treasure on earth, meticulous in preparation for our *golden years,* even as our physical body continues to systematically fail. We prepare for old age, but not for eternity. Relative to eternity, 70 or 80, or even 90 years, is a drop in a bucket – or a drop in an ocean.

The best of us might spend 15 minutes in the morning for prayer, or to read some devotion. If my math is correct, that is 15 of 1440 minutes in the day. Yes, the ratio is abysmal.

Genuine faith recognizes that striving for material possessions is vanity, fuel for the pride of this temporal life, a distraction and strong delusion. It is an anesthetic, a narcotic to keep us from thinking about eternity. While some possessions are a temporary necessity, the majority of us are drunk on their accumulation.

This temporal life and it's appetites strive for ascendancy, suppression and domination of my spirit man. Life is not about luxuries and the hoarding of wealth; true life is that spark that makes me an eternal entity created in the likeness and image of GOD. That *Breath of Life* belongs to GOD, his for assessment and judgment. Christian, we are *hardwired* to GOD, his for astute evaluation and eternal disposition.

(I can imagine) GOD saying: I sent you a way out of the madness; I sent you a way to stop the cycle of mania and despondency – what have you done with the Gift of my only Son, Jesus?

Our reckoning shall be a fastidious individual assessment – of loving GOD and loving our neighbor. We will be One with GOD in his kingdom, or cast into the hopelessness and abyss of the lake of fire. We have an immutable appointment to keep.

✳

*If a man die, shall he live again? all the days of my
"appointed" time will I wait, till my "change" come.*

*Thou shalt call, and I will answer thee: thou wilt
have a desire to the work of thine hands.*
– JOB 14:14-15

＊

Yes, there is a change coming: the redemption and gathering of the redeemed, mere mortals assuming immortality. The above scriptures are the sublime utterance of raw faith, the patriarch Job, speaking the character and promises of GOD into his circumstances.

(IF I may), this is Job assessing the sovereign will and motives of the Almighty, essentially agreeing with GOD: I know you are going to want to see me again, to see what I have done with (or how I have *spent*), the gift of life and breath you have graciously bestowed upon me.

Such as I am, afflicted, and assailed by untenable contrary circumstance, still, I am your handiwork, *in your image and after your likeness*. I wait upon the redemption of this fallen nature which never ceases to afflict and fail – I am yours to abase, and yours to exalt.

My days are appointed according to faith, according to the prescient foreknowledge of GOD: *"Though you slay me, yet will I trust in you"* (re. Job 13:15). Until I hear my name upon your lips, I will work with what is left to me. I shall stand silent before your assessment, all complaint and excuses forsaken as vanity – as you afford me a glimpse of your glory by greater grace.

✹

*I have heard of thee by the hearing of the
ear: but now mine eye seeth thee.*

Wherefore I abhor myself, and repent in dust and ashes.
– JOB 42:5-6

✹

We have little (or no) comprehension of *Infinity*, little (or no) functional understanding of our own insignificance. We conveniently forget our inevitable end is dust unto dust.

We still presume that the universe revolves around our needs and wants, that the world exists to accommodate and facilitate our pleasures. Our ego subsists upon the imagined wealth of worldly things, our consciousness taken willful prisoner of strong delusion. And when we are not ministered unto satisfactorily, and placated with shiny new toys, we become disillusioned, petulant, bitter.

We are an infinitesimal entity with an insatiable appetite and preposterous expectations, dust demanding glory, our own idolatrous self-serving, self-obsessed god, (little g).

Just one glimpse of GOD by greater grace and Job abhorred his own pretentions, acknowledged and despised dust vying for ascendancy, his own self-righteous (absurd) human ideology. In the presence of GOD, our negligible wisdom (and worth) are illuminated, silence and repentance are indicated.

In the presence of GOD proper perspective is restored; my sinful nature is revealed relative to holiness. The most righteous among us walk humbly with GOD, always affording the next fellow grace. Love is an action verb, if I may express it like that. His name is Jesus.

That man is created out of dust (or out of earth), exacerbates the greatness of GOD. The greatest expression of love in the universe, is that GOD would share with man his own Breath of Life – that man would become a living soul, and an eternal one. That GOD would take our sins upon himself defies all finite description.

Indeed. The Holy Spirit shared with me some years ago that the essence and character of GOD, and his own preeminent commandment for man, is one and the same – it is Love. Love, not in the expression of empty religious platitudes and soundbites or Sunday morning smarm and supercilious smiling faces, but Love in action.

✳

Hereby perceive we the love of GOD, because he laid down his life for us: and we ought to lay down our lives for the brethren.

But whoso hath this world's good, and seeth his brother have need, and shutteth up his bowels of compassion from him, how dwelleth the love of GOD in him?
– 1 John 3:16-17

✳

Many of us postulate that *"if"* there *"is"* a creative Genius or unspecified higher power and intelligence who brings order and balance to the universe (namely GOD), that he is too much love to cast hordes of humanity into hell, or delegate his creative masterpiece into a lake of fire and eternal torment.

We then seamlessly proceed to dismiss not only the idea of GOD (or his existence), but the entire discussion of eternity.

You see, we think too highly of ourselves, and too little of GOD. In fact, we have no fear (or reverence) of GOD; we are unthankful, unholy.

Our thoughts do not rise far above our own appetites and pleasures; our eyes look to the fruit upon the tree. We do not ask, or give thanks or acknowledgement to anyone. We take. We eat when we are not even hungry, willfully oblivious that a large population of people with whom we share the earth are starving.

How can we not know that we are an eternal being? Well, I call it volitional ignorance; the Word of GOD calls it (spiritual) blindness.

＊

In whom the god of this world hath blinded the minds of them which believe not, lest the light of the glorious gospel of Christ, who is the image of GOD, should shine unto them.
– 2 CORINTHIANS 4:4

＊

The Truth of GOD's Word would sanctify (or separate) us from our love of this world system, provided of course, that we submit ourselves to its One commandment of loving GOD and loving our neighbor as ourself. This would necessitate a radical transformation of mind and heart and soul, and an intense (even militant) character conversion. This is a heavenly phenomenon that the LORD Jesus Christ calls being *born again.* In contemporary vernacular, the LORD Jesus tells Nicodemus, and each of us, as well: Don't look so surprised.

✳

Marvel not that I said unto thee, Ye must be born again.
– John 3:7

✳

Why would we be so startled, so contentious and defiant? We cannot realistically refuse to know . . . well, what we already know. Indeed. Our awareness must be rigorously suppressed, and at great effort. We know this being born again is the strait gate and narrow way of a cross, of self-denial and austerity. Frankly, this is suffering association with the Son of man, the way of death and resurrection.

Being born again is the reality (and the agony) and oftentimes inexpressible joy of being birthed anew into the love of GOD in Christ Jesus, not only for our own soul, but for the soul of the world – one neighbor at a time. Christian, we will know (realize and apprehend) the selfless love of as exemplified in the cross of Jesus Christ, or we shall have no part in its resurrection glory and power. This is the gospel.

What does it say about us (the preponderance of Christianity), that we would rather be blinded to the Truth, willfully surrendering our consciousness and heart to a self-imposed unbelief? We submit to an abject servitude, denying and rejecting the Gift of GOD, giving our love (our first love) to the world and its temporary riches.

GOD's love in Christ Jesus seeks our *"highest good,"* but we would rather grovel for what does not satisfy or endure. We think we are laying up treasure as we strive for gold and silver, and things – just things, selling our soul to have them. It is not just blindness; it is insanity – evil.

We do not watch or wait or tarry; we do not pray or look for his coming. We look to tomorrow and our own feeble abilities in pursuit of transient unstable gain. Not believing in his return presupposes that we do not really believe in hell or eternity either.

The love and honor we deny GOD to espouse (and enslave) ourselves to another has eternal consequences. Those who truly love GOD and are preparing and looking for his coming, (what the Word of GOD calls our first love), is a prerequisite commandment to enter the kingdom of heaven. The Apostle Paul expresses this phenomenon to his protege Timothy as follows:

✳

> *Henceforth there is laid up for me a crown of*
> *righteousness, which the LORD, the righteous judge,*
> *shall give me at that day: and not to me only, but*
> *unto all them also that love his appearing.*
> **– 2 TIMOTHY 4:8**

✳

But are we thinking about *that day,* with anticipation: with awe and wonder and preparation, with prayer and fasting and tarrying with the Holy Spirit, our comforter and advocate, our helper unto sanctification and holiness? Those who really believe and genuinely love the LORD Jesus Christ are eagerly awaiting his coming; but to the scoffer and the infidel, to the dead – all things are dead.

✳

Behold, he cometh with clouds; and every eye shall see him, and they also which pierced him: and all the kindreds of the earth shall wail because of him. Even so, Amen.
– Revelation 1:7

✳

(I believe) his glory and his visage will be so awe-inspiring as to instill absolute terror in them that do not know him, and know him as LORD. The LORD Jesus Christ is the embodiment of the Truth they have denied. Instantaneous terror, inescapable exposure – spiritual nakedness, dread and conviction upon them that rejected him; this is what pierced him more than a Roman soldier's spear. The wail of infidels and hypocrites, and all who ridiculed and despised the Son of GOD, shall fill the earth.

An estimated 750 years or so before Jesus was born in Bethlehem of Judea, the prophet Isaiah spoke of him, attesting to his existence and majesty and his omnipotence before recorded time began.

✳

Have ye not known? have ye not heard? hath it not been told you from the beginning? Have ye not understood from the foundations of the earth?

It is he that sitteth upon the circle of the earth, and the inhabitants thereof are as grasshoppers;

*that stretcheth out the heavens as a curtain, and
spreadeth them out as a tent to dwell in.*
– Isaiah 40:21-22

✳

Only a fool would presume that there is no GOD and no Creator who brings order and balance to the universe; we call them atheists and agnostics and infidels. Simply put, we deny GOD and reject Truth so that we can continue to indulge our appetites, serving ourselves instead of serving GOD, adamantly and arrogantly withholding the honor and worship and the allegiance due him, spending it upon the lust of the flesh in our illicit love affair with the world.

Christian, these current Perilous Times are preamble to that great Day (meaning season, or era) of the LORD's wrath. (It needs to be said) that we willfully misinterpret the love of GOD, viewing it relevant to our sticky-sweet Sunday affectatious smarm, an imposter. Our interpretation of love leaves us some leniency for our lust. You understand.

GOD's love is a *"holy"* love, a pure, consuming fire intolerant of wood, hay, and stubble; religious form, self-celebratory, self-inflating superficial service. The love of GOD is perfect, it's exemplification is his only begotten Son nailed to a merciless cross; it can also be said that the cross of Jesus Christ is the personification (and expectations) of the love of GOD, the commands (and conditions) of his espousals.

The LORD Jesus Christ *"is"* Truth. In fact, he is the Way, the Truth, and the Life (re. John 14:6). There are dire and eternal consequences for rejecting the Truth. Many of us expend great and convoluted effort attempting to persuade ourselves that we do not know . . . uh, well, what we already know. Our denial is a grievous personal insult to the honor and integrity of the LORD of Glory.

GOD's sacrifice to liberate and exonerate humanity could not have been greater than the Lamb of GOD crucified, mocked, spit upon. Our rejection of the Gift of GOD (of himself) renders us complicit in the deplorable disrespect and inhumane crucifixion of the only begotten Son of GOD, *"as a Lamb to the slaughter"* (re. Isaiah 53:7). Our volitional disrespect and disregard of the LORD of Creation shall elicit a most terrible recompense of the wrath of GOD.

That *Day of the LORD* within the depths of our consciousness, that day of which we anesthetize ourselves in a vain attempt to forget, is coming. That day (of which) we are deliberately remiss to prepare ourselves for, is upon the horizon. By the Holy Ghost and revelation, John the Beloved Elder describes *"that Day."*

✳

And the heaven departed as a scroll when it is rolled together;
and every mountain and island were moved out of their places.

And the kings of the earth, and the great men, and the
rich men, and the chief captains, and the mighty men,
and every bond man, and every free man, hid themselves
in the dens and in the rocks of the mountains.

And said to the mountains and rocks, Fall on us,
and hide us from the face of him that sitteth on
the throne, and from the wrath of the Lamb.

For the Great Day of his Wrath is come;

and who shall be able to stand?
– REVELATION 6:14-17

❋

Many of us that believe in GOD peripherally, as it were, assume that his grace and benevolence are his predominant (or only) characteristic. We couldn't be more wrong.

❋

For the LORD thy GOD is a consuming
fire, even a jealous GOD.
– DEUTERONOMY 4:24, (SEE ALSO HEBREWS 12:29)

❋

GOD gave us the Breath of Life that makes us a living soul – his own Spirit and essence, likeness and image. Hardwired to GOD, if you will allow the comparison, this is a covenant relationship which makes us a moral agent, obligated, accountable.

We reject this accountability in favor of our appetites and lusts, the pride of our lives in wanton abandon despising the love overtures and tender espousals of the GOD that gives us life and breath and health. Essentially, we mistrust GOD to be our patron, suspecting his portion to be insufficient – intuitively knowing that a Most Holy GOD will not minister to (or fulfill) our aberrant desires and abject perversities. Our indifference and denial of the love of GOD in preference to pride and depraved appetites is a most odious and horrendous insult. We incite the wrath of GOD upon ourselves; and he shall have his Day (or season).

✳

*The Great Day of the LORD is near, it is near, and
hasteth greatly, even the Voice of the Day of the
LORD: the mighty man shall cry there bitterly.*

*That day is a Day of wrath, a day of trouble and distress,
a day of wasteness and desolation, a day of darkness
and gloominess, a day of clouds and thick darkness.*
– ZEPHANIAH 1:14-15

✳

Even we superficial Christians, if we actually knew GOD
as we purport and posture to do, we would understand the
wrath of GOD that our spiritual adultery and illicit love of
the world engenders – that we prefer the basest lusts rather
than acquiesce to the Gift of his only begotten Son, Jesus. We
pierce him again and again, and crucify him afresh. This is the
prophetic reality of the Word of GOD, that we are complicit
in his suffering and shame because the preponderance of us
(contemporary Christians) prefer the love of the world (toys
and trinkets) to the love of GOD.

He could not have given more than himself; and we have no
respect to the sacrifice. On that Day, he will tell many of us:
"I never knew you" (re. Matt. 7:23).

We never took the time nor gave of ourselves. We have many
lovers. Many of us never separated (or sanctified) ourselves
from the lust of the flesh or the pride of our lives, from the
love of things, just things in the illusion of wealth. We presume the Word of GOD as a one-dimensional inanimate
historical document – but He is a living entity. His name is
Jesus, the Author of life and Creator of universes.

We have no reverence or godly fear because we have no faith. Our depraved lifestyles and reckless spiritual (and physical) fornication testify against us. Our hearts do not corroborate the boasting of our mouths – they condemn us as hypocrites.

✳

And blessed is he, whosoever shall not be offended in me.
– **MATTHEW 11:6**

✳

There is a mass delusion rampant, progressive and deadly infectious among the ranks of Christianity in America: we presume the love of GOD will rapture us, rescuing us from tribulation and GOD's incendiary recompense upon the world system that rejected and crucified his Son. We smugly and arrogantly assume a proprietary knowledge of Jesus, hoarding him within the four walls of our denominational enclave. The wrath of GOD shall be our fair wages.

Christian, the LORD Jesus Christ will not submit to self-celebratory religious ceremony, to being essentially imprisoned within our presumptions, our coveting the honor of men more wicked than ourselves, purveyors of worldly counsel, wise men and witch doctors. In review, a taste of the reality (or Truth) of GOD:

✳

*Shall not the Day of the LORD be darkness, and not
light? even very dark, and no brightness in it?*

*I hate, I despise your feast days, and I will
not smell in your solemn assemblies.*

*Though ye offer me burnt offerings and your meat
offerings, I will not accept them: neither will I regard
the peace offerings of your fat beasts.*

*Take thou away from me the noise of thy songs;
for I will not hear the melody of thy viols.*

*But let judgment run down as waters, and
righteousness as a mighty stream.*
– AMOS 5:20-24

＊

We know that we *"look"* (relatively) good on Sunday, but are
we smiling and spouting religious speak and "we'll pray for
Y'all" the other six days? Am I kind and forgiving and generous
with grace (and money) Monday through Saturday; do I speak
of ministering to the poor and the lost and the downtrodden,
or do I actually put in the work of the face-to-face encounter?

Is the love I espouse on Sunday a tangible reality on Tuesday,
or maybe Thursday, or when all hell breaks loose during the
week? Can I freely give my time and undivided attention
and (again, oftentimes money) to help resolve or lessen the
impact of another person's crisis; can I speak the virtues
and comforts of Jesus Christ into someone else's sorrow, or
do I speak empty (and inedible) religious platitudes as I pass
by on the other side?

Well, some of us write a check, and that is needful. For many of us, the Word of GOD spoken Sunday (or any day, for that matter) does not penetrate our consciousness, change our mind, or touch our hearts. Someone must say it again and again: if I am not the same fellow or a converted one 24/7 365, then I am an imposter on the LORD's day. (That is a kinder synonym for hypocrite).

Re-read what the prophet Amos is speaking by the Holy Ghost. And let's remember that this Word is a *"living"* Word, a universal and instantaneous Word, a very present Word, (in fact) spoken Now. This terrible portend and excruciating Word is specifically spoken to GOD's elect of every generation.

Frankly, God is speaking to the Church: his people, his body, his inheritance, his betrothed (or Bride). GOD is referencing the three major feast days that are the backbone or heart of the religion Judaism: mandatory religious observation.

Some would say that by default or inference or suggestion that GOD is referencing ALL religious observation in EVERY era or dispensation.

(But) it is not even a *figure* or a *type;* this Word of GOD is a prophetic *Reality* laid against the soul of a comprehensive (or global) heart and *ALL* religious expression, assembly and/or congregation.

Perhaps it will help to place this text in contemporary vernacular (or laymen's terms). Well, after all, it is spoken *Now.* This is the nature of the eternal Word of GOD; to be perpetually pertinent to our very present circumstances – his name is Jesus.

Dearest Christian, faithful reader, I ask for your forbearance as I speak my personal faith. Please, remember that this chronicle, this manuscript, is the expression and power (and admonition and rebuke) of GOD unto me, first: the first offender, as it were: the very worst of a sinner saved by Grace and sustained by Mercy. . . a mere scribe.

All this (and much more) to say: I trust what the Holy Ghost gives me of Christ Jesus: of what the LORD Jesus knew that the Father had given him.

IF (or as) you can receive it by your measure of faith, I write for GOD upon the edge of revelation, at times nigh unto trespass. As the Apostle Paul would say, there are many adversaries. Nonetheless, I write by stripes and mandate and with the Word of GOD pressed hard upon me personally, out of the crushing and sifting of my own conversion.

＊

(inspirational)

Thus saith the LORD:

Many presuppose sunny, leisurely days,

angels ministering fine wine and delicacies,

sweetmeats and heavenly excess, if you will –

the glory and radiance of a religious type

highlighting and exalting them:

eternal bliss in exchange for a mindless,

heartless ceremonial service.

They already have their wages:

their carnal love of the world in all its delightful delusion,

encasing and entrapping and delegating them

into an eternal darkness.

In that they rejected Light (enlightenment and liberty) in their lifetime, it shall eternally be withheld from them in hell.

Frankly, your feast days, and your comprehensive religious observation, stinks.

Your most solemn assembly or (righteous) congregation is to me a religious stench – it reeks of hypocrisy and impersonation.

My prophet Amos scribed it most eloquently (re. Amos 5:21-24).

Self-celebratory religious routine is spiritually dead.

It does not touch my senses or resonate with my heart.

It has no viable witness, no living faith.
It has the distinct odor of decay.

I AM not the GOD of the dead; I AM the GOD of the Living.

I will not smell a rotting corpse, partake of pretense, or consider the fleeting vapor of posturing pride.

You sacrifice unto me a pittance of your wealth: your distracted and disjointed perfunctory time, lifeless substance – stale bread: what you neither want nor condescend to eat – the leftovers of a preoccupied consciousness, a mindless, thoughtless, religious thing.

*You approach me with pretentious, tedious, religious
terminology, your "idea" of worship, your forefathers
hand me downs, an antiquated repetitious religious
litany, prayers, only for yourself, but in the very shadow
of your neighbor's hunger and struggle for the basics.*

I have no respect for plated gold or tarnished silver.

You know not that I AM the LORD.

*But I know you, that ye have not the
love of GOD in you. (John 5:42)*

*Take away from me the discordant sounding brass and
tinkling cymbals of your songs: the selfish transient
incantations which convince your insecurities that you have
worshipped well: an imposter and a liar ensconced within
the heart of your assembly – the cancer of the body.*

*The melody has gone out of your songs; you minister
to yourself with corrupt and toneless instruments.*

What you presume to return to me was never mine.

I AM the LORD.

*Child, you are intended to be an overflowing reservoir
of Living Waters quenching the thirst of the orbit I have
given you to occupy; to bring equity and an all-inclusive
love to your neighborhood, hydration, hope.*

*You are my catalyst for change, the facilitator of
floods – one drop at a time, and I give the increase.*

I AM He who sits upon the waves of righteousness – my name is Jesus, the Christ of GOD, thy Creator, thy Savior and LORD.

I AM the Holy One.

*Worship is not a place or an event; worship in Spirit
and in Truth is the harmonious beating of the rhythm
of your heart beating along with mine in One song:
the undivided consciousness and attention of One
Love: a 24/7 – 365 day covenant relationship.*

*It is I who write the lyrics; it is I, the giver
of songs and greater grace.*

*How is it? that you have not known? that the sun and the
moon and the stars do my bidding, even as the universe
sings my praises – everything created is my personal
orchestra, thousands times a thousand thousand viols, and
I, even I, raising the trumpet in the Day of the LORD.*

If only you knew that I AM GOD.

✳

*And take heed to yourselves, lest at any time your hearts be
overcharged with surfeiting, and drunkenness, and cares
of this life, and so THAT DAY come upon you unaware.*

*For as a snare shall it come on all them that
dwell on the face of the whole earth.*

*Watch ye therefore, and pray always, that ye may be
accounted worthy to escape all these things that shall
come to pass, and to stand before the Son of man.*
– **LUKE 21:34-36**

– rdb